Financial Innovation

Financial Innovation

Too Much or Too Little?

edited by Michael Haliassos

The MIT Press
Cambridge, Massachusetts
London, England

MIT Press books may be purchased at special quantity discounts for business or sales promotional use. For information, please email special_sales@mitpress.mit.edu or write to Special Sales Department, The MIT Press, 55 Hayward Street, Cambridge, MA 02142.

This book was set in Times Roman by Toppan Best-set Premedia Limited, Hong Kong. Printed and bound in the United States of America.

Library of Congress Cataloging-in-Publication Data

Financial innovation : too much or too little? / edited by Michael Haliassos.
   p. cm.
Includes bibliographical references and index.
ISBN 978-0-262-01829-6 (hbk. : alk. paper)
1. Financial engineering. 2. Financial crises. 3. Finance. I. Haliassos, Michael.
HG176.7.F56   2013
331—dc23
                                                2012014694

10 9 8 7 6 5 4 3 2

Contents

FINANCIAL INNOVATION AND CRISIS: PERSPECTIVES FROM POLICY AND PRACTICE

Financial Innovation and Economic Crisis: An Introduction

Michael Haliassos

The basic mission of finance is to set up arrangements whereby people may pursue risky opportunities without themselves being destroyed by this risk, and arrangements that incentivize people to behave in a socially constructive manner.
— *Robert Shiller*

This collective volume is about financial innovation, its history, and its potential to cause or to prevent financial crises. It conveys the message that financial innovation is typically not inherently beneficial or harmful but derives its qualities from the uses to which it is put. Contrary to often voiced opinions, the book promotes the view that it was too little and too unbalanced rather than too much financial innovation that lay behind the global financial crisis that began in 2007. Correspondingly, preventing future financial crises neither requires nor is assisted by regulation that stifles financial innovation but is aided by policies and a regulatory and legal framework that helps broaden the informed use of financial innovation and distills its positive impact on the economy.

The preliminary versions of most of the essays included in this volume were prepared for a symposium organized by the Center for Financial Studies at Goethe University Frankfurt to honor Robert Shiller, the recipient of the 2009 Deutsche Bank Prize in Financial Economics. The papers were substantially developed after the conference in an effort to produce a coherent, but by no means single-minded, analysis of the complex issues involved, and one that would be accessible to the educated public. The published volume is neither a festschrift nor a compilation of conference proceedings but a book presenting issues highly relevant for research and policy in an accessible and lucid way. In this introduction, I attempt to synthesize some of the arguments brought up in individual contributions in a way that develops some central themes. As I do not attempt to summarize each chapter, the reader is bound to find a wealth of further ideas in the book. Unless

otherwise indicated, references to names of authors point to their respective book chapters.

How Is Financial Innovation Generated?

Financial innovation is a product of the complex interaction between and among the saving and borrowing needs of households, the financing needs of firms, the need to manage risks, developments in financial theory and related fields, and the profit motives of the financial sector. Unlike most forms of innovation, financial innovation is not particularly helped by the patent system: it is difficult to prevent others from copying new financial instruments. Nevertheless, a broader use of new instruments is not necessarily bad for the innovator, as attractiveness increases with widespread use.

What are the key ingredients of financial innovation? Shiller stresses the importance of good theory and econometrics, but also an understanding of the intricacies of human behavior. While this seems to point to a strong academic background as a prerequisite for innovation, Josef Ackermann points out that banks are in a very good position to facilitate innovation, as they are in constant contact with clients, improve risk management processes, and have a strong reputation in the market. Combining the two views, this appears to be an area where research and practice can usefully interact in the production, dissemination, and ultimately standardization of key new products. Shiller gives an interesting account of financial innovators through time, and Karl E. Case adds to it Shiller's own contributions. Robin Greenwood and Luis M. Viceira present a case study of Shiller's most insightful and versatile innovation, MacroMarkets, relevant not only for housing markets but also for the management of other important risks.

The policy and regulatory environment is crucial to the process of financial innovation. Regulation can prevent useful innovation from happening but, interestingly, it can also encourage beneficial innovation aimed at circumventing regulations. Ackermann points out that the now time-honored money market funds and the eurodollar market stemmed from efforts to avoid Regulation Q in the United States. He describes the crucial stages in the financial innovation process, as well as key incentives and trade-offs.

Floating a new product on the market does not necessarily mean that households or firms will pick it up, even when it could be used to manage important risks they objectively face. In their contributions, Shiller, Case,

and Greenwood and Viceira document cases of the limited use of new financial products by actors who find them too complicated or who do not perceive as important the risks that the products are intended to manage. For example, home owners who have come to believe that house prices can only go up are not likely to buy assets providing insurance against house price drops.

What Are Some Inherent Dangers and Risks of Financial Innovation?

It is by now commonplace to argue that financial innovation is risky, in the sense that its outcomes can lead to the financial distress of individuals, firm and bank failures, and general financial instability. What is stressed less is that financial products have something in common with building materials. One can use a brick to build a house or to smash a window. Similarly, predicting the possible role of a new financial instrument prior to its introduction in the financial market is often close to impossible.

The recent crisis provides some telling examples. Shiller points out that the securitization of mortgages, even of subprime mortgages, and their breakdown into different risk classes that could be disseminated to portfolios around the world was an a priori positive development. It was subsequent bad use, lack of transparency, and the failure of rating agencies to assess the risk of securitized products that contributed to the ensuing crisis. Even a long history of good past use is no safeguard against poor future use. Ackermann points out that the precursors of asset-backed securities, now associated with the subprime crisis, were German covered bonds, which have effectively survived for three hundred years or so.

It sounds almost like a tautology to say that use is determined by the user, and indeed this may be true for bricks. However, with financial innovation, producers can sometimes influence the identity of the user and the particular use to which their product is put. The channel of influence might run, as usual, via conventional marketing targeted to specific groups, but it also runs via financial advice given to customers by advisers linked to financial institutions that have specific products to promote.

Financially sophisticated consumers are more likely to make use of new financial products, and this differential tendency may limit the risks of unsophisticated agents running into financial distress. Innovators themselves need to figure out whether it is more profitable to standardize and popularize their innovations so as to operate in a lower-cost,

wider-access environment or whether it is more profitable to move to new markets for more advanced potential customers. It is not a priori clear that optimal choices for innovators are also optimal from the point of view of minimizing the risks of exposure of unsophisticated users to new products they do not fully understand and are likely to misuse.

This type of influence of producers on user and use is not unique to financial innovation. Medicines exhibit many of the same inherent risks. Medicines are often dangerous if they are not taken by the right patients or if they are taken in bigger doses than appropriate. This has not led us to ban the production of new medicines but rather to set up agencies, such as the Food and Drug Administration in the United States, whose main mission is to test and authorize the release of new drugs. Moreover, a requirement for prescriptions is in place, to ensure that drugs are used by patients for whom they are appropriate. Why should we worry about financial innovation if we can set up an agency authorizing new financial products before they hit the market, as was recently suggested; and if we restrict the access of inexperienced customers to complicated products following directives such as the Markets in Financial Instruments Directive?

Despite the attractiveness of the analogy with medicines, there are differences that should not be underestimated. As several contributors point out, the laboratory testing of new financial products may not be feasible or reliable. Maybe testing could be substituted by field experiments, run by financial institutions among their customers, but these have real financial consequences and reputational effects, limiting the scope of experimentation. Unlike doctors, financial advisers often lack the information or expertise to assess the true needs of their clients and how these are affected by new financial products. Even if they have the necessary knowledge, they may not have the incentives to promote the most suitable financial products (see Inderst and Ottaviani [2009] on the various conflicts of interest). Finally, although medical doctors may also face conflicts of interest (given that pharmaceutical companies usually fund their conferences and may support their research), they have also taken the Hippocratic oath, an equivalent of which is hard to imagine for the financial industry; and they face malpractice suits, while misselling suits are still hard to undertake.

The matching process, between those in need of advice and the providers of such advice, also differs. When it comes to complex financial products, many "patients" may choose not to go to the "doctor," and this is likely to be particularly true for those who need the "doctor" most. For example, households that exhibit overconfidence and can end up hurting

their wealth positions through bad asset or debt selection or through overtrading are least likely to seek financial advisers precisely because they are overconfident. Small, inexperienced investors may not only fail to perceive the risks but may also not draw the attention of financial advisers interested in maximizing commissions per unit time spent on providing advice. Indeed, Hackethal, Haliassos, and Jappelli (2012) find that those who use financial advisers tend to be more sophisticated, experienced, older clients rather than those who are in greater need of advice.

Even if matching takes place and those who need sound advice are willing and able to receive it (a good "prescription"), sellers of financial products ("pharmacists") should refuse to sell dangerous products to those who have not received sound financial advice and have not been diagnosed as needing the product. For this, the right incentives and penalties need to be in place. While there is an elaborate legal framework defining the obligations of doctors, the rights of patients, and procedures for handling malpractice, and although its counterpart for consumer protection is also available, a legal framework for investor and borrower protection has yet to be fully articulated and implemented. The absence of such a framework contributes to risky financial innovation and to society's inability to deal with its adverse consequences.

A further layer of difficulty emerges because the optimal response to bad practices of financial innovators or users, whether legally mandated or dictated by policy considerations, is difficult to establish. For example, there are important systemic consequences of letting the institutions that contributed to the overexposure of households or firms to risk fail, but also moral hazard issues associated with bailing them out. The debate over the issue of financial institutions that are "too big to fail" is a case in point. Otmar Issing provides a lucid exposition of the issues and makes clear the risks involved in having governments create the impression that very big banks will not be allowed to fail and that all bondholders will be largely bailed out of risky investments. In a nutshell, since bailouts of financial institutions are typically funded with taxpayer money, it is a matter of debate whether society should bear the burden of losses when profits are kept in private hands.

What Were the Likely Causes of the Recent Financial Crisis?

The recent subprime crisis was produced with ingredients that could be described as individually inert and, in some cases, welfare-enhancing.

First, we had substantial drops in interest rates as a result of inflation containment, combined with fixed-rate mortgages allowing refinancing and lower mortgage payments. Second, improvements in mortgage refinancing technology and enhanced possibilities for borrowing against home equity (such as home equity lines of credit) meant that households had a greater potential for consumption smoothing, as it became easier to liquidate part of the house while still living in it. Third, the spread of mortgage securitization was originally intended to increase liquidity in the mortgage market and ultimately the financial inclusion of households other than prime borrowers.

Who was responsible for the shift away from cost containment, consumption smoothing, and financial inclusion and toward a subprime crisis? It is not unfair to say that all participants had a share in the creation of the crisis: households that were intrigued by the possibilities of lower debt-service costs and completely ignored the risks of house price drops and resulting negative equity, loan officers who ignored the questionable credentials of their customers and approved large loans because their institutions had managed to transfer risks to others, rating agencies that were willing to rate mortgage-backed securities with AAA ratings they did not deserve, and policy makers and regulators who failed to monitor and prevent the escalation of such practices.

What may have coordinated such a range of diverse actors to behave in a way that created the crisis, while at the same time leaving no traces to be picked up by financial economists and market analysts? This is a thorny and as yet unresolved question on which this book provides ample food for thought and for debate. The contrast between the contributions of Maria Vassalou, on the one hand, and those of Nicholas C. Barberis and Susan J. Smith on the other is a telling example.

Vassalou argues forcefully that developments in the subprime market are no proof of the failure of efficient markets or of investor rationality, and they do not necessarily lend support to behavioral theories of financial behavior. Bubbles are discovered only after the fact, and failure to predict them does not constitute proof of irrationality. Tests of efficient markets hinge as much on individual rationality as on the asset pricing model used to assess it. Assuming that the crisis uncovered a new risk factor that was not incorporated in asset pricing and yielded risk-adjusted excess returns because it was not known or was unknowable prior to the crisis may be a much better working hypothesis, according to Vassalou, than postulating that financial market participants are irrational or subject to an arbitrary variety of behavioral biases.

A concrete example of the debate between rationality-based and behavioral explanations is related to what caused the subprime crisis. A key factor that almost everybody ignored was the behavior of house prices, and in particular their potential to go not only up but also down. As Case points out, between 1975 and 2005, house prices in the United States never fell nationally, not for any single quarter (based on the Office of Federal Housing Enterprise Oversight purchase index). Based on this 120-quarter sample, households could form a belief that house prices never go down, and thus fail to incorporate the risk of negative equity into their decisions regarding mortgage levels and the optimal use of home equity borrowing. Correspondingly, loan officers could fail to take house price risk into account when approving mortgages, even for households with shaky finances.

Using the framework of Vassalou, and based on these data observations, house price risk and the limited ability of households to respond to downturns were largely irrelevant to the pricing of mortgage-backed securities and could be ignored by the sellers and buyers of these securities. Asset pricing models could ignore this risk factor, as they ignore other risks not deemed empirically relevant for the issue at hand. Once house price slumps entered the sample and became empirically relevant, asset pricing models could incorporate them.

In my view, the essence of the debate between this rationality-based viewpoint and the behavioral one lies in whether the failure to incorporate this particular risk factor was a rational response to its absence from a long span of data or a result of some behavioral bias that prevented market participants from recognizing its relevance. Barberis argues forcefully that the latter is more credible.

Barberis goes through an impressive range of potential behavioral explanations for the crisis, both belief- and preference-based, and focuses on a single most promising mechanism, namely, belief manipulation based on cognitive dissonance (see below). He considers this a mechanism that could potentially contribute to bad models, or models that fail to incorporate all the relevant factors.

Barberis stresses the "representativeness heuristic," namely, the belief that what we have just experienced will go on. This applies directly to the behavior of house prices. It is conceivable that more sophisticated market participants, mostly those working in the financial sector and supplying mortgages and asset-backed securities, may have had moments of doubt, but cognitive dissonance did not allow them to pursue these doubts and to alter their behavior. Cognitive dissonance is "the discomfort

we feel when we take an action that conflicts with our typically positive self-image." This discomfort led loan suppliers and rating agency employees to manipulate their beliefs into thinking that trends in house prices could not be reversed and that what they were doing was right.

Barberis points to three factors that may have contributed to this process: the long history of price increases, the complexity of new financial products, and the representativeness heuristic. The reprinted article by Barberis and Shleifer provides an example of bubble formation based on extrapolation of past returns associated with the representativeness heuristic. This behavioral idea is very different from the argument that the long history of price increases imparted a "stealth quality" to house price risk, making it essentially undetectable by rational agents employing state-of-the-art methods.

On the household side, there is the big question of why U.S. households decided to borrow to the hilt, thus exposing themselves to serious risks of developing negative equity in the face of a downturn in home prices. Smith argues that an important explanation for the overindebtedness of households is the use of equity lines as precautionary buffers, activated during "bridgeable" periods of financial stress. She points to evidence from the UK and Australia consistent with the idea that equity borrowing is used to provide a financial buffer for unforeseen events, including spells of unemployment thought to be temporary but excluding events such as health deterioration or widowhood. Certain events, such as permanent transitions out of the labor force or a discontinued job search, actually reduce the likelihood of equity borrowing.

Although such tendencies were observed in a number of countries, there is now evidence that the use of mortgages in the United States prior to the subprime crisis was much larger in comparison with major European countries, even controlling for household characteristics. Christelis, Georgarakos, and Haliassos (forthcoming) studied microdata from 2004 on households aged fifty-plus in the United States, eleven European countries, and England. One of their several findings is that mortgage holders in the United States owed, prior to the crisis, much more than European mortgage holders did, throughout the mortgage distribution, even after controlling for numerous household characteristics.

Shiller observes that mortgage market participants did not make effective use of the best principles of risk management that were already available, or of financial innovation aimed at enhancing the potential for such risk management. He calls this a failure to "democratize the best principles of risk management," namely, to spread the ideas originally

used by the privileged few who are sophisticated enough to the broad masses of less sophisticated investors. Although the supply side must have played a role, Case and Greenwood and Viceira point out that an important part of the problem may well be that home owners, faced with a long history of house price increases, were not perceiving the risk of house price downturns, rather than the intricacies of new financial instruments available to hedge against such downturns. Indeed, this would be consistent with the observation that U.S. households borrowed so much and also did not bother to hedge house price risk.

How Did Financial Innovation Contribute to the Crisis?

There is a long literature on how financial development can contribute to growth and to crises, and the chapter by Alexander Popov and Frank R. Smets goes through an impressive set of arguments and results. Perhaps the most striking relevant lesson from this literature is that financial development, beyond any effects on growth rates, increases growth variability and especially tail risk because of large output contractions during recessions resulting from financial crises. Financial innovation is only one aspect of financial development, but it has considerable potential to create crises. The pace of financial innovation is cyclical and can amplify fluctuations and instability. During boom times, excessive optimism often leads to too much experimentation with new financial products, leaving lots of failures to be absorbed during the subsequent downturns.

The basic link between financial innovation and crisis has to do with the nature and pace at which innovation proceeds, the use of new financial products by users and providers, and the mechanisms available for monitoring and regulating such use. Smith argues forcefully that, leading up to the recent crisis, financial innovation was unbalanced across the debt and asset sides. It focused mostly on providing new types of mortgages and possibilities for borrowing on home equity, but this was not balanced by innovation on the asset side aimed at providing the means of hedging and sharing house price risks across potentially interested parties, such as between home owners and real estate developers. Popov and Smets point out that excess world savings and interest in channeling them into safe debt instruments contributed to this frenzy of creating debt-related products and to the wave of securitizations.

Institutional and behavioral factors were decisive for the provision of new financial products and its regulation. In principle, securitization

helps transfer the risk to those most willing to bear it, provided they understand what they are buying and how to price the instrument. In cases of mispricing or lack of transparency, one would expect regulatory agencies to intervene and rating agencies to provide appropriate signals to market participants. As Shiller and Smith point out, during the recent crisis, they appeared to lack the expertise or the incentives or the instruments to intervene to an appropriate extent to avert the crisis.

Lack of transparency and lack of proper incentives may have been amplified by behavioral factors described by Barberis. The complexity of new financial products may have induced providers to convince themselves that these products were appropriate, if only because they lacked the analytical tools to reach a different conclusion, and cognitive dissonance prevented them from thinking they were doing anything wrong. In addition, based on the "competence hypothesis" of Heath and Tversky, a perception of lack of competence to deal with the new products may have enhanced ambiguity aversion, that is, aversion to not understanding how the mechanism worked. The experience of losses can enhance loss aversion, and a disproportionate concern with the potential for losses may not be matched by the consideration of potential gains.

Another potential link between financial innovation and economic crisis runs through the lack of financial literacy among households faced with new and complicated products, coupled with the lack of sound financial advice. This link is beyond the scope of the present book but is among the most active areas of current research in household finance.

How Can Innovation-Linked Crises Be Avoided in the Future?

It is tempting to think that the best way to avoid future crises is for the government to "just say no" to financial innovation. For one thing, as Shiller points out, to ask governments to solve the problem of financial risks and crises is like asking them to build a supersonic jet: they simply do not have the expertise to do this. For another, stopping all financial innovation kills potentially beneficial new products, or product uses, along with preventing potentially harmful ones.

Recognizing the limitations of government does not mean that unfettered markets could deliver socially optimal outcomes on their own. Case is very careful to describe the inherent instabilities in markets and the potential of government to control, regulate, and steer to better outcomes, a view also shared by Shiller. The underlying premise of most of the contributions in this book is that prevention of future financial crises

should be the result of the combined efforts of governments, regulators, and private markets; and that efforts should be targeted toward fostering further useful innovation while preventing excesses and harmful side effects.

Part of the problem in designing such an approach has to do with our limited understanding of how assets are priced. Vassalou writes about factors that are potentially missing from our rational models and need to be incorporated. Scientific ignorance spills over to financial practitioners, who need reliable models with which to price assets and against which to measure mispricing and exploitable anomalies. Vassalou describes at length the perils of using a state-of-the-art (in her case, fully rational) model that fails to incorporate a risk factor relevant for pricing. Using such a model, the practitioner is led to believe that there is an anomaly and to then strive to exploit it in order to earn excess returns, instead of appropriately incorporating the factor in risk management processes.

Coming from a behavioral perspective and a different discipline, Smith shares the concern that, with all the modern theoretical and econometric advances, we are unlikely to have an adequate understanding of house price determinants. However, she pushes for greater interdisciplinarity in the analysis of house prices and related risks.

Smith points out that the combination of economics, finance, and psychology has enhanced our understanding of how home owners value various attributes of a house, but important further insights can be had if we also explore links to sociology, anthropology, and geography: "Prices are sensitive to hopes rather than fears, pragmatism as much as overconfidence, affection or attachment alongside hedonism, and sociality as much as psychology."

In our quest to prevent future crises, we are confronted not only with our limited understanding of asset pricing but also with the unpredictability of how financial products are actually used. Still, dangerous drugs are not banned because of their potential to be abused, specifically because those who can use them wisely can benefit. So, they are only given by prescription to people whose condition qualifies their use. By analogy, dangerous financial products could be given only to those who can establish that they know how to use them, even going as far as requiring a "prescription" from a sound financial adviser.

Ackermann goes a step further and stresses that regulation should not be product- but process-specific. In other words, it needs to take account of the financial institution that issues the financial product in question. Financial institutions themselves have their own management and robust

control processes to contain the risk of their productive activities, and these processes could be regulated and supervised by the government, using its superior access to data. The risk is also different for an undercapitalized bank than for a well-managed institution, and applying blanket regulations to the product rather than to the characteristics of the banks that can issue it may lead to suboptimal outcomes. Given the possibilities for regulatory arbitrage, Ackermann insists on a level playing field across countries and regulators of bank processes and characteristics.

Skeptics might worry that requiring banks to adopt approved processes and to go through the right motions may still not be enough, if the underlying objectives of financial innovators are not aligned with those of society at large. Issing points out that if those who innovate think they cannot be held responsible for the effects of innovations on other agents, they will ultimately not care enough about adverse effects. Requiring reward schemes with longer horizons for financial managers or retention of part of the risk on the balance sheet of originators of new financial products could be steps in this direction.

Governments can also encourage institutions and innovation that foster transparency and discourage those that block it. For example, Issing proposes that credit default swaps be standardized and traded on central counterparty exchanges to boost transparency and to lower spreads for market participants. According to an Issing Commission proposal, a risk map could also be constructed, a diagram of the financial system that captures interdependencies among the most important institutions, based on lists, provided to the macroprudential supervisor, of all larger claims and liabilities of banks on other financial institutions. Yet a point of Popov and Smets should be borne in mind: the purpose of macroprudential regulation is to reduce the costs generated by financial fragility and to address the procyclicality of the financial system without limiting the beneficial effects of developed and interconnected financial systems on long-term growth.

Finally, in addition to establishing a proper regulatory framework, the legal framework itself should be augmented. Adequate investor and borrower protection is needed against sales of inappropriate products to unsuspecting customers, especially if these products are new and largely unknown to potential users. Shiller points out that improvements in mathematics and statistics have often led to new financial products whose introduction necessitated the transformation of corporate structures and of the law. He provides limited liability as an example of a provision that increased risk capital and allowed portfolio diversifica-

tion by removing worries about lawsuits from multiple sources. One could also add the example of shareholder protection, which varies across countries and has been linked to greater participation of households in the stock market and to home bias in stock investments (Giannetti and Koskinen 2010). A well-designed framework of investor and borrower protection not only punishes those with misaligned objectives but can also serve to align objectives more closely with those of society at large.

Should We Have Less or More Financial Innovation in the Future?

In view of proposals for a new regulatory and legal framework governing financial innovation, it will not come as a surprise that the contributors to this book argue for more financial innovation in the future. In the years leading up to the crisis, innovation seems to have focused on the mortgage side, partly in an effort to raise home ownership, but, as Smith points out, it was unable to raise this rate by more than five percentage points in the United States until 2005, and hardly at all in the UK and Australia. The doubling of the overall mortgage debt in the United States between 2001 and 2007 did not occur because of developments on the extensive margin but mostly because of improvements in the potential of home owners to borrow against home equity.

Contributors point to a lot that could be done to enable households to manage some of the most important risks they face, such as inflation risk and house price risk. The reprinted article by Campbell, Shiller, and Viceira lucidly describes the properties of inflation-indexed bonds that could serve the former purpose. Shiller himself has proposed, under the general heading "MacroMarkets," a versatile set of instruments linked to an underlying index. These could help households manage a number of important risks, from oil price risk to housing price risk and even to GDP risk.

The overall philosophy is explained by Smith: home owners need to be able to enjoy housing services but share the risks of house prices with those more willing and able to bear them; they should also be able to hedge house price risk. Developers and institutional investors should be able to get a share of the pie, namely, capital gains, without having to own property in the first place. This leads not only to risk management but also to inclusion, by allowing younger or poorer home owners to pay a lower price for the house in exchange for sharing some of the prospects of future capital gains.

Experiences with this instrument, first applied to oil prices and then to house prices, are explained in detail in the contributions by Case and by Greenwood and Viceira. Although MacroMarkets applied to oil prices experienced reasonable success, the application to house prices failed to generate enough volume to sustain a market for the instrument. The exchange-traded funds Up Major Markets and Down Major Markets, with a simple structure that let those who believed house prices would rise essentially bet with those who thought they were likely to fall, started trading on the New York Stock Exchange in August 2009 but lasted only until the end of 2010. Case and Greenwood and Viceira attribute this failure to deeply rooted beliefs of households that house prices have to rise, as well as to a preference of institutional investors to trade Mac-roShares for liquid or "arbitrageable" assets or indices.

The road to introducing any such instrument in the future is quite bumpy, as regulators first need to understand and authorize it, institutional investors must figure it out, and also get permissions to invest in it, and households have to expect future movements in the underlying index that make them concerned enough about risk to invest in the instrument. Smith adds to those the problem of provider avoidance to get involved in new housing products in the wake of the subprime crisis. In the face of all these obstacles, Greenwood and Viceira speculate that MacroShares can gain a bigger clientele in the future by first tapping the market for vanilla asset classes (at the liquid end of the spectrum) and then moving on to more advanced concepts, such as managing inflation and housing risk, or, even further, managing health care cost and GDP risk.

The process of financial innovation is one that may also involve creative destruction. As Vassalou puts it, it is common in science to discard some innovations when they become obsolete or their shortcomings become obvious. If certain instruments are shown to be harmful, this itself does not speak to the usefulness of financial innovation.

Conclusion

Financial innovation is an incremental, targeted, but still random process that responds to developments in financial theory and related fields, but also to the evolution of regulatory and legal structures and to its own failures. The overall thrust of the contributions in this book is that this process needs to be fostered and monitored, rather than banned or assigned to the government.

Financial innovation relies heavily on practitioners, who design and launch the products. The success of financial products and their potential for crisis are difficult for anyone to predict, as they are not only a matter of their design but also of the use to which products are put. Policy and regulation need to ensure that the incentives of producers are closely aligned with those of users. Where this is not possible, the processes that producers follow need to be monitored, as opposed to imposing blanket restrictions on new financial products.

User access also needs to be monitored in many cases. Given the well-documented lack of financial literacy among various, mostly disadvantaged, demographic groups, and the various conflicts of interest that arise between financial advisers and their clients, it is important to make sure that users access products suitable for them. The process of ensuring suitability involves not only access restrictions but also measures to encourage people who are unaware of or hesitant to use new products to actually utilize the ones suitable for them. Part of what has gone wrong in the past could have been avoided if people had made more use of opportunities that were available, if unfamiliar and novel.

In some cases, this process will go wrong, mistakes will be made, and crises may develop. If they do, crises should be used as an impetus for more and better financial innovation that helps eliminate or manage the risks that contributed to the previous ones, and for finding ways to shield the real economy from wrongdoings in the financial sector.

The chapters of this book take the reader on a journey through past innovations, missed opportunities, and crises to future challenges. Some of the best minds in the profession have come together to guide the reader in this journey, to suggest new paths, and to navigate some uncharted territory. I can only thank them for joining forces, on behalf of all those who will benefit from reading their collective wisdom as much as I benefited from coordinating their remarkable individual efforts. I would especially like to thank Bob Shiller, whose work and sheer enthusiasm brought all of us together and inspired this collective volume.

Acknowledgments

I am grateful to Lut De Moor, without whose dedication, devotion to detail, and tough discipline with respect to deadlines, this volume would not have been produced. I would also like to thank Lutz Erkens, Laura Moretti, and Lulu Wang for their assistance.

References

Christelis, D., D. Georgarakos, and M. Haliassos. Forthcoming. Differences in Portfolios across Countries: Economic Environment versus Household Characteristics. *Review of Economics and Statistics.*

Giannetti, M., and Y. Koskinen. 2010. Investor Protection, Equity Returns, and Financial Globalization. *Journal of Financial and Quantitative Analysis* 45: 135–168.

Hackethal, A., M. Haliassos, and T. Jappelli. 2012. Financial Advisors: A Case of Babysitters? *Journal of Banking & Finance* 36 (2): 509–524.

Inderst, R., and M. Ottaviani. 2009. Misselling through Agents. *American Economic Review* 99: 883–908.

INVENTORS, PRODUCTS, AND INVESTORS IN FINANCE

1 Inventors in Finance: An Impressionistic History of the People Who Have Made Risk Management Work

Robert J. Shiller

It may seem inopportune to talk about the creations of finance at the present time. After the biggest financial crisis since the Great Depression, which started in 2007 with the subprime crisis, was worsened after 2010 with the European sovereign debt crisis, and is still smoldering today, there is great anger and disappointment in our financial institutions. But I think we must keep to a larger perspective so that we can understand that our financial institutions are ultimately the support of our entire economy today, and of the many great things that are happening. This financial crisis might even be viewed as only one relatively small glitch in the grand scheme of things.

The basic mission of finance is to set up arrangements whereby people may pursue risky opportunities without themselves being destroyed by this risk, and arrangements that incentivize people to behave in a socially constructive manner. Finance provides incentives to entreprencurship, and hence to socially useful invention. The incentivization is made effective because it is deeply responsive to financial prices. Price discovery in financial markets provides the information that drives the incentivization properly. The financial arbitrage that ensures that prices for the same thing are roughly the same across markets differing in space and time horizons has the important consequence that real resources flow to the places and times where they are more needed. As arbitrage grows more sophisticated, the flow of resources to uses becomes more effective, and so the use of scarce resources becomes more efficient. Without finance, we would all be left behind in the world. Finance makes possible processes that are the major source of our economic growth.

It is especially important to talk about the process of innovation in finance, for this is the process that might extricate the world's economy from the problems we are in. The G-20 nations, in their joint statement following the Pittsburgh Summit of September 24–25, 2009,

acknowledged their joint responsibility to "promote entrepreneur-ship and innovation across countries" (Leaders' Statement 2009, annex, paragraph 5). One might hope that this responsibility will be inter-preted as including financial innovation as well as other kinds of innovation.

But the question is just *what* is to be done. I want to emphasize that the best process in fixing the economy after this crisis, or after any crisis, consists of moving ahead by all forms of new invention, including finan-cial invention. Financial crises are often tied up with the uncertainties associated with the recent application of some financial innovation. The process of innovation creates the potential for accidents. But the response to accidents shouldn't be to reverse the innovation. The re-sponse should be moving the economy ahead to be even better, not to patch holes in an existing theory. Here I want to consider what kind of process that is.

Challenges That Confront Financial Innovators

Financial organizations and instruments are inventions, just like engi-neering inventions. They are part of the same process of invention that brought us railroads and computers, and in fact, they have interacted along the way with these other inventions. Moreover, successful inven-tion requires the assimilation of various aspects of technology, including the relative prices of different inputs to the invention, or the public support that there can be for social inventions. Our financial institutions and instruments incorporate inventive ideas that were in turn responses to the information technology we have: our computers, our databases, and our news media and their outlets.

Inventions are ideas that usually can be copied, and good inventions are eventually copied all around the world. Patent law gives the inventor a period of time to benefit before this copying process begins. But patent law has rarely restricted the ability of others to copy financial ideas, a fact that has reduced the incentives to innovate in finance. It has raised the speed of transmission of ideas, once created, but also slowed the creation of these ideas.

The spread of inventive ideas is also slowed by the fact that the defects of financial inventions are perceived only with a time lag—often only after decades, when the next financial crisis occurs.

That is why it is so important to react to financial crises with encour-agement, on the part of the government or financial organizations, for

the development and application of new financial ideas. We must now take this opportunity to do this.

Financial inventions require a suitable basic theory, and this theory must develop on an abstract plane to make possible some of the innovations. Some of the authors represented in this volume, among them Nicholas C. Barberis, John Y. Campbell, Andrei Shleifer, Frank R. Smets, and Luis M. Viceira, have made important contributions both to mathematical finance and to the econometric implementation of it.

Financial inventions also sometimes require advances in statistical theory. Here I am pleased to see in this book my long-time partner, Karl E. Case, who independently invented the repeat-sales econometric concept that was the underlying idea for the repeat-sales index that we developed together, now called the S&P/Case-Shiller Home Price Index.

Financial inventions also require an attention to human behavior and institutions. We need human-factors engineering, as it is called in engineering schools. This means a working out of the complexities of human foibles and their interrelation with actual economic mechanisms. The work and life history of other authors in this book fit very well into this dimension. I am glad to see such a diversity of expertise brought together to common purpose.

Democratizing Finance

Historically, financial inventions have over the centuries had the effect of democratizing finance, making it work better *for* the people. Financial ideas at first work to the advantage only of the privileged few who understand and have the right opportunities to access the technology. But as time goes by, these inventions become more and more available to everyone. This is a historical principle and one that is already far advanced, but the process is not over.

The current financial crisis is substantially the result of a failure to democratize the best principles of risk management. I am thinking notably of the spectacle in the United States of home mortgages, coupled with a housing debacle that has put over fifteen million households in the United States underwater, with mortgages being defaulted on in the millions. It may seem that our only hope is that the recent declines in home prices are at last behind us, and that prices are starting to pick up. But basing our future on such a hope is not enlightened finance.

Progress means bringing financial principles to all these people. In their "Core Values for a Sustainable Economy," adopted as an annex to the Pittsburgh Declaration, the G-20 nations said, following up on Angela

Merkel's proposal of a Global Charter for a Sustainable Economy: "We commit to taking responsible actions to ensure that every stakeholder— consumers, workers, investors, entrepreneurs—can participate in a balanced, equitable, and inclusive global economy" (Leaders' Statement 2009, annex, paragraph 2). We have to ask what this means, how it can be compatible with incentives and with the proper allocation of resources. Answering this question requires inventiveness. The process of changing the system to fulfill this commitment means developing and implementing new financial ideas.

Just as inventiveness a century ago put the automobile gradually into the hands of everyone and democratized our highway system, this goal cannot be achieved by governments alone. It must be achieved by facilitating creativeness among private sector actors as well as governments.

Inventions are made by *people*, and by people who have a natural curiosity and the energy to do repeated experiments. Only that process will solve real problems. Invention is akin to entrepreneurship, something that requires a certain kind of animal spirits.

The historian of technology Jacob Schmookler, in his book *Invention and Economic Growth* (1966), stressed that advances in technology are mostly the incremental efforts of individual people, usually making small advances that achieve little notice. Making things work right takes a long sequence of experimentation and thought, and more experimentation and more thought, between the initial germ of an idea and the ultimate practical device. He used the example of horseshoes in the late nineteenth and early twentieth centuries: the U.S. Patent Office lists hundreds of patents for horseshoes. You might think that something as simple as a horseshoe would not need a patent: not so. Horseshoes were constantly being improved.

Inventions in one realm of technology often open up opportunities in other realms, either through showing new possibilities or by creating new necessities. Thus, Schmookler found, the invention of the automobile did not initially slow down these horseshoe patents. For automobiles brought with them paved roads, and horses were slipping and falling on those paved roads, which was injuring them. This necessitated a flurry of inventions, after the automobile, of horseshoes with caulk.

Financial Innovation in History

Because there are so many incremental improvements, we never hear about most of the people who advance technology. We only hear of those few who were present at major turning points.

The chapter by Josef Ackermann in this book serves to remind us of part of the recent history of financial innovation, with his examples of recent financial innovations and analysis of the phases these innovations went through.

Taking then a longer view, we see that the invention of financial theory has occurred over centuries and in parallel with many inventions in mathematics and economic theory. The first beginnings of the mathematical theory of probability in the seventeenth century led to the first insurance companies in that same century that based their operations on sound statistical risk analysis. The mathematical thinking that led to the Laplace transform in the mathematics of the eighteenth century also led to the concept of present value of a flow of income, and to modern investment theory. Advances in the theory of stochastic processes in the nineteenth century led to the concepts of statistical innovations and of the random walk, and hence to the twentieth-century concept of efficient markets. Advances in theoretical physics in the twentieth century led to the mathematics of the Black-Scholes option pricing theory.

Over these same centuries there were significant changes in our corporate structures, our society, and our laws that went hand in hand with innovations in finance. The invention of the modern multinational corporation came about with the Dutch East India Company, created in Holland in 1602 to pursue the spice trade around the world. It was an important invention in that prior trading business ventures were customarily short-term ventures, dissolved after the voyage was over. The long-term nature of the Dutch East India Company was an invention of some consequence, for it allowed the development of long-term capital, in the form of trading posts around the world, and distribution channels, and long-term contracts. The large size of the company allowed the pursuit of economies of scale. The joint-stock ownership form allowed investors to minimize the enormous risks.

The running of the Dutch East India Company was challenged by corruption. These problems were held off for a while under the draconian strictness of such men as Jan Pieterszoon Coen. This strictness staved off the decline of this company long enough that it was able to establish to the world the potential importance of multinational corporations. But the controls against corruption were not good enough. The Dutch East India Company eventually failed as a result of agency and moral hazard problems that could not be effectively controlled with the financial technology of the time.

The first central bank was the Bank of England, founded by William Paterson in 1694. It was initially founded with no idea of its becoming

a systemic regulator that would prevent financial crises from getting out of control. Its function as lender of last resort was invented over the centuries as it encountered one crisis after another, tried to survive, and tried to preserve a healthy banking sector for its own and others' benefit.

The Bank of England encountered a lot of systemic instability that, though on a smaller scale, was just as bad as the instability that brought us the current crisis. It had to deal, for example, with the first international stock market bubbles and bursts, the South Sea Bubble in the UK and the Mississippi Bubble in France. The beginnings of central bank understanding of how to deal with such crises were laid down then.

The free charter of a large national corporation was enhanced by another invention, embodied in the New York State corporate law of 1811, which established two fundamental principles (then for New York State only): the right of anyone to set up a corporation, automatically on establishing certain conditions, and the principle of limited liability, which meant that no shareholder could ever be pursued for the transgressions of a company. The creation of the New York State corporate law was criticized at the time as one that would promote speculation, irresponsibility, and greed. Perhaps it did do just that, but it also produced some wonderful and powerful new companies, and the world watched the New York experience, and virtually every country later copied the New York principles of free incorporation and limited liability.

David Moss, in his book *When All Else Fails: The Government as Ultimate Risk Manager* (2004), argues that the invention of the broad principle of limited liability, which had the effect of reassuring investors, was behaviorally very important in generating a supply of risk capital. People then began to *enjoy* investing in limited liability stocks. Limited liability was an example of human-factors engineering of a risk management device. Limited liability prevents unnecessary worry about possible lawsuits against stockholders. Even though lawsuits against shareholders were rarely successful before 1811, they were always a possibility. The human mind can easily dwell on low-probability events, partly because of a psychological propensity to exaggerate their probability (as documented by psychologists Daniel Kahneman and Amos Tversky), but also because the probability of a wave of lawsuits in the future cannot be reliably linked to the incidence of such lawsuits in the past. Limited liability gave investors peace of mind, and made investing fun. It thereby greatly increased the supply of risk capital available for entrepreneurship and propelled economic growth.

Moreover, the New York law made it possible to establish the principle of portfolio diversification, something we all take for granted today but which was new then. Before limited liability was a basic legal principle, people rationally would not diversify their portfolios, fearing the reprisals they might face if any one of their investments turned out badly.

Inventions also accompany major social changes, and this relates to the founding of the Deutsche Bank in 1870, just one year before the founding of the modern German nation in 1871. According to the book *Die Deutsche Bank 1870–1995*, by Lothar Gall, Gerald D. Feldman, Harold James, and colleagues (1995), the motivation of the Deutsche Bank's founders, Adelbert Delbrück and Ludwig Bamberger, was tied to the development of the German nation-state under Bismarck.

According to the historian Benedict Anderson, the large nation-state was itself a mostly nineteenth-century invention. The nation-state involved a new psychology, what Anderson called (as in the title of his 1983 book) an *imagined community* of people who cannot possibly know each other personally but who feel as if they do know each other, as an extension of our primitive sense of family. The imagined community allows cooperation on the scale of a nation, opening up many possibilities. The nation-state was based, in his words, on "a deep, horizontal comradeship" (Anderson 1983, 22).

The concept of the nation-state grew out of a number of revolutions, such as the English Civil War of 1642–1651, the Glorious Revolution of 1688, the American Revolutionary War of 1776–1783, the French Revolution of 1789–1899, and the revolutions of 1848—the so-called Spring of Nations—throughout much of Europe. The revolutions had their effect gradually: states were eventually based squarely on the concept of equal citizenship rather than on feudal hierarchies, whose vestiges had been slow to disappear over much of Europe. The nation-state replaced the monarchy, which had a hierarchical view of society that was not as effective at producing cooperative action.

The invention of the nation-state required the adoption of a standard language. In France, at the time of the French Revolution in 1789, there was a hodgepodge of dialects, not a unified French language. One of the things that had to be done after the Revolution was to teach the French to speak French. Similarly, over the years, the German-speaking people of Europe gradually became united on the concept of High German.

These language advances were paralleled by advances in bureaucratic procedures, and in business entity forms, standardized at the level of the

nation. These bureaucratic standardizations accelerated the economies of scale of the larger national economies.

The modern Olympic Games (which had been suspended after AD 393) were an invention of Pierre de Coubertin, who conceived the idea of participation by countries and of rotating the host from country to country, thereby showcasing the nation-states, not just the individual athletes. The first modern games occurred in 1896. This was part of the nation-state movement, for it created a sense of nation as a cooperative element of a world order.

The economies of scale in operations for nation-states were enhanced in the late nineteenth century by the rapid advances in information technology. The development of a modern postal system in the nineteenth century was an important advance, involving innovations such as the attaching of numeric addresses to homes and businesses and the spreading of post offices into every neighborhood. The invention of the typewriter, the filing cabinet, and carbon paper sped up and expanded the application of information technology and made it possible to develop procedures whereby a very large organization could monitor corruption.

The motivation of the founders of Deutsche Bank was tied to the development of the German nation-state (Gall et al. 1985). A new nation built on a large scale would create opportunities for a grander multinational, with many offices domestically and abroad, exploiting local knowledge and enjoying scale economies. Germany was an ideal place to launch such an endeavor, with its advanced information technology and high bureaucratic tradition. Delbrück and Bamberger reasoned, based on ideas about the functioning of large multinationals, that such a firm would be a huge success, and what we see today is evidence that they were absolutely right.

Opportunities and Challenges for Financial Innovation

We are starting to see activities that go beyond the economies of scale of the nation-state to encompass world organizations. The EU, with its Economic and Monetary Union, established in the 1990s, is a recent example, facilitating business arrangements that can operate on a large scale.

The development of English language instruction for young people around the world has created a new lingua franca that facilitates even more the development of new forms of business, and on a larger scale. The recognition of the importance of a world language, despite our con-

tinuing commitment to our regional languages, is an important sign of a new enlightenment that will produce many economic benefits and facilitate the adoption of important new financial forms.

The achievements of the G-20 Pittsburg Summit in 2009 are historic in that they represent a compact among the peoples of the leading countries of the world, moving even further beyond the nation-state. "Our Framework for Strong, Sustainable and Balanced Growth is a compact that commits us to work together to assess how our policies fit together, to evaluate whether they are collectively consistent with more sustainable and balanced growth, and to act as necessary to meet our common objectives." (Leaders' Statement 2009, preamble, paragraph 15)

The Summit Declaration also establishes that there is a new enlightenment afoot in the world today regarding the sources of economic fluctuations: "We pledge to avoid destabilizing booms and busts in asset and credit prices and adopt macroeconomic policies, consistent with price stability, that promote adequate and balanced global demand." (Leaders' Statement 2009, preamble, paragraph 14)

In thinking about these things, we have to recognize that it is the inventiveness of our people that should be fostered and facilitated. The economies of the world have reached a high level of performance by means of a wide variety of financial inventions. We also must be aware that the very process of invention carries with it the risk of accidents that can set back the entire process, with the public demanding better controls over financial innovation.

The Chernobyl nuclear disaster in 1986, for example, reduced public support for nuclear power and put a virtual halt to the construction of new nuclear power facilities for years. But an international regulatory response, notably the Early Notification and Assistance Convention of 1986, signed in Vienna, and the Convention on Nuclear Safety of 1994, also signed in Vienna, made possible the resumption and expansion of nuclear power facilities. This regulatory response went hand in hand with innovations in nuclear power plant structures and procedures. Nuclear power suffered yet another setback with the 2011 Tōhoku earthquake and tsunami in Japan, but once again an innovative regulatory response to that event has begun (World Nuclear Association 2012). I am hopeful that the same kind of international regulatory response is happening today in response to the current financial crisis.

The world financial crisis that began in the United States in 2007 is a bit like these nuclear disasters in that it involved relatively untested financial innovations escaping the firm hand of regulators. The securitization of

mortgages, including subprime mortgages, and the breakdown of these into risk classes suitable for dissemination to portfolios around the world were genuine advances, but the safety measures were inadequate. Financial institutions either were effectively unregulated or were able to hide their exposure to systemic risks from their regulators. There was a decline in the integrity of many real estate appraisals. There were faulty estimates of the risk of these securities by the credit rating agencies. These institutions, designed to promote the safety of investors, were faulty.

The regulatory response to date, including the Basel III bank reforms and the Dodd-Frank Act in the United States, are impressive beginnings of a rational response to this crisis. But the implementation of these reforms has been proceeding slowly, and much more remains to be done. Many of the responses will take the form of new financial innovations, propelled by our understanding of the financial theory that is evolving and responding to the crisis.

I trust that the examples here have illustrated that financial innovation is an incremental process that has been going on for centuries and that brings together creative ideas from people with many different perspectives. This supports the idea that the final solution to the world financial crises must come from the further encouragement of just this process. The solution cannot come just from the government or just from a political process. That would be like asking the political leaders for a design for a new locomotive or supersonic jet.

I see the essays collected in this book as wonderful examples of some of the best such thinking, representing the financial progress that is going on around the world today, progress that can contribute ultimately to yield just such new designs.

I am very honored by this set of essays on the occasion of my receiving the Deutsche Bank Prize in Financial Economics. I feel unworthy of the prize. I am reminded of Isaac Newton's statement, "If I have seen a little further it is by standing on the shoulders of Giants." I thought I would consider here the many, many others who have created the foundations of financial theory and made financial institutions work as well as they do today.

References

Anderson, Benedict. 1983. *Imagined Communities: Reflections on the Origin and Spread of Nationalism*. London: Verso.

Gall, Lothar, Gerald D. Feldman, Harold James, Carl-Ludwig Holtfrerich, and Hans E. Büschgen. 1995. *Die Deutsche Bank 1870–1995*. Munich: Verlag C. H. Beck.

Leaders' Statement. 2009. Leaders' Statement, G-20 Pittsburgh Summit. Available at http://ec.europa.eu/commission_2010-2014/president/pdf/statement_20090826_en_2.pdf.

Moss, David. 2004. *When All Else Fails: The Government as Ultimate Risk Manager*. Cambridge, MA: Harvard University Press.

Schmookler, Jacob. 1966. *Invention and Economic Growth*. Cambridge, MA: Harvard University Press.

World Nuclear Association. 2012. Nuclear Power Plants and Earthquakes. Available at http://www.world-nuclear.org/info/inf18.html.

FINANCIAL INNOVATION: TOO MUCH OR TOO LITTLE?;
ED. BY MICHAEL HALIASSOS.
                              Cloth   252 P.
CAMBRIDGE: MIT PRESS, 2013

ED: GOETHE UNIVERSITY FRANKFURT. NEW COLLECTION
ON CAUSES OF RECENT FINANCIAL CRISIS.
LCCN 2012-14694
  ISBN 0262018292   **Library PO#** AP-SLIPS

                                   List   35.00   USD
  9395 NATIONAL UNIVERSITY LIBRAR   **Disc**   14.0%
  App. Date   5/07/14   SOC-SCI   8214-09 **Net**   30.10   USD

SUBJ: 1. FINANCIAL ENGINEERING. 2. FINANCIAL
CRISES. 3. FINANCE.

CLASS HG176.7   DEWEY# 331.   LEVEL ADV-AC

YBP Library Services

FINANCIAL INNOVATION: TOO MUCH OR TOO LITTLE?;
ED. BY MICHAEL HALIASSOS.
                              Cloth   252 P.
CAMBRIDGE: MIT PRESS, 2013

ED: GOETHE UNIVERSITY FRANKFURT. NEW COLLECTION
ON CAUSES OF RECENT FINANCIAL CRISIS.
  LCCN 2012-14694
  ISBN 0262018292   **Library PO#** AP-SLIPS

                                   List   35.00   USD
  9395 NATIONAL UNIVERSITY LIBRAR   **Disc**   14.0%
  App. Date   5/07/14   SOC-SCI   8214-09 **Net**   30.10   USD

SUBJ: 1. FINANCIAL ENGINEERING. 2. FINANCIAL
CRISES. 3. FINANCE.

CLASS HG176.7   DEWEY# 331.   LEVEL ADV-AC

2

Psychology and the Financial Crisis of 2007–2008

Nicholas C. Barberis

The field of behavioral finance investigates whether certain financial phenomena are the result of less than fully rational behavior on the part of some agents in the economy. For guidance on *how* people deviate from full rationality, it advocates a close reading of research in psychology. The field has focused, with some success, on three areas of application: the pricing of financial assets, the portfolio choice and trading decisions of investors, and the behavior of firm managers.

Can behavioral finance offer a useful perspective on the financial crisis of 2007–2008? In particular, can ideas from psychology help us make sense of the crisis? I suspect they can, but it is still too early to be sure. The process of gathering and analyzing data from the crisis period is far from over. Researchers may eventually conclude that psychological factors *were* important during the crisis, but they may also conclude that they were not of first-order significance. In this chapter, I speculate about some ways in which concepts from psychology *may* be helpful for understanding the crisis. I do not attempt a comprehensive discussion but simply sketch a few specific ideas.[1]

Bubbles

A central element in many discussions of the financial crisis is the idea that there was a real estate "bubble": that, by 2006, owing to a friction of some kind, or to irrational thinking, real estate prices had been pushed up to unsustainably high levels. According to a common narrative, the bubble burst, triggering widespread defaults on subprime loans, dragging down the value of banks' subprime-linked holdings, and setting off a run on the banking system.[2]

While many commentators are very confident that we witnessed a bubble, it is hard to know for sure that this was the case. Still, it is a

reasonable hypothesis. And the fact that a bubble may have played a critical role in recent events has, not surprisingly, led many observers to call for more research on why bubbles form.

I agree with this call for action. At the same time, it is important to note that there is *already* a lot of research, some of it done by behavioral finance scholars, about the formation of bubbles—in short, about why an asset class might become overvalued. The problem may not be that we lack theories of bubble formation but rather that we have too many such theories. As a result, rather than rushing to develop entirely new theories of bubbles, we should perhaps first test and refine the theories we already have.

It may be useful to list some of the theories of asset market overvaluation that already exist in the behavioral finance literature. The theories can be categorized based on whether they focus on investor *beliefs* or on investor *preferences*.

On the beliefs side, there are perhaps three main theories. The first argues that a bubble forms when investors disagree sharply about an asset's future prospects *and* there are short-sale constraints (Miller 1977; Harrison and Kreps 1978; Scheinkman and Xiong 2003; Hong and Stein 2007). The logic is straightforward. Suppose that some investors are very bullish about an asset's prospects, while others are very bearish. In the presence of short-sale constraints, the price of the asset will only reflect the views of the bullish: bearish investors will stay out of the market. In other words, the asset will be overvalued.[3]

Another belief-based theory of overvaluation argues that bubbles arise because investors extrapolate past outcomes—returns, earnings growth, or default rates—too far into the future (Lakonishok, Shleifer, and Vishny 1994; Barberis, Shleifer, and Vishny 1998; Greenwood and Hanson 2010). This assumption is usually motivated by Kahneman and Tversky's (1974) representativeness heuristic. According to this heuristic, people expect even small samples of data to reflect the properties of the parent population. As a result, they draw overly strong inferences from these small samples, and this can lead to overextrapolation. Chapter 5, a reprint of Barberis and Shleifer (2003), presents a model of bubble formation based on overextrapolation of past returns, itself motivated by representativeness.

A third belief-based theory of bubble formation is based on overconfidence—specifically, on the idea that people overestimate the precision of their forecasts (Daniel, Hirshleifer, and Subrahmanyam 1998). According to this theory, when investors, in an effort to estimate an asset's

fundamental value, gather and analyze information, they become over-confident about the usefulness of this information. For example, if they uncover favorable information about the asset, their overconfidence about how reliable the information is leads them to push the price of the asset up too high.

While most models of bubble formation are belief-based, there are also some preference-based models. One theory, for example, argues that, after investors experience gains in their holdings of an asset, they become less risk averse because of a "house money" effect: in short, having experienced gains, they are less concerned about future losses because any losses will be cushioned by the prior gains. Their reduced risk aversion leads them to buy the asset even more enthusiastically, thereby pushing its price up even further (Thaler and Johnson 1990; Barberis, Huang, and Santos 2001).

Another, quite different preference-based model of overvaluation argues that bubbles are particularly likely to occur in stocks related to a new technology (Barberis and Huang 2008). The reason is that investors view these stocks as lottery-like: should the new technology deliver on its early promise, some of the stocks may experience huge increases in value. Given that many people have a strong preference for lottery-like payoffs—perhaps because, as Kahneman and Tversky (1979) argue, the brain overweights low probabilities—they may overvalue these stocks. A theory of this type may be particularly suited to thinking about the high valuations of U.S. technology stocks in the late 1990s.

Of all these models, the one that may be most useful for understanding the recent behavior of the real estate market is the second type of belief-based model: the model that argues that bubbles occur because, perhaps owing to the representativeness heuristic, people overextrapolate the past when making forecasts about the future. On one level, we can apply this idea to home buyers and say that, when forecasting the future growth in house prices, they overextrapolated the past growth in these prices. This led them to overpay for their new homes and to take out loans with excessively high loan-to-value ratios.

In order to generate a real estate bubble, however, it is not enough to assume that households were overextrapolating. Since homes are usually purchased with the help of outside financing, we need to argue that the people involved in the provision of this outside financing were *also* over-extrapolating. In more detail, the story might go as follows. A real estate bubble formed because of an oversupply of credit to home buyers, principally in the form of subprime loans. This in turn occurred because,

through the process of securitization, the subprime loans could be used to manufacture securities that investors were very enthusiastic about, namely, securities with AAA ratings. Crucially, investors were *too* enthusiastic about these securities, because the AAA ratings were often not truly deserved.

It is here, in the rating agencies, that overextrapolation may have had its greatest impact. The agencies may have given AAA ratings to securities that did not truly deserve them because they extrapolated the past growth in home prices too far into the future, which in turn led them to severely underestimate the level of future subprime defaults. The overextrapolation may have occurred because analysts naively applied the representativeness heuristic; but it may also have occurred because they *wanted* to believe that house prices would keep rising, a belief that the representativeness heuristic made particularly easy to embrace. I return to this last idea below.[4]

In summary, then, while an account of the recent behavior of the real estate market sounds different, in many of its details, from accounts of other perceived bubbles—the U.S. stock market in the 1920s and the 1990s, the Japanese real estate and stock markets in the late 1980s, not to mention the South Sea Bubble of 1720 and the tulip mania of the 1630s—all of these episodes may nonetheless have at least one important driving force in common: a tendency on the part of some market participants to extrapolate past price increases too far into the future.

Cognitive Dissonance and Risks in the Banking System

The recent plunge in real estate prices was far more devastating to the U.S. economy than the plunge in technology stock prices a few years earlier. One possible reason for this outcome is that, in the one case, the banking system was largely unaffected, while in the other, it was severely compromised. In particular, over the course of several years leading up to 2007, banks built up large holdings of subprime loans and of subprime-linked securities. When house prices started falling, the value of these holdings also fell, triggering what Gorton (2010) describes as a crippling run on the banking system. This in turn led to a reduction in the supply of credit to the economy. By contrast, when technology stock prices collapsed, banks were barely affected: their exposure to these stocks was relatively small.

How can we understand banks' large holdings of subprime loans and of related securities? On one level, we can try to explain these holdings

by saying that they were simply the inventory that inevitably accumulates over the many weeks it can take to complete a securitization deal; that the securities were the "skin in the game" that banks were required to have in order to satisfy investors; or that, since the securities were earning a return that was higher than their funding cost, it was profitable to hold them, at least in the short term.

The problem with these explanations, of course, is that banks' sub-prime-linked holdings also carried some very significant risks. If house prices were to fall, the value of these holdings would drop precipitously. Given that the banks were highly levered, often with short-term debt, this could have severe consequences. A crucial puzzle therefore remains: why, in spite of the risk, did banks take on the exposures they did?

There are perhaps three broad answers to this last question. The first, which I label the "bad incentives" view, posits that people on the mort-gage desks of banks were *aware* that, through their activities, they were exposing their institutions to significant risk, but that they simply did not care, because their compensation schemes did not force them to face the consequences of the risks they were taking (Acharya et al. 2009). In many cases, they were compensated largely on the size of the deals they were structuring, and not on the long-term performance of those deals.

The second explanation for banks' large holdings of subprime-linked securities can be labeled the "bad models" view. It says that the people on the mortgage desks of banks were genuinely unaware of the risk embedded in their subprime holdings, and that this lack of awareness was due to faulty reasoning. For example, they, too, may have extrapo-lated the past growth in real estate prices too far into the future. The models they used to value their positions incorporated this faulty belief and, as a result, did not reveal any alarming risks.

In appealing to faulty reasoning, the "bad models" view is implicitly assuming that in 2006, say, a *rational* individual with the right incentives would have known that banks' subprime-linked holdings were very risky. A third view, the "bad luck" view, disputes this. According to this view, expressed by Maria Vassalou in chapter 11, a rational individual, even one with the right incentives, would *not* have assigned a high probability, ex ante, to the poor subsequent performance of subprime-linked securi-ties. This poor performance was simply bad luck: the realization of a state of the world that a rational observer in 2006 would have deemed very unlikely.

While all three of these views are defensible, I am skeptical of the bad luck view. If a rational observer had carefully and exhaustively examined

the quality of the subprime loans being extended in the run-up to the crisis, it seems likely that he would have raised at least a few red flags.[5]

The bad incentives and bad models views, by contrast, seem more plausible. At the same time, even these hypotheses are not quite satisfactory. After all, the mortgage desks of the largest banks were generally staffed by highly intelligent and capable individuals. How could they allow sloppy reasoning to mislead them about the risks they were taking? In other words, how plausible is the bad models view?

It is also unclear how plausible it is that traders *knowingly* exposed their banks and the broader financial system to risk simply because of bad incentives, in other words, simply because they wanted a larger end-of-year bonus. A fundamental idea in social psychology is that people do not only want to make money; they also want to feel good about themselves, and it is hard to feel good about oneself if one is knowingly doing something that is potentially ruinous to others. So if a trader was aware that his business model posed serious risks to his firm, he might limit the scale of his activities, even if he could earn more money by expanding it further.

If the bad incentives and bad models views do not tell the whole story, how *can* we understand the large subprime positions that banks built up? Here is an alternative hypothesis. Under this hypothesis, traders on mortgage desks were vaguely aware that their business model might entail serious risks. However, by *manipulating their beliefs*, they deluded themselves into thinking that their business model was *not* risky but, rather, worth pursuing.

One way to put this idea on firmer psychological footing is through the concept of cognitive dissonance. Cognitive dissonance is the discomfort we feel when we take an action that conflicts with our typically positive self-image. Of particular importance is what people often do to remove the feeling of discomfort: they manipulate their beliefs.

For example, smokers often experience cognitive dissonance. A smoker will say to himself, "I am a sensible person, so why am I doing something that is bad for my health?" To reduce the dissonance that he feels, he can stop smoking—but that is hard to do. Instead, he manipulates his beliefs and convinces himself that smoking is *not*, after all, as risky as some say. He may, for example, remind himself of the eighty-five-year old man who lives down the street and who, despite smoking for much of his life, seems to be doing just fine.

How can we use cognitive dissonance to formalize the story I told above? If a trader on the mortgage desk of a bank begins to sense that the holdings of subprime securities he is building up may pose serious

risks to his institution and to the broader financial system, this will threaten his positive self-image—specifically, his self-image as an upstanding person whose work is valuable to society—and will therefore create uncomfortable dissonance. After all, he does not want to believe that, while enriching himself, he is putting many others at risk. To remove the dissonance, he could resign his position—but that would be financially costly. Instead, he manipulates his beliefs, telling himself that his business model is *not* that risky. For example, he might stop himself from inspecting the quality of the subprime loans he is working with too closely lest he stumble on some disturbing information.[6]

A similar mechanism may have been at work in the credit rating agencies. On the one hand, an analyst at a rating agency who was being asked, by an issuing bank, to give a subprime-linked product an AAA rating had a strong financial incentive to do so, even if the rating seemed undeserved: by rating the product AAA, he would avoid losing the business to another rating agency, thereby allowing both himself and his firm to earn more money that quarter. On the other hand, the analyst would also want to be able to maintain a positive self-image: to be able to think of himself as a responsible person providing a useful service to society. Giving an AAA rating to a product that did not deserve one would make it hard to maintain a positive self-image and would immediately induce dissonance.

As with the traders on the mortgage desks of banks, the analyst may have reacted to the uncomfortable feeling of dissonance by manipulating his beliefs: by telling himself that the product he was analyzing was perhaps not that risky after all, and therefore deserving of the AAA rating. For example, he may have told himself that, since house prices had been rising for years, they were likely to keep rising, thereby ensuring that subprime defaults would remain low. The representativeness heuristic would have made this argument seem quite plausible: after all, according to that heuristic, people have a natural tendency to believe that past trends *will* continue into the future.

It is worth noting that, for at least two reasons, subprime securitization may have lent itself particularly well to belief manipulation. The first reason is that subprime-linked products were often complex. Given their intricacies, it would have taken considerable effort to disprove the claim that they were relatively safe. This may have made it easier for people to delude themselves about their risks.

The second reason why it may have been easy for people to hold distorted beliefs about the risks of subprime securities is because there was

a plausible-sounding argument that appeared to justify these beliefs. The argument was simply that, since house prices had been rising for many years, they were likely to keep rising—and if they did keep rising, then subprime defaults would be low, as would the risks of subprime-linked securities. As I noted above, the representativeness heuristic made this a particularly seductive argument.

The belief manipulation hypothesis can be thought of as an alternative to the bad incentives, bad models, and bad luck views. But it can also be thought of as a foundation for the bad models view. In the belief manipulation view, as in the bad models view, mortgage traders are unaware of the risks they are taking. The belief manipulation view tries to explain *why* they are unaware. In short, they are unaware because they choose to be.[7]

Psychological Amplification Mechanisms

A striking feature of the crisis was that, during the crisis period, many kinds of risky assets experienced dramatic price declines—price declines that were surprisingly large, given the relatively small delinquencies among subprime loans.

To explain these large price drops, researchers have focused on *institutional* amplification mechanisms. For example, if a bank's holdings of subprime-related securities decline in value, then, in order to deleverage or to meet more stringent margin requirements, the bank will have to sell some of its risky asset holdings. This will push down the value of *other* banks' holdings of risky assets, forcing them into sales of their own, thereby pushing the prices of risky assets down even further, and so on.

These loss spirals and margin spirals, described in detail by Shleifer and Vishny (1997), Gromb and Vayanos (2002), and Brunnermeier (2009), among others, were probably important in transforming relatively small subprime losses into much larger price declines on many kinds of risky assets. However, *psychological* amplification mechanisms —specifically, mechanisms related to loss aversion and ambiguity aversion, two concepts that have been extensively studied in behavioral finance—may also have played a role. In short, the idea is that, after suffering losses in their risky asset holdings, both institutional and individual investors experienced increases in loss aversion and ambiguity aversion. This led them to reduce their holdings of risky assets, thereby pushing the prices of these assets down even further.

The idea that an increase in ambiguity aversion was central to the crisis has already been put forward (see, e.g., Caballero and Krishnamurthy 2008; Easley and O'Hara 2010; Krishnamurthy 2010). My goal here is to emphasize that this idea has strong psychological foundations. Many economists are familiar with ambiguity aversion—the notion that people are averse to situations where they do not feel able to assign probabilities to future outcomes—and are aware of the basic evidence for it, the Ellsberg paradox. However, economists are typically much less aware of a literature in psychology—one that is potentially very relevant to finance—on how ambiguity aversion can *change* over time. Two particularly insightful papers in this literature are those of Heath and Tversky (1991) and Fox and Tversky (1995).

Heath and Tversky (1991) present a theory of ambiguity aversion that they label the "competence hypothesis." The idea is that an individual can be either ambiguity averse *or* ambiguity seeking, depending on how *competent* he feels at analyzing the situation at hand. Here, "competence" refers to how much the person feels he knows about a situation relative to what could be known. According to the competence hypothesis, if the individual does not feel competent at analyzing some situation, he will be ambiguity averse. Conversely, if he does feel competent at analyzing the situation, he will be ambiguity seeking.

Through a series of ingenious studies, Heath and Tversky (1991) and Fox and Tversky (1995) acquired evidence for the competence hypothesis. One of their most striking findings is that they can alter subjects' degree of ambiguity aversion by manipulating their feelings of competence. Specifically, they are able to increase subjects' aversion to an ambiguous situation by reminding them of *another* situation that is easier to analyze; or by telling subjects that another, seemingly more able group of people, is also analyzing the same situation. For example, in one experiment, they tell their undergraduate student subjects at San Jose State University that the situation they are analyzing is also being studied by a group of graduate students at Stanford University. This news significantly increases the San Jose State students' ambiguity aversion.

These results, while fascinating in their own right, may also be useful to financial economists because they suggest a way of understanding the large declines in risky asset prices during the crisis. In the language of Heath and Tversky (1991) and Fox and Tversky (1995), once investors suffered some initial losses in their holdings of risky assets—losses that coincided with surprising and confusing developments in the market for subprime-linked securities—they felt less *competent* at analyzing

these assets. This made them more ambiguity averse, leading them to reduce their holdings of risky assets, thereby further lowering the prices of these assets.[8]

Loss aversion—Kahneman and Tversky's (1979) observation that people are much more sensitive to losses than to gains of the same magnitude—is perhaps even more familiar to economists than ambiguity aversion. Of particular relevance here, however, is some evidence that economists are less aware of, namely, evidence that the degree of loss aversion can change over time, depending on experienced gains and losses. Specifically, in a series of experiments, Thaler and Johnson (1990) showed that subjects who experienced a loss subsequently became *more* loss averse, refusing to take gambles that, in the absence of the prior loss, they would have taken. It is still not fully understood what drives this effect, but a natural interpretation is that, after suffering through one painful loss, people cannot face the idea of going through another loss. In short, their loss aversion increases.

It is clear how changes in loss aversion could have aggravated the collapse in risky asset prices during the crisis. The initial price declines forced many investors to endure painful losses. As suggested by Thaler and Johnson (1990), these losses may have made investors more loss averse, leading them to reduce their risky asset holdings and thereby causing further price declines.[9]

Conclusion

This book is, in part, about financial innovation. In general, the field of behavioral finance takes a favorable view of financial innovation. After all, a major theme of behavioral finance research is that people often make suboptimal financial decisions. If this is the case, then financial innovations can play a useful role in helping people make better decisions. Indeed, over the past few years, a new branch of behavioral finance has emerged—a branch sometimes known as "prescriptive behavioral finance"—whose goal is precisely to design innovations that can help people achieve better financial outcomes (Thaler and Sunstein 2008).

While financial innovations can be useful in preventing psychological factors from leading people astray, the discussion above suggests that the same psychological factors can make certain innovations dangerous. This may be particularly true for innovations that are *complex*. If an innovation is complex, it is easier for people supplying the innovation to convince themselves that it is *not* flawed, even if, in fact, it is; this may then

lead them to market the innovation too aggressively. Moreover, the failure of a complex financial innovation may have large amplifying effects because it may cause investors to feel less competent at analyzing risky assets in general, and hence to drive the prices of these assets down.

Most of the ideas for financial reform that have been proposed over the past few years are aimed at the *institutional* failures that contributed to the crisis. While it is too early to be sure, it is very possible that psychological factors were also central to the crisis. As such, it may be important to think about reforms that can address both the institutional *and* the psychological failures. In short, the financial crisis presents finance researchers, and perhaps behavioral finance researchers in particular, with a challenge: to design a financial system that can mute the impact of irrational thinking and prevent it from adversely affecting the real economy in the way that it may recently have done. This is a difficult challenge—but it may be one of the most important facing us today.

Acknowledgments

I am grateful to Malcolm Baker, James Choi, Kent Daniel, Xavier Gabaix, Michael Haliassos, Jonathan Ingersoll, Augustin Landier, Steven Malliaris, Andrew Metrick, and Andrei Shleifer for very helpful comments.

Notes

1. See Akerlof and Shiller (2009) and Shefrin (2009) for more extensive psychology-based accounts of the crisis.

2. The term "bubble" is widely used but rarely defined, probably because it is hard to define. A working definition for the purposes of this note is: a bubble is an episode in which irrational thinking or a friction causes the price of an asset to rise to a level that is higher than it would be in the absence of the friction or the irrationality; and, moreover, the price level is such that a rational observer, armed with all available information, would forecast a low long-term return on the asset.

3. There is a second channel through which disagreement and short-sale constraints can lead to overvaluation. If there is disagreement about an asset's future prospects, the asset's price will be higher than its holders' valuation of its future cash flows because these holders believe they can sell to other more optimistic investors in the near future. This dynamic channel is the focus of Harrison and Kreps (1978) and Scheinkman and Xiong (2003).

4. Some countries, of course, experienced dramatic increases in real estate prices even in the absence of much securitized finance. In these cases, the overextrapolation hypothesis, while essentially the same, may take a simpler form: that banks extrapolated the low past rates of mortgage default too far into the future and, as a result, made many imprudent loans.

5. There is some preliminary evidence consistent with the claim that the poor performance of subprime-linked securities was predictable through careful analysis. In an interview reported by McLean and Nocera (2010), a prominent hedge fund manager stated that a significant number of fixed-income hedge funds bet against subprime securities. And according to several accounts of the crisis, the two banks with perhaps the most respected risk management organizations, Goldman Sachs and J.P. Morgan, reduced their exposure to subprime loans before the worst of the crisis hit. Much more data on these issues is clearly needed, however.

6. I am by no means the first to propose that belief manipulation played a role in the crisis. Many accounts of recent events, both academic and non-academic, have also suggested it. In particular, see Benabou (forthcoming) for a formalization of ideas related to those I present here. For a discussion of the research in psychology on cognitive dissonance, see Kunda (1999) and chapter 6 of Aronson, Wilson, and Akert (2005).

7. See Gennaioli, Shleifer, and Vishny (2012) for another possible foundation for the bad models view, namely, that market participants neglect unlikely bad scenarios.

8. More generally, the findings of Heath and Tversky (1991) and Fox and Tversky (1995) may be useful for understanding the high empirical return volatility of many risky asset classes. If an asset class performs poorly, investors may feel less competent at analyzing it, increasing their ambiguity aversion and triggering selling and further price declines. Conversely, if an asset class performs well, investors may feel *more* competent at analyzing it, decreasing their ambiguity aversion and leading to purchases and further price increases.

9. The argument in this section is related to that of Cochrane (2009). He argues that the initial declines in risky asset prices brought investors' consumption closer to their habit level of consumption. This increased their risk aversion, leading to further declines in risky asset prices.

References

Acharya, V., T. Cooley, M. Richardson, and I. Walter. 2009. Manufacturing Tail Risk: A Perspective on the Financial Crisis of 2007–2009. *Foundations and Trends in Finance* 4: 247–325.

Akerlof, G., and R. Shiller. 2009. *Animal Spirits*. Princeton, NJ: Princeton University Press.

Aronson, E., T. Wilson, and R. Akert. 2005. *Social Psychology*. Englewood Cliffs, NJ: Prentice Hall.

Barberis, N., and M. Huang. 2008. Stocks as Lotteries: The Implications of Probability Weighting for Security Prices. *American Economic Review* 98: 2066–2100.

Barberis, N., M. Huang, and T. Santos. 2001. Prospect Theory and Asset Prices. *Quarterly Journal of Economics* 116: 1–53.

Barberis, N., and A. Shleifer. 2003. Style Investing. *Journal of Financial Economics* 68: 161–199.

Barberis, N., A. Shleifer, and R. Vishny. 1998. A Model of Investor Sentiment. *Journal of Financial Economics* 49: 307–343.

Benabou, R. Forthcoming. Groupthink: Collective Delusions in Organizations and Markets. *Review of Economic Studies*.

Brunnermeier, M. 2009. Deciphering the Liquidity and Credit Crunch 2007–2008. *Journal of Economic Perspectives* 23: 77–100.

Caballero, R., and A. Krishnamurthy. 2008. Musical Chairs: A Comment on the Credit Crisis. *Banque de France Financial Stability Review* 11: 1–3.

Cochrane, J. 2009. Asset Pricing after the Crash. Manuscript, University of Chicago.

Daniel, K., D. Hirshleifer, and A. Subrahmanyam. 1998. Investor Psychology and Security Market Under- and Overreactions. *Journal of Finance* 53: 1839–1885.

Easley, D., and M. O'Hara. 2010. Liquidity and Valuation in an Uncertain World. *Journal of Financial Economics* 97: 1–11.

Fox, C., and A. Tversky. 1995. Ambiguity Aversion and Comparative Ignorance. *Quarterly Journal of Economics* 110: 585–603.

Gennaioli, N., A. Shleifer, and R. Vishny. 2012. Neglected Risks, Financial Innovation, and Financial Fragility. *Journal of Financial Economics* 104: 452–468.

Gorton, G. 2010. *Slapped by the Invisible Hand: The Panic of 2007*. Oxford: Oxford University Press.

Greenwood, R., and S. Hanson. 2010. Issuer Quality and the Credit Cycle. Working paper, Harvard University.

Gromb, D., and D. Vayanos. 2002. Equilibrium and Welfare in Markets with Financially Constrained Arbitrageurs. *Journal of Financial Economics* 66: 361–407.

Harrison, M., and D. Kreps. 1978. Speculative Investor Behavior in a Stock Market with Heterogeneous Expectations. *Quarterly Journal of Economics* 92: 323–336.

Heath, C., and A. Tversky. 1991. Preference and Belief: Ambiguity and Competence in Choice under Uncertainty. *Journal of Risk and Uncertainty* 4: 5–28.

Hong, H., and J. Stein. 2007. Disagreement and the Stock Market. *Journal of Economic Perspectives* 21: 109–128.

Kahneman, D., and A. Tversky. 1974. Judgment under Uncertainty: Heuristics and Biases. *Science* 185: 1124–1131.

Kahneman, D., and A. Tversky. 1979. Prospect Theory: An Analysis of Decision under Risk. *Econometrica* 47: 263–291.

Krishnamurthy, A. 2010. Amplification Mechanisms in Liquidity Crises. *American Economic Journal: Macroeconomics* 2: 1–30.

Kunda, Z. 1999. *Social Cognition: Making Sense of People*. Cambridge, MA: MIT Press.

Lakonishok, J., A. Shleifer, and R. Vishny. 1994. Contrarian Investment, Extrapolation, and Risk. *Journal of Finance* 49: 1541–1578.

McLean, B., and J. Nocera. 2010. *All the Devils Are Here: The Hidden History of the Financial Crisis*. London: Penguin Group.

Miller, E. 1977. Risk, Uncertainty, and Divergence of Opinion. *Journal of Finance* 32: 1151–1168.

Scheinkman, J., and W. Xiong. 2003. Overconfidence and Speculative Bubbles. *Journal of Political Economy* 111: 1183–1219.

Shefrin, H. 2009. How Psychological Pitfalls Generated the Global Financial Crisis. Working paper, Santa Clara University.

Shleifer, A., and R. Vishny. 1997. The Limits of Arbitrage. *Journal of Finance* 52: 35–55.

Thaler, R., and E. Johnson. 1990. Gambling with the House Money and Trying to Break Even: The Effects of Prior Outcomes on Risky Choice. *Management Science* 36: 643–660.

Thaler, R., and C. Sunstein. 2008. *Nudge: Improving Decisions about Health, Wealth, and Happiness*. New Haven, CT: Yale University Press.

3 Understanding Inflation-Indexed Bond Markets

John Y. Campbell, Robert J. Shiller, and Luis M. Viceira

In recent years, government-issued inflation-indexed bonds have become available in a number of countries and have provided a fundamentally new instrument for use in retirement saving. Because expected inflation varies over time, conventional, nonindexed (nominal) Treasury bonds are not safe in real terms, and because short-term real interest rates vary over time, Treasury bills are not safe assets for long-term investors. Inflation-indexed bonds fill this gap by offering a truly riskless long-term investment (Campbell and Shiller 1997; Campbell and Viceira 2001, 2002; Brennan and Xia 2002; Campbell, Chan, and Viceira 2003; Wachter 2003).

The UK government first issued inflation-indexed bonds in the early 1980s, and the U.S. government followed suit by introducing Treasury inflation-protected securities (TIPS) in 1997. Inflation-indexed government bonds are also available in many other countries, including Canada, France, and Japan. These bonds are now widely accepted financial instruments. However, their history raises some new puzzles that deserve investigation.

First, given that the real interest rate is determined in the long run by the marginal product of capital, one might expect inflation-indexed bond yields to be extremely stable over time. But whereas ten-year annual yields on UK inflation-indexed bonds averaged about 3.5 percent during the 1990s (Barr and Campbell 1997), and those on U.S. TIPS exceeded 4 percent around the turn of the millennium, by the mid-2000s, yields on both countries' bonds averaged below 2 percent, bottoming out at around 1 percent in early 2008 before spiking to near 3 percent in late 2008. The massive decline in long-term real interest rates from the 1990s to the 2000s is one puzzle, and the instability in 2008 is another.

Second, in recent years inflation-indexed bond prices have tended to move opposite to stock prices, so that these bonds have a negative "beta" with respect to the stock market and can be used to hedge equity risk.

This has been even more true of prices on nominal government bonds, although these bonds behaved very differently in the 1970s and 1980s (Campbell, Sunderam, and Viceira 2009). The reason for the negative beta on inflation-indexed bonds is not well understood.

Third, given integrated world capital markets, one might expect that inflation-indexed bond yields would be similar around the world. But this is not always the case. During the first half of 2000, the yield gap between U.S. and UK inflation-indexed bonds was more than two percentage points, although yields have since converged. In January 2008, ten-year yields were similar in the United States and the UK, but elsewhere yields ranged from 1.1 percent in Japan to almost 2.0 percent in France (according to Bloomberg data). Yield differentials were even larger at long maturities, with UK yields well below 1 percent and French yields well above 2 percent.

To understand these phenomena, it is useful to distinguish three major influences on inflation-indexed bond yields: current and expected future short-term real interest rates, differences in expected returns on long-term and short-term inflation-indexed bonds caused by risk premiums (which can be negative if these bonds are valuable hedges), and differences in expected returns on long-term and short-term bonds caused by liquidity premiums or technical factors that segment the bond markets. The expectations hypothesis of the term structure, applied to real interest rates, states that only the first influence is time-varying, whereas the other two are constant. However, there is considerable evidence against this hypothesis for nominal Treasury bonds, so it is important to allow for the possibility that risk and liquidity premiums are time-varying.

The path of real interest rates is undoubtedly a major influence on inflation-indexed bond yields. Indeed, before TIPS were issued, Campbell and Shiller (1997) argued that one could anticipate how their yields would behave by applying the expectations hypothesis of the term structure to real interest rates. A first goal of this chapter is to compare the history of inflation-indexed bond yields with the implications of the expectations hypothesis, and to explain how shocks to short-term real interest rates are transmitted along the real yield curve.

Risk premiums on inflation-indexed bonds can be analyzed by applying theoretical models of risk and return. Two leading paradigms deliver useful insights. The consumption-based paradigm implies that risk premiums on inflation-indexed bonds over short-term debt are negative if returns on these bonds covary negatively with consumption, which will be the case if consumption growth rates are persistent (Backus and Zin

1994; Campbell 1986; Gollier 2007; Piazzesi and Schneider 2007; Wachter 2006). The capital asset pricing model (CAPM) implies that risk premiums on inflation-indexed bonds will be negative if their prices covary negatively with stock prices. The second paradigm has the advantage that it is easy to track the covariance of inflation-indexed bonds and stocks using high-frequency data on their prices, in the manner of Viceira and Mitsui (2007) and Campbell, Sunderam, and Viceira (2009).

Finally, it is important to take seriously the effects of institutional factors on inflation-indexed bond yields. Plausibly, the high TIPS yields in the first few years after their introduction were due to the slow development of TIPS mutual funds and other indirect investment vehicles. Currently, long-term inflation-indexed yields in the UK may be depressed by strong demand from UK pension funds. The volatility of TIPS yields in the fall of 2008 appears to have resulted in part from the unwinding of large institutional positions after the failure of the investment bank Lehman Brothers in September. These institutional influences on yields can alternatively be described as liquidity, market segmentation, or demand-and-supply effects (Greenwood and Vayanos 2008).

This chapter is organized as follows. Section 3.1 presents a graphical history of the inflation-indexed bond markets in the United States and the UK, discussing bond supplies, the levels of yields, and the volatility and covariances with stocks of high-frequency movements in yields. Section 3.2 asks what portion of the TIPS yield history can be explained by movements in short-term real interest rates, together with the expectations hypothesis of the term structure. This section revisits the vector autoregression (VAR) analysis of Campbell and Shiller (1997). Section 3.3 discusses the risk characteristics of TIPS and estimates a model of TIPS pricing with time-varying systematic risk, a variant of the model in Campbell, Sunderam, and Viceira (2009), to see how much of the yield history can be explained by changes in risk. Section 3.4 discusses the unusual market conditions that prevailed in the fall of 2008 and the channels through which they might have influenced inflation-indexed bond yields. Section 3,5 draws implications for investors and policy makers. An appendix available online presents technical details of our bond pricing model and of data construction.[1]

3.1 The History of Inflation-Indexed Bond Markets

Figure 3.1a shows the growth of the outstanding supply of TIPS during the period 1997–2008. From modest beginnings in 1997, TIPS grew to

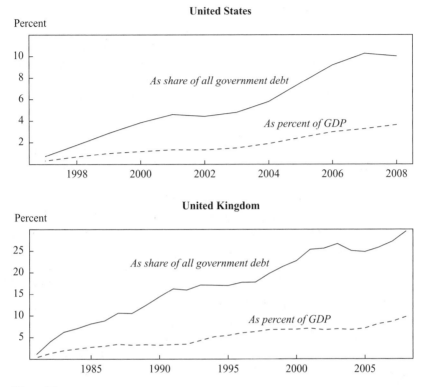

Figure 3.1
Stocks of inflation-indexed government bonds outstanding, United States (a) and United Kingdom (b). *Source:* Treasury Bulletin, various issues, table FD-2; Heriot-Watt/Faculty and Institute of Actuaries Gilt Database (http://www.ma.hw.ac.uk/~andrewc/gilts, file BGSAmounts.xls).

around 10 percent of the marketable debt of the U.S. Treasury, and more than 3.5 percent of U.S. GDP, in 2008. This growth was fairly smooth, with a minor slowdown in 2001–2002. Figure 3.1b shows a comparable history for UK inflation-indexed gilts (government bonds). From equally modest beginnings in 1982, the stock of these bonds grew rapidly and accounted for almost 30 percent of the British public debt in 2008, equivalent to about 10 percent of GDP. Growth in the inflation-indexed share of the public debt slowed in 1990–1997 and reversed in 2004–2005, but otherwise proceeded at a rapid rate.

Figure 3.2a plots yields on ten-year nominal and inflation-indexed U.S. Treasury bonds from January 1998, a year after their introduction, through March 2009.[2] The figure shows a considerable decline in both nominal and real long-term interest rates since TIPS yields peaked early

Figure 3.2
Yields on ten-year nominal and inflation-indexed government bonds, 1991–2009, United States (a) and United Kingdom (b). *Note:* Yields are calculated from spliced yields and price data of individual issuances. *Source:* Authors' calculations using data from Bloomberg and Heriot-Watt/Faculty and Institute of Actuaries Gilt Database; see the online appendix (http://kuznets.fas.harvard.edu/~campbell/papers.html) for details.

in 2000. Through 2007 the decline was roughly parallel, as inflation-indexed bond yields fell from slightly above 4 percent to slightly above 1 percent, while yields on nominal government bonds fell from around 7 percent to 4 percent. Thus, this was a period in which both nominal and inflation-indexed Treasury bond yields were driven down by a large decline in long-term real interest rates. In 2008, in contrast, nominal Treasury yields continued to decline, while TIPS yields spiked above 3 percent toward the end of the year.

Figure 3.2b shows a comparable history for the UK since the early 1990s. To facilitate comparison of the two plots, the beginning of the U.S.

sample period is marked with a vertical line. The downward trend in inflation-indexed yields is even more dramatic over this longer period. UK inflation-indexed gilts also experienced a dramatic yield spike in the fall of 2008.

Figure 3.3a plots the ten-year breakeven inflation rate, the difference between ten-year nominal and inflation-indexed Treasury bond yields. The breakeven inflation rate was fairly volatile in the first few years of the TIPS market; it then stabilized at between 1.5 and 2.0 percent a year in the early years of the 2000s before creeping up to about 2.5 percent from 2004 through 2007. In 2008 the breakeven inflation rate collapsed, reaching almost zero at the end of the year. The figure also shows, for the early years of the sample, the subsequently realized three-year inflation rate. After the first couple of years, in which there is little relationship between breakeven and subsequently realized inflation, a slight decrease in breakeven inflation between 2000 and 2002, followed by a slow increase from 2002 to 2006, is matched by similar gradual changes in realized inflation. Although this is not a rigorous test of the rationality of the TIPS market—apart from anything else, the bonds are forecasting inflation over ten years, not three years—it does suggest that inflation forecasts influence the relative pricing of TIPS and nominal Treasury bonds. We explore this issue in greater detail in the next section.

Figure 3.3b depicts the breakeven inflation history for the UK. It shows a strong decline in the late 1990s, probably associated with the granting of independence to the Bank of England by the newly elected Labour government in 1997, and a steady upward creep from 2003 to early 2008, followed by a collapse in 2008 comparable to that in the United States. Realized inflation in the UK also fell in the 1990s, albeit less dramatically than the breakeven inflation rose, and rose in the mid-2000s.

Figure 3.4b examines the short-run volatility of TIPS returns. Using daily government bond prices, with the appropriate correction for coupon payments, we calculate daily nominal return series for the on-the-run ten-year TIPS. This graph plots the annualized standard deviation of this series within a centered moving one-year window. For comparison, it also shows the corresponding annualized standard deviation for ten-year nominal Treasury bond returns, calculated from Bloomberg yield data on the assumption that the nominal bonds trade at par. The striking message of this graph is that TIPS returns have become far more volatile in recent years. In the early years, until 2002, the short-run volatility of ten-year TIPS was only about half that of ten-year nominal Treasury bonds, but

Figure 3.3
Breakeven inflation rates implied by ten-year nominal inflation-indexed bond yields, and actual three-year inflation, 1991–2009, U.S. realized and breakeven inflation rates (a) and UK realized and breakeven inflation rates (b). *Notes:* Bond yields are computed from spliced yields and price data of individual issuances. a. Annualized percent change in the Consumer Price Index over the preceding three years. b. Difference between ten-year yields of nominal and inflation-indexed bonds; monthly data. *Source:* Authors' calculations from Bloomberg and Bureau of Labor Statistics data; see the online appendix for details.

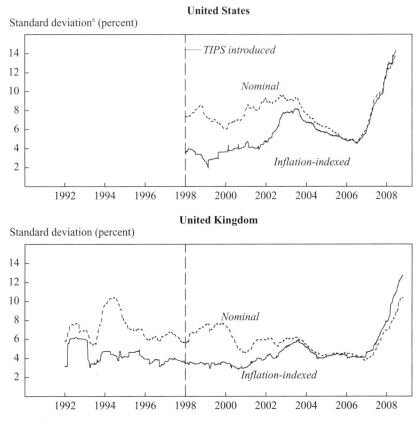

Figure 3.4
Volatility of ten-year nominal and inflation-indexed government bond returns, 1992–2009, United States (a) and United Kingdom (b). *Notes:* Bond yields are computed from spliced yields and price data of individual issuances. a. Standard deviation of daily returns on government bonds with ten years to maturity, over a one-year centered moving window. *Source:* Authors' calculations from Bloomberg data; see the online appendix for details.

the two standard deviations converged between 2002 and 2004 and have been extremely similar since then. The annualized standard deviations of both bonds ranged between 5 percent and 8 percent between 2004 and 2008, and then increased dramatically to almost 14 percent.

Mechanically, two variables drive the volatility of TIPS returns. The more important of these is the volatility of TIPS yields, which has increased over time; in recent years it has been very similar to the volatility of nominal Treasury bond yields as breakeven inflation has stabilized. A second, amplifying factor is the duration of TIPS, which has increased

as TIPS yields have declined.[3] The same two variables determine the very similar volatility patterns shown in figure 3.4b for the UK.

Figure 3.5a plots the annualized standard deviation of ten-year break-even inflation (measured in terms of the value of a bond position long a ten-year nominal Treasury bond and short a ten-year TIPS). This standard deviation trended downward from 7 percent in 1998 to about 1 percent in 2007 before spiking above 13 percent in 2008. To the extent that breakeven inflation represents the long-term inflation expectations of market participants, these expectations stabilized during most of the sample period but moved dramatically in 2008. Such a destabilization of inflation expectations should be a matter of serious concern to the Federal Reserve, although, as we discuss in section 3.4, institutional factors may have contributed to the movements in the breakeven inflation rate during the market disruption of late 2008. Figure 3.5b suggests that the Bank of England should be equally concerned by the recent destabilization of the yield spread between nominal and inflation-indexed gilts.

Figures 3.5a and 3.5b also plot the correlations of daily inflation-indexed and nominal government bond returns within a one-year moving window. Early in the period, the correlation for U.S. bonds was quite low, at about 0.2, but it increased to almost 0.9 by the middle of 2003 and stayed there until 2008. In the mid-2000s TIPS behaved like nominal Treasuries and did not exhibit independent return variation. This coupling of TIPS and nominal Treasuries ended in 2008. The same patterns are visible in the UK data.

Although TIPS have been volatile assets, this does not necessarily imply that they should command large risk premiums. According to rational asset pricing theory, the risk premium on an asset should be driven by the covariance of its returns with the marginal utility of consumption rather than by the variance of returns. One common proxy for marginal utility, used in the CAPM, is the return on an aggregate equity index. Figures 3.6a and 3.6b plot the correlations of daily inflation-indexed bond returns, nominal government bond returns, and breakeven inflation returns with daily returns on aggregate U.S. and UK stock indexes, again within a centered moving one-year window. Figures 3.7a and 3.7b repeat this exercise for betas (regression coefficients of daily bond returns and breakeven inflation on the same stock indexes).

All these figures tell a similar story. During the 2000s there was considerable instability in both countries in the correlations between government bonds of both types and stock returns, but these correlations

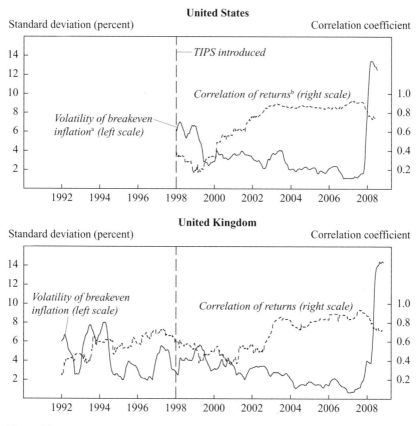

Figure 3.5
Volatility of ten-year breakeven inflation and correlation of nominal and inflation-indexed government bond returns, 1992–2009, United States (a) and United Kingdom (b). *Notes:* Bond yields are computed from spliced yields and price data of individual issuances. a. Standard deviation of daily ten-year breakeven inflation rate, measured in terms of the value of position long a ten-year nominal government bond and short a ten-year inflation-indexed bond, over a one-year moving window. b. Correlation of daily inflation-indexed and nominal bond returns within a one-year moving window. *Source:* Authors' calculations from Bloomberg data; see the online appendix for details.

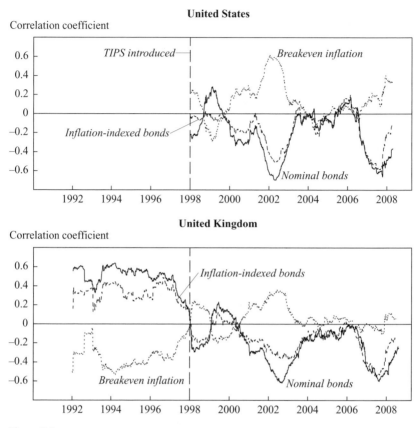

Figure 3.6
Correlations of ten-year government bond returns and breakeven inflation rates with
equity returns, 1992–2009, United States (a) and United Kingdom (b). *Notes:* Correlations
between nominal returns on the stock index of the indicated country (CRSP Value-
Weighted Index for the United States, FTSE 100 index for the UK) and either nominal
ten-year returns on the indicated bond type (computed from spliced yields and price data
of individual issuances) or returns in the breakeven inflation rate (the difference between
nominal bond returns and inflation-indexed bond returns). *Source:* Authors' calculations
from Bloomberg and Center for Research on Security Prices data; see the online appendix
for details.

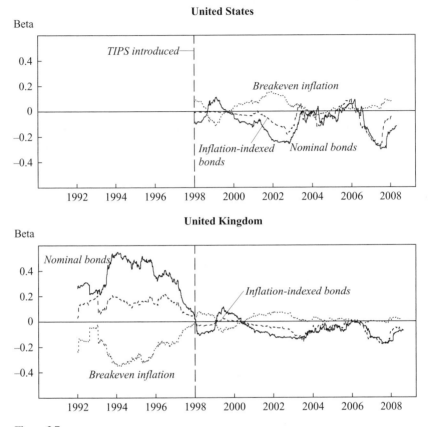

Figure 3.7
Betas of ten-year government bond returns and breakeven inflation rates with equity returns, 1992–2009, United States (a) and United Kingdom (b). *Notes:* Coefficients from a regression of either nominal ten-year returns on the indicated bond type (computed from spliced yields and price data of individual issuances) or the breakeven inflation rate (the difference between nominal bond returns and inflation-indexed bond returns) on nominal returns on the stock index of the indicated country (CRSP Value-Weighted Index for the United States, FTSE 100 index for the UK). *Source:* Authors' calculations from Bloomberg and Center for Research on Security Prices data; see the online appendix for details.

were predominantly negative, implying that government bonds can be used to hedge equity risk. To the extent that the CAPM describes risk premiums across asset classes, government bonds should have had predominantly negative rather than positive risk premiums. The negative correlation was particularly strong for nominal government bonds, because breakeven inflation was positively correlated with stock returns, especially during 2002–2003 and 2007–2008. Campbell, Sunderam, and Viceira (2009) build a model in which a changing correlation between inflation and stock returns drives changes in the risk properties of nominal Treasury bonds. That model assumes a constant equity market correlation for TIPS and thus cannot explain the correlation movements shown for TIPS in figures 3.6 and 3.7. In section 3.3 we explore the determination of TIPS risk premiums in greater detail.

3.2 Inflation-Indexed Bond Yields and the Dynamics of Short-Term Real Interest Rates

To understand the movements of inflation-indexed bond yields, it is essential first to understand how changes in short-term real interest rates propagate along the real term structure. Declining yields for inflation-indexed bonds in the 2000s may not be particularly surprising given that short-term real interest rates have also been low in this decade.

Before TIPS were introduced in 1997, Campbell and Shiller (1997) used a time-series model for the short-term real interest rate to create a hypothetical TIPS yield series under the assumption that the expectations theory of the term structure in logarithmic form, with zero log risk premiums, describes inflation-indexed bond yields. (This does not require the assumption that the expectations theory describes nominal bond yields, a model that has often been rejected in U.S. data.) In this section we update Campbell and Shiller's analysis and ask how well the simple expectations theory describes the twelve-year history of TIPS yields.

Campbell and Shiller (1997) estimated a VAR model on quarterly U.S. data over 1953–1994. Their basic VAR included the ex post real return on a three-month nominal Treasury bill, the nominal bill yield, and the once-lagged one-year inflation rate. They solved the VAR forward to create forecasts of future quarterly real interest rates at all horizons, and then aggregated the forecasts to generate the implied long-term inflation-indexed bond yield.

Table 3.1 repeats this analysis for 1982–2008. The top panel reports the estimated VAR coefficients, and the bottom panel reports selected sample

Table 3.1
Results of VAR Estimation and Observed and Hypothetical Moments of 10-Year Inflation-Indexed Bonds, United States[a]

Independent Variable	Dependent Variable		
	Inflation-Indexed Bill Return	Nominal Bill Yield	Inflation[b]
Inflation-indexed bill return	−0.06	0.01	−0.21
	(0.10)	(0.02)	(0.10)
Nominal bill yield	0.62	0.95	0.57
	(0.17)	(0.04)	(0.16)
Inflation	0.09	−0.04	0.58
	(0.08)	(0.02)	(0.08)
Constant	−0.005	0.001	0.007
	(0.002)	(0.0005)	(0.002)
R^2	0.26	0.91	0.63

Moments of 10-Year Inflation-Indexed Bonds	Observed		Hypothetical
Mean	2.66		1.04
Standard deviation	0.95		0.39
Correlation		0.71	

Notes: a. Numbers in parentheses are standard errors. b. Non-seasonally adjusted all-urban consumer price index (NSA CPI-U).
Source: Authors' regressions. Independent variables are lagged one period.

moments of the hypothetical VAR-implied ten-year TIPS yields, and for comparison the same moments of observed TIPS yields, over the period since TIPS were introduced. The table delivers several interesting results.

First, the hypothetical yields are considerably lower on average than the observed yields, with a mean of 1.04 percent compared with 2.66 percent. This implies that on average, investors demand a risk or liquidity premium for holding TIPS rather than nominal Treasuries. Second, hypothetical yields are more stable than observed yields, with a standard deviation of 0.39 percent as opposed to 0.95 percent. This reflects the fact that observed yields have declined more dramatically since 1997 than have hypothetical yields. Third, hypothetical and observed yields have a relatively high correlation of 0.71, even though no TIPS data were used to construct the hypothetical yields. Real interest rate movements do have an important effect on the TIPS market, and the VAR system is able to capture much of this effect.

Figure 3.8a shows these results in graphical form, plotting the history of the observed TIPS yield, the hypothetical VAR-implied TIPS yield,

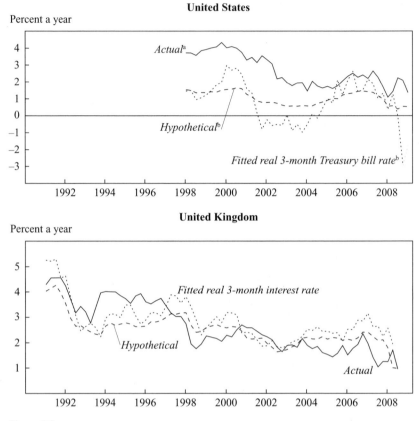

Figure 3.8
Hypothetical and actual yields on ten-year inflation-indexed bonds, United States (a) and United Kingdom (b). *Notes:* a. Quarterly averages of ten-year TIPS yields (from figure 3.2a). b. Extracted from an estimated VAR(1) model in quarterly U.S. data over 1953–1994 on the ex post real return on a three-month nominal Treasury bill, the nominal bill yield, and the lagged one-year inflation rate. *Source:* Authors' calculations from Bloomberg, Center for Research on Security Prices, and Bureau of Labor Statistics data; see the online appendix for details.

Table 3.2
Results of VAR Estimation and Observed and Hypothetical Moments of 10-Year Inflation-Indexed Bonds, United Kingdom[a]

	Dependent variable		
Independent Variable	Inflation-Indexed Bill Return	Nominal Bill Yield	Inflation[b]
Inflation-indexed bill return	0.09	–0.04	–0.39
	(0.09)	(0.03)	(0.09)
Nominal bill yield	0.42	1.07	0.82
	(0.19)	(0.05)	(0.18)
Inflation	0.02	–0.03	0.66
	(0.07)	(0.02)	(0.07)
Constant	0.0001	0.0002	0.0007
	(0.0019)	(0.0005)	(0.0018)
R^2	0.22	0.93	0.87

Moments of 10-Year Inflation-Indexed Bonds	Observed	Hypothetical
Mean	2.64	2.49
Standard deviation	1.00	0.61
Correlation	0.77	

Notes: a. Numbers in parentheses are standard errors. b. Retail price index.
Source: Authors' regressions. Independent variables are lagged one period.

and the VAR estimate of the ex ante short-term real interest rate. The sharp decline in the real interest rate in 2001 and 2002 drives down the hypothetical TIPS yield, but the observed TIPS yield is more volatile and declines more strongly. The gap between the observed TIPS yield and the hypothetical yield shrinks fairly steadily over the sample period until the very end, when the 2008 spike in the observed yield widens the gap again. These results suggest that when they were first issued, TIPS commanded a high risk or liquidity premium, which then declined until 2008.

Table 3.2 and figure 3.8b repeat these exercises for the UK. Here the hypothetical and observed yields have similar means (2.64 and 2.49 percent, respectively), but again, the standard deviation is lower for the hypothetical yield, at 0.61 percent, than for the observed yield, at 1.00 percent. The two yields have a high correlation of 0.77. The graph shows that the VAR model captures much of the decline in inflation-indexed gilt yields since the early 1990s. It is able to do this because the estimated process for the UK ex ante real interest rate is highly persistent, so that

the decline in the real rate over the sample period translates almost one for one into a declining yield on long-term inflation-indexed gilts. However, for the same reason the model cannot account for variations in the spread between the short-term expected real interest rate and the long-term inflation-indexed gilt yield.

It is notable that the expectations hypothesis of the real term structure does not explain the decline in inflation-indexed gilt yields from 2005 through 2008. A new UK accounting standard introduced in 2000, FRS17, may account for this. As Viceira and Mitsui (2003) and Dimitri Vayanos and Jean-Luc Vila (2007) explain, FRS 17 requires UK pension funds to mark their liabilities to market, using discount rates derived from government bonds. The standard was implemented, after some delay, in 2005, and it greatly increased the demand for inflation-indexed gilts from pension funds seeking to hedge their inflation-indexed liabilities.

3.3 The Systematic Risks of Inflation-Indexed Bonds

The yield history and VAR analysis presented in the previous two sections suggest that U.S. and UK inflation-indexed bonds had low risk premiums in the mid-2000s, but the former, at least, had higher risk premiums when they were first issued. In this section we use asset pricing theory to ask what fundamental properties of the macroeconomy might lead to high or low risk premiums on inflation-indexed bonds. We first use the consumption-based asset pricing framework and then present a less structured empirical analysis that relates bond risk premiums to changing covariances of bonds with stocks.

3.3.1 Consumption-Based Pricing of Inflation-Indexed Bonds

A standard paradigm for consumption-based asset pricing assumes that a representative investor has Epstein-Zin (Epstein and Zin 1989, 1991) preferences. This preference specification, a generalization of power utility, allows the coefficient of relative risk aversion γ and the elasticity of intertemporal substitution (EIS) ψ to be separate free parameters, whereas power utility restricts one to be the reciprocal of the other. Under the additional assumption that asset returns and consumption are jointly log normal and homoskedastic, the Epstein-Zin Euler equation implies that the risk premium RP on any asset i over the short-term safe asset is

$$RP_i \equiv E_t[r_{i,t+1}] - r_{f,t+1} + \frac{\sigma_i^2}{2} = \theta \frac{\sigma_{ic}}{\psi} + (1-\theta)\sigma_{iw}. \tag{3.1}$$

In words, the risk premium is defined to be the expected excess log return on the asset over the risk-free log return r_f, plus one-half its variance to convert from a geometric average to an arithmetic average, that is, to correct for Jensen's inequality. The preference parameter $\theta \equiv (1 - \gamma)/[1 - (1/\psi)]$; in the power utility case, $\gamma = 1/\psi$, so that $\theta = 1$. According to this formula, the risk premium on any asset is a weighted average of two conditional covariances, the consumption covariance σ_{ic} (scaled by the reciprocal of the EIS), which gets full weight in the power utility case, and the wealth covariance σ_{iw}. The risk premium is constant over time by the assumption of homoskedasticity.

It is tempting to treat the consumption covariance and the wealth covariance as two separate quantities, but this ignores the fact that consumption and wealth are linked by the intertemporal budget constraint and by a time-series Euler equation. By using these additional equations, one can substitute either consumption (Campbell 1993) or wealth (Restoy and Weil 1998) out of the formula for the risk premium.

The first approach explains the risk premium using covariances with the current market return and with news about future market returns; this might be called "CAPM+," as it generalizes the insight about risk that was first formalized in the CAPM. Campbell (1996) and Campbell and Tuomo Vuolteenaho (2004) pursue this approach, which can also be regarded as an empirical version of Robert Merton's (1973) intertemporal CAPM.

The second approach explains the risk premium using covariances with current consumption growth and with news about future consumption growth; this might be called "CCAPM+," as it generalizes the insight about risk that is embodied in the consumption-based CAPM with power utility. This approach has generated a large asset pricing literature in recent years (e.g., Bansal and Yaron 2004; Bansal, Khatchatrian, and Yaron 2005; Piazzesi and Schneider 2007; Bansal, Kiku, and Yaron 2007; Bansal, Dittmar, and Kiku 2009; Hansen, Heaton, and Li 2008). Some of this recent work adds heteroskedasticity to the simple homoskedastic model discussed here.

The CAPM+ approach delivers an approximate formula for the risk premium on any asset as

$$RP_i = \gamma\sigma_{iw} - (\gamma-1)\sigma_{i,TIPS},$$

where σ_{iw} is the covariance of the unexpected return on asset i with the return on the aggregate wealth portfolio, and $\sigma_{i,TIPS}$ is the covariance with the return on an inflation-indexed perpetuity.

The intuition, which dates back to Merton (1973), is that conservative long-term investors value assets that deliver high returns at times when investment opportunities are poor. Such assets hedge investors against variation in the sustainable income stream that is delivered by a given amount of wealth. In a homoskedastic model, risk premiums are constant, and the relevant measure of long-run investment opportunities is the yield on an inflation-indexed bond. Thus, the covariance with the return on an inflation-indexed perpetuity captures the intertemporal hedging properties of an asset. In equilibrium, an asset that covaries strongly with an inflation-indexed perpetuity will offer a low return as the price of the desirable insurance it offers.

Applying this formula to the inflation-indexed perpetuity itself, we find that

$$RP_{TIPS} = \gamma\sigma_{TIPS,w} - (\gamma - 1)\sigma^2_{TIPS}.$$

In words, the risk premium on a long-term inflation-indexed bond is increasing in its covariance with the wealth portfolio, as in the traditional CAPM, but decreasing in the variance of the bond return whenever the risk aversion of the representative agent is greater than 1. Paradoxically, the insurance value of inflation-indexed bonds is higher when these bonds have high short-term volatility, because in this case they hedge important variability in investment opportunities. In a traditional model with a constant real interest rate, inflation-indexed bonds have constant yields; but in this case there is no intertemporal hedging to be done, and the traditional CAPM can be used to price all assets, including inflation-indexed bonds.

The CCAPM+ approach can be written as

$$RP_i = \gamma\sigma_{ic} + \left(\gamma - \frac{1}{\psi}\right)\sigma_{ig}, \tag{3.2}$$

where σ_{ig} is the covariance of the unexpected return on asset i with revisions in expected future consumption growth $\tilde{g}_{t+1}$, defined by

$$\tilde{g}_{t+1} \equiv (E_{t+1} - E_t)\sum_{j=1}^{\infty}\rho^j \Delta c_{t+1+j}. \tag{3.3}$$

In equation (3.2) the risk premium on any asset is the coefficient of risk aversion γ times the covariance of that asset with consumption growth,

plus $(\gamma - 1/\psi)$ times the covariance of the asset with revisions in expected future consumption growth, discounted at a constant rate ρ. The second term is zero if $\gamma = 1/\psi$, the power utility case, or if consumption growth is unpredictable so that there are no revisions in expected future consumption growth. Evidence on the equity premium and the time-series behavior of real interest rates suggests that $\gamma > 1/\psi$. This implies that controlling for assets' contemporaneous consumption covariance, investors require a risk premium to hold assets that pay off when expected future consumption growth increases. Ravi Bansal and Amir Yaron (2004) use the phrase "risks for the long run" to emphasize this property of the model.

What does this model imply about the pricing of an inflation-indexed perpetuity? When expected real consumption growth increases by one percentage point, the equilibrium real interest rate increases by $1/\psi$ percentage points, and thus the return on the inflation-indexed perpetuity is given by[4]

$$r_{TIPS,t+1} = -\frac{1}{\psi}\tilde{g}_{t+1}. \tag{3.4}$$

Combining equation (3.2) with equation (3.4), one can solve for the risk premium on the inflation-indexed perpetuity:

$$RP_{TIPS} = \gamma\left(-\frac{1}{\psi}\right)\sigma_{cg} + \left(\gamma - \frac{1}{\psi}\right)\left(-\frac{1}{\psi}\right)\sigma_g^2. \tag{3.5}$$

With power utility, only the first term in equation (3.5) is nonzero. This case is described by Campbell (1986). In a consumption-based asset pricing model with power utility, assets are risky if their returns covary positively with consumption growth. Since bond prices rise when interest rates fall, bonds are risky assets if interest rates fall in response to consumption growth. Because equilibrium real interest rates are positively related to expected future consumption growth, this is possible only if positive consumption shocks drive expected future consumption growth downward, that is, if consumption growth is negatively autocorrelated. In an economy with temporary downturns in consumption, equilibrium real interest rates rise and TIPS prices fall in recessions, and therefore investors require a risk premium to hold TIPS.

In the presence of persistent shocks to consumption growth, by contrast, consumption growth is positively autocorrelated. In this case recessions not only drive down current consumption but also lead to prolonged periods of slow growth, driving down real interest rates. In such an economy

the prices of long-term inflation-indexed bonds rise in recessions, making them desirable hedging assets with negative risk premiums.

This paradigm suggests that the risk premium on TIPS will fall if investors become less concerned about temporary business-cycle shocks and more concerned about shocks to the long-term consumption growth rate.

It is possible that such a shift in investor beliefs did take place during the late 1990s and 2000s, as the Great Moderation mitigated concerns about business-cycle risk (Bernanke 2004; Blanchard and Simon 2001; McConnell and Perez-Quiros 2000; Kim and Nelson 1999; Stock and Watson 2003) while long-term uncertainties about technological progress and climate change became more salient. Of course, the events of 2007–2008 have brought business-cycle risk to the fore again. The movements of inflation-indexed bond yields have been broadly consistent with changing risk perceptions of this sort.

The second term in equation (3.5) is also negative under the plausible assumption that $\gamma > 1/\psi$, and its sign does not depend on the persistence of the consumption process. However, its magnitude does depend on the volatility of shocks to long-run expected consumption growth. Thus, increasing uncertainty about long-run growth drives down inflation-indexed bond premiums through this channel as well.

Overall, the Epstein-Zin paradigm suggests that inflation-indexed bonds should have low or even negative risk premiums relative to short-term safe assets, consistent with the intuition that these bonds are the safe asset for long-term investors.

3.3.2   Bond Risk Premiums and the Bond-Stock Covariance

The consumption-based analysis of the previous section delivers insights but also has weaknesses. The model assumes constant second moments and thus implies constant risk premiums; it cannot be used to track changing variances, covariances, or risk premiums in the inflation-indexed bond market. Although one could generalize the model to allow time-varying second moments, as in the long-run risks model of Bansal and Yaron (2004), the low frequency of consumption measurement makes it difficult to implement the model empirically. In this section we follow a different approach, writing down a model of the stochastic discount factor (SDF) that allows us to relate the risk premiums on inflation-indexed bonds to the covariance of these bonds with stock returns.

To capture the time-varying correlation of returns on inflation-indexed bonds with stock returns, we propose a highly stylized term structure

model in which the real interest rate is subject to conditionally heteroskedastic shocks. Conditional heteroskedasticity is driven by a state variable that captures time variation in aggregate macroeconomic uncertainty.
We build our model in the spirit of Campbell, Sunderam, and Viceira
(2009), who emphasize the importance of changing macroeconomic conditions for an understanding of time variation in systematic risk and
in the correlations of returns on fundamental asset classes. Our model
modifies their quadratic term structure model to allow for heteroskedastic shocks to the real rate.

We assume that the log of the real SDF, $m_{t+1} = \log M_{t+1}$, can be
described by

$$-m_{t+1} = x_t + \frac{1}{2}\sigma_m^2 + \varepsilon_{m,t+1}, \tag{3.6}$$

where x_t follows a conditionally heteroskedastic AR(1) process,

$$x_{t+1} = \mu_x(1-\varphi_x) + \varphi_x x_t + v_t \varepsilon_{x,t+1} + \varepsilon'_{x,t+1}, \tag{3.7}$$

and v_t follows a standard AR(1) process,

$$v_{t+1} = \mu_v(1-\varphi_v) + \varphi_v v_t + \varepsilon_{v,t+1}. \tag{3.8}$$

The shocks $\varepsilon_{m,t+1}$, $\varepsilon_{x,t+1}$, $\varepsilon'_{x,t+1}$, and $\varepsilon_{v,t+1}$ have zero means and are jointly
normally distributed with a constant variance-covariance matrix. We
assume that $\varepsilon'_{x,t+1}$ and $\varepsilon_{v,t+1}$ are orthogonal to each other and to the other
shocks in the model. We adopt the notation σ_i^2 to describe the variance
of shock ε_i, and σ_{ij} to describe the covariance between shock ε_i and shock
ε_j. The conditional volatility of the log SDF (σ_m) describes the price of
aggregate market risk, or the maximum Sharpe ratio in the economy,
which we assume to be constant.[5]

The online appendix to this chapter (see note 1) shows how to solve
this model for the real term structure of interest rates. The state variable
x_t is equal to the log short-term real interest rate, which follows an AR(1)
process whose conditional variance is driven by the state variable v_t.

In a standard consumption-based power utility model of the sort discussed in the previous subsection, v_t would capture time variation in the
dynamics of consumption growth. When v_t is close to zero, shocks to the
real interest rate are uncorrelated with the SDF; in a power utility model,
this would imply that shocks to future consumption growth are uncorrelated with shocks to the current level of consumption. As v_t moves
away from zero, the volatility of the real interest rate increases and its
covariance with the SDF becomes more positive or more negative. In a

power utility model, this corresponds to a covariance between consumption shocks and future consumption growth that is either positive or negative, reflecting either momentum or mean reversion in consumption. Broadly speaking, one can interpret v_t as a measure of aggregate uncertainty about long-run growth in the economy. At times when that uncertainty increases, real interest rates become more volatile.

Solving the model for the real term structure of interest rates, we find that the log price of an n-period inflation-indexed bond is linear in the short-term real interest rate x_t, with coefficient $B_{x,n}$, and quadratic in aggregate economic uncertainty v_t, with linear coefficient $B_{v,n}$ and quadratic coefficient $C_{v,n}$. An important property of this model is that bond risk premiums are time varying. They are approximately linear in v_t, where the coefficient on v_t is proportional to σ_m^2.

A time-varying conditional covariance between the SDF and the real interest rate implies that the conditional covariance between inflation-indexed bonds and risky assets such as equities should also vary over time as a function of v_t. To see this, we now introduce equities into the model.

To keep things simple, we assume that the unexpected log return on equities is given by

$$r_{e,t+1} - E_t r_{e,t+1} = \beta_{em} \varepsilon_{m,t+1}. \tag{3.9}$$

This implies that the equity premium equals $\beta_{em} \sigma_m^2$, the conditional standard deviation of stock returns is $\beta_{em} \sigma_m$, and the Sharpe ratio on equities is σ_m. Equities deliver the maximum Sharpe ratio because they are perfectly correlated with the SDF. Thus, we are imposing the restrictions of the traditional CAPM, ignoring the intertemporal hedging arguments stated in the previous subsection.

The covariance between stocks and inflation-indexed bonds is given by

$$Cov_t(r_{e,t+1}, r_{n,t+1}) = B_{x,n-1} \beta_{em} \sigma_{mx} v_t, \tag{3.10}$$

which is proportional to v_t. This proportionality is also a reason why we consider two independent shocks to x_t. In the absence of a homoskedastic shock $\varepsilon'_{x,t}$ to x_t, our model would imply that the conditional volatility of the short-term real interest rate would be proportional to the conditional covariance of stock returns with returns on inflation-indexed bonds. However, although the two conditional moments appear to be correlated in the data, they are not perfectly correlated, still less proportional to one another.

We estimate this term structure model by applying the nonlinear Kalman filter procedure described in Campbell, Sunderam, and Viceira

(2009) to data on zero-coupon inflation-indexed bond yields, from Refet Gürkaynak, Brian Sack, and Jonathan Wright (2008), for the period 1999–2008, and total returns on the value-weighted U.S. stock market portfolio, from CRSP data.[6] Because the U.S. Treasury does not issue TIPS with short maturities, and there are no continuous observations of yields on near-to-maturity TIPS, this data set does not include short-term zero-coupon TIPS yields. To approximate the short-term real interest rate, we use the ex ante short-term real interest rate implied by our VAR approach described in section 3.2.

Our estimation makes several identifying and simplifying assumptions. First, we identify σ_m using the long-run average Sharpe ratio for U.S. equities, which we set to 0.23 on a quarterly basis (equivalent to 0.46 on an annual basis). Second, we identify β_{em} as the sample standard deviation of equity returns in our sample period (0.094 per quarter, or 18.9 percent per year) divided by σ_m, for a value of 0.41. Third, we exactly identify x_t with the ex ante short-term real interest rate estimated from the VAR model of the previous section, which we treat as observed, adjusted by a constant. That is, we give the Kalman filter a measurement equation that equates the VAR-estimated short-term real interest rate to x_t with a free constant term but no measurement error. The inclusion of the constant term is intended to capture liquidity effects that lower the yields on Treasury bills relative to the longer-term real yield curve. Fourth, because the shock $\varepsilon_{x,t+1}$ is always premultiplied by v_t, we normalize σ_x to 1. Fifth, we assume that there is perfect correlation between the shock $\varepsilon_{x,t+1}$ and the shock $\varepsilon_{m,t+1}$ to the SDF; equivalently, we set σ_{mx} equal to 0.23. This delivers the largest possible time variation in inflation-indexed bond risk premiums and thus maximizes the effect of changing risk on the TIPS yield curve. Sixth, we treat equation (3.10) as a measurement equation with no measurement error, where we replace the covariance on the left-hand side of the equation with the realized monthly covariance of returns on ten-year zero-coupon TIPS with returns on stocks. We estimate the monthly realized covariance using daily observations on stock returns and on TIPS returns from the Gürkaynak-Sack-Wright data set. Since β_{em} and σ_{mx} have been already exactly identified, this is equivalent to identifying the process v_t with a scaled version of the covariance of returns on TIPS and stocks.

We include one final measurement equation for the ten-year zero-coupon TIPS yield using the model's solution for this yield and allowing for measurement error. The identifying assumptions we have made imply that we are exactly identifying x_t with the ex ante short-term real interest

Table 3.3
Parameter Estimates for Alternative Risk Models

| Parameter | Full Model | Restricted Models | |
		Constant-Covariance Model	Persistent-Risk Model
φ_x	0.94	0.93	0.95
μ_x	0.0028	0.0104	0.0034
φ_v	0.77	NA[a]	Set to 1
μ_v	-2.01×10^{-5}	NA	0.0010
σ_m	Set to 0.23	Set to 0.23	Set to 0.23
σ_x	Set to 1	0.0031	Set to 1
σ_{mx}	0.23	7.23×10^{-4}	0.23
$\sigma_{x'}$	0.0048	NA	0.0031
σ_v	0.0003	NA	0.0004
β_{em}	Set to 0.41	NA	Set to 0.41
σ_{yield}	1.16×10^{-6}	1.12×10^{-4}	9.14×10^{-6}
σ_{cov}	4.74×10^{-4}	NA	5×10^{-4}
Premium	0.0157	0.0016	0.00160

Notes: a. NA, not applicable. See the text for descriptions of the models.
Source: Authors' calculations.

rate, v_t with the realized covariance of returns on TIPS and stocks, and the log SDF with stock returns. Thus, our estimation procedure in effect generates hypothetical TIPS yields from these processes and compares them with observed TIPS yields.

Table 3.3 reports the parameter estimates from our full model and two restricted models. The first of these two models, reported in the second column, drops the measurement equation for the realized stock-bond covariance and assumes that the stock-bond covariance is constant, and hence that TIPS have a constant risk premium, as in the VAR model of section 3.2. The second restricted model, reported in the last column, generates the largest possible effects of time-varying risk premiums on TIPS yields by increasing the persistence of the covariance state variable v_t from the freely estimated value of 0.77, which implies an eight-month half-life for covariance movements, to the largest permissible value of 1.

Figure 3.9 shows how these three variants of our basic model fit the history of the ten-year TIPS yield. The yields predicted by the freely estimated model of changing risk and by the restricted model with a constant bond-stock covariance are almost on top of one another, diverging only slightly in periods such as 2003 and 2008 when the realized bond-stock covariance was unusually negative. This indicates that changing TIPS risk is not persistent enough to have a large effect on TIPS

Percent a year

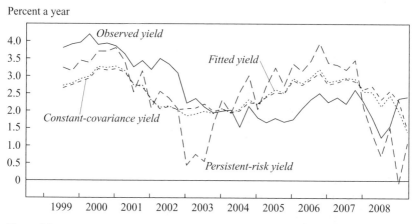

Figure 3.9
Real ten-year inflation-indexed bond yields implied by alternative risk models, United States, 1998–2009. *Source:* Authors' calculations based on data for yields from Gürkaynak, Sack, and Wright (2005) and for stock returns from the Center for Research on Security Prices.

yields. Only when we impose a unit root on the process for the bond-stock covariance do we obtain large effects of changing risk. This model implies that TIPS yields should have fallen more dramatically than they did in 2002–2003, and again in 2007, when the covariance of TIPS with stocks turned negative. The persistent-risk model does capture observed TIPS movements in the first half of 2008, but it dramatically fails to capture the spike in TIPS yields in the second half of 2008.

Over all, this exploration of changing risk, as captured by the changing realized covariance of TIPS returns and aggregate stock returns, suggests that variations in risk play only a supporting role in the determination of TIPS yields. The major problem with a risk-based explanation for movements in the inflation-indexed yield curve is that the covariance of TIPS and stocks has moved in a transitory fashion, and thus should not have had a large effect on TIPS yields unless investors were expecting more persistent variation and were surprised by an unusual sequence of temporary changes in risk.

These results contrast with those reported by Campbell, Sunderam, and Viceira (2009), who find that persistent movements in the covariance between inflation and stock returns have had a powerful influence on the nominal U.S. Treasury yield curve. They find that U.S. inflation was negatively correlated with stock returns in the late 1970s and early 1980s, when the major downside risk for investors was stagflation; it was posi-

tively correlated with stock returns in the 2000s, when investors were more concerned about deflation.[7] As a result, Campbell, Sunderam, and Viceira argue that the inflation risk premium was positive in the 1970s and 1980s but was negative in the 2000s, implying even lower expected returns on nominal Treasury bonds than on TIPS. The movements in inflation risk identified by Campbell, Sunderam, and Viceira are persistent enough to have important effects on the shape of the nominal U.S. Treasury yield curve, reducing its slope and concavity relative to what was typical in the 1970s and 1980s.

3.4 The Crisis of 2008 and Institutional Influences on TIPS Yields

In 2008, as the subprime crisis intensified, the TIPS yield became highly volatile and appeared to become suddenly disconnected from the yield on nominal Treasuries. At the beginning of 2008, the thirty-year TIPS yield as reported by the Federal Reserve Bank of St. Louis fell to extremely low levels, as low as 1.66 percent on January 23, 2008. Shorter-maturity TIPS showed even lower yields, and in the spring and again in the summer of 2008 some of these yields became negative, falling below –0.5 percent, reminding market participants that zero is not the lower bound for inflation-indexed bond yields. The fall of 2008 then witnessed an unprecedented and short-lived spike in TIPS yields, peaking at the end of October 2008, when the thirty-year TIPS yield reached 3.44 percent.

These extraordinary short-run movements in TIPS yields are mirrored in the ten-year TIPS yield shown in figure 3.2. The extremely low TIPS yield in early 2008 was given a convenient explanation by some market observers, namely, that investors were panicked by the apparently heightened risks in financial markets due to the subprime crisis and sought safety at just about any price. But if this is the correct explanation, the massive surge in the TIPS yield later in that year remains a mystery. This leap upward was puzzling, since it was not observed in nominal bond yields and so marked a massive drop in the breakeven inflation rate, as seen in figure 3.3. The UK market behaved in similar fashion.

The anomalous sudden jump in inflation-indexed bond yields came as a total surprise to market participants. Indeed, just as the jump was occurring in October 2008, some observers were saying that because inflation expectations had become extremely stable, TIPS and nominal Treasury bonds were virtually interchangeable. For example, Marie

Brière and Ombretta Signori concluded, in a paper published in March 2009, that "although diversification was a valuable reason for introducing IL [inflation-linked] bonds in a global portfolio before 2003, this is no longer the case" (279). The extent of this surprise suggests that the rise in the TIPS yield, and its decoupling from nominal Treasury yields, had something to do with the systemic nature of the crisis that beset U.S. financial institutions in 2008.

Indeed, the sharp peak in the TIPS yield and the accompanying steep drop in the breakeven inflation rate occurred shortly after an event that some observers blame for the anomalous behavior of TIPS yields. This was the bankruptcy of the investment bank Lehman Brothers, announced on September 15, 2008. The unfolding of the Lehman bankruptcy proceedings also took place over the same interval of time during which the inflation-indexed bond yield made its spectacular leap upward.

Lehman's bankruptcy was an important event, the first bankruptcy of a major investment bank since that of Drexel Burnham Lambert in 1990. That is not to say that other investment banks did not also get into trouble in the meantime, especially during the subprime crisis. But the federal government had always stepped in to allay fears. Bear Stearns was sold to the commercial bank J.P. Morgan in March 2008 in a deal arranged and financed by the government. Bank of America announced its purchase of Merrill Lynch on September 14, 2008, again with government financial support. Yet the government decided to let Lehman fail, and investors may have interpreted this event as indicative of future government policy that might spell major changes in the economy.

One conceivable interpretation of the events that followed the Lehman bankruptcy announcement is that the market viewed the bankruptcy as a macroeconomic indicator, a sign that the economy would be suddenly weaker. This could have implied a deterioration in the government's fiscal position, justifying an increase in expected future real interest rates and therefore in the long-term real yield on Treasury debt, as well as a decline in inflation expectations, thus explaining the drop in breakeven inflation.

However, many observers doubt that the perceived macroeconomic impact of just this one bankruptcy could bring about such a radical change in expectations about real interest rates and inflation. At one point in 2008 the breakeven seven-year inflation rate reached −1.6 percent. According to Gang Hu and Mihir Worah (2009, 1), bond traders at PIMCO, "The market did not believe that it was possible to realize that kind of real rate or sustained deflation."

Another interpretation is that there was a shift in the risk premium for inflation-indexed bonds. In terms of our analysis above, this could be a change in the covariance of TIPS returns with consumption or wealth. But such a view sounds even less plausible than the view that the Lehman effect worked through inflation expectations. We have shown that the observed fluctuations in the covariances of TIPS returns with other variables are hard to rationalize even after the fact, and so it is hard to see why the market would have made a major adjustment in this covariance.

Hu and Worah (2009, 1, 3) conclude instead that "the extremes in valuation were due to a potent combination of technical factors. . . . Lehman owned Tips as part of repo trades or posted Tips as counterparty collateral. Once Lehman declared bankruptcy, both the court and its counterparty needed to sell these Tips for cash." The traders at PIMCO saw then a flood of TIPS on the market for which there appeared to be few buyers. Distressed market makers were not willing to risk taking positions in these TIPS; their distress was marked by a crisis-induced sudden and catastrophic widening, by October 2008, in TIPS bid-ask spreads. Making the situation worse was the fact that some institutional investors in TIPS had adopted commodity overlay strategies that forced them to sell TIPS because of the fall at that time in commodity prices. Moreover, institutional money managers had to confront a sudden loss of client interest in relative value trades. Such trades, which take advantage of unusual price differences between securities with related fundamentals, might otherwise have exploited the abnormally low breakeven inflation.

An important clue about the events of fall 2008 is provided by the diverging behavior of breakeven inflation rates in the TIPS cash market and breakeven inflation rates implied by zero-coupon inflation swaps during the months following the Lehman bankruptcy. Zero-coupon inflation swaps are derivatives contracts in which one party pays the other cumulative CPI (consumer price index) inflation over the term of the contract at maturity, in exchange for a predetermined fixed rate. This rate is known as the "synthetic" breakeven inflation rate, because if inflation grew at this fixed rate over the life of the contract, the net payment on the contract at maturity would be zero. As with the "cash" breakeven inflation rate implied by TIPS and nominal Treasury bonds, this rate reflects both expected inflation over the relevant period and an inflation risk premium.

Figure 3.10 plots the cash inflation breakeven rate implied by off-the-run (as opposed to newly issued, or on-the-run) TIPS and nominal Treasury bonds maturing on July 2017, and the synthetic inflation breakeven

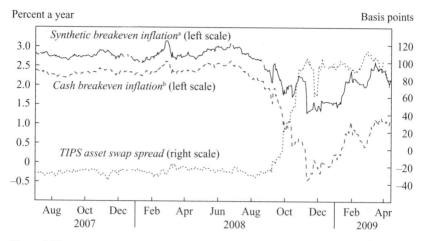

Figure 3.10
Breakeven inflation rates and asset swap spreads on TIPS, July 2007–April 2009. *Notes:* a. Synthetic breakeven inflation rate derived from interest rates on zero-coupon inflation swaps. b. Breakeven inflation rate derived from differences in yields on nominal government bonds and TIPS. *Source:* Authors' calculations based on data from Barclays Capital.

rate for the ten-year zero-coupon inflation swap, from July 2007 through April 2009. The figure also plots the TIPS asset swap spread, explained below. The two breakeven rates track each other very closely until mid-September 2008, with the synthetic inflation breakeven rate about 35 to 40 basis points above the cash breakeven inflation rate on average.

This difference in breakeven rates is typical under normal market conditions. According to analysts, it reflects, among other things, the cost of manufacturing pure inflation protection in the United States. Most market participants supplying inflation protection in the United States inflation swap market are leveraged investors such as hedge funds and banks' proprietary trading desks. These investors typically hedge their inflation swap positions by simultaneously taking long positions in TIPS and short positions in nominal Treasuries in the asset swap market. A buying position in an asset swap is functionally similar to a leveraged position in a bond. In an asset swap, one party pays the cash flows on a specific bond and receives in exchange interest at the London interbank offer rate (LIBOR) plus a spread known as the asset swap spread. Typically this spread is negative and larger in absolute magnitude for nominal Treasuries than for TIPS. Thus, leveraged investors selling inflation protection in an inflation swap face a positive financing cost derived from their long-TIPS, short-nominal Treasuries position.

Figure 3.10 shows that starting in mid-September 2008, cash breakeven inflation rates fell dramatically while synthetic rates did not fall nearly as much; at the same time TIPS asset swap spreads increased from their normal level of about −35 basis points to about +100 basis points. Although not shown in the figure, nominal Treasury asset swap spreads remained at their usual levels. That is, financing long positions in TIPS became extremely expensive relative to historical levels just as their cash price fell abruptly.

There is no reason why declining inflation expectations should directly affect the cost of financing long positions in TIPS relative to nominal Treasuries. The scenario that these two simultaneous changes suggest instead is one of intense selling in the cash market and insufficient demand to absorb those sales—as described by Hu and Worah—and simultaneously another shortage of capital to finance leveraged positions in markets other than that for nominal Treasuries; that is, the bond market events of the fall of 2008 may have been a "liquidity" episode.

Under this interpretation, the synthetic breakeven inflation rate was at the time a better proxy for inflation expectations in the marketplace than the cash breakeven inflation rate, despite the fact that in normal times the inflation swap market is considerably less liquid than the cash TIPS market. The synthetic breakeven inflation rate declined from about 3 percent a year to about 1.5 percent at the trough. This long-run inflation expectation is perhaps more plausible than the ten-year expectation of zero inflation reflected in the cash market for off-the-run bonds maturing in 2017.

Interestingly, cash breakeven inflation rates also diverged between on-the-run and off-the-run TIPS with similar maturities during this period. The online appendix shows that breakeven rates based on on-the-run TIPS were lower than those based on off-the-run TIPS. This divergence reflected another feature of TIPS that causes cash breakeven inflation rates calculated from on-the-run TIPS to be poor proxies for inflation expectations in the face of deflation risk. Contractually, TIPS holders have the right to redeem their bonds at maturity for the greater of either par value at issuance or that value plus accrued inflation during the life of the bond. Thus, when there is a risk of deflation after a period of inflation, new TIPS issues offer better deflation protection than older ones. Accordingly, on-the-run TIPS should be more expensive than off-the-run TIPS, and thus their real yields should be lower. Breakeven inflation rates derived from on-the-run TIPS must be adjusted upward for this deflation protection premium to arrive at a measure of inflation expectations.

We view the experience with TIPS yields after the Lehman bankruptcy as reflecting a highly abnormal market situation, where liquidity problems suddenly created severe financial anomalies. This may seem to imply that one can regard the recent episode as unrepresentative and ignore the observations from these dates. However, investors in TIPS who would like to regard them as the safest long-term investment must consider the extraordinary short-term volatility that such events have given their yields.

3.5   The Uses of Inflation-Indexed Bonds

We conclude by drawing out some implications of the recent experience with inflation-indexed bonds for both investors and policy makers.

3.5.1   Implications for Investors

The basic case for investing in inflation-indexed bonds, stated by Campbell and Shiller (1997) and further developed by Michael Brennan and Yihong Xia (2002), Campbell and Viceira (2001, 2002), Campbell, Yeung Lewis Chan, and Viceira (2003), and Jessica Wachter (2003), is that these bonds are the safe asset for long-term investors. An inflation-indexed perpetuity delivers a known stream of real spending power to an infinite-lived investor, and a zero-coupon inflation-indexed bond delivers a known real payment in the distant future to an investor who values wealth at that single horizon. This argument makes no assumption about the time-series variation in yields, and so it is not invalidated by the gradual long-term decline in inflation-indexed bond yields since the 1990s, the mysterious medium-run variations in TIPS yields relative to short-term real interest rates, the spike in yields in the fall of 2008, or the high daily volatility of TIPS returns.

There are, however, two circumstances in which other assets can substitute for inflation-indexed bonds to provide long-term safe returns. First, if the breakeven inflation rate is constant, as will be the case when the central bank achieves perfect anti-inflationary credibility, then nominal bonds are perfect substitutes for inflation-indexed bonds, and conventional government bonds will suit the preferences of conservative long-term investors. For a time in the mid-2000s, it looked as if this nirvana of central bankers was imminent, but the events of 2008 dramatically destabilized inflation expectations and reaffirmed the distinction between inflation-indexed and nominal bonds.

Second, if the ex ante real interest rate is constant, as Eugene Fama (1975) famously asserted, then long-term investors can roll over short-term Treasury bills to achieve almost perfectly certain long-term real returns. Because inflation uncertainty is minimal over a month or a quarter, Treasury bills expose investors to minimal inflation risk. In general, they do expose investors to the risk of persistent variation in the real interest rate, but this risk is absent if the real interest rate is constant over time.

Investors can tell whether this happy circumstance prevails by forecasting realized real returns on Treasury bills and measuring the movements of their forecasts, as we did in figure 3.8, or more simply by measuring the volatility of inflation-indexed bond returns. If inflation-indexed bonds have yields that are almost constant and returns with almost no volatility, then Treasury bills are likely to be good substitutes.[8] Seen from this point of view, the high daily volatility of inflation-indexed bond returns illustrated in figure 3.4, far from being a drawback, demonstrates the value of inflation-indexed bonds for conservative long-term investors.

A simple quantitative measure of the usefulness of inflation-indexed bonds is the reduction in the long-run standard deviation of a portfolio that these bonds permit. One can estimate this reduction by calculating the long-run standard deviation of a portfolio of *other* assets chosen to minimize long-run risk (what we call the global minimum variance, or GMV, portfolio). This is the smallest risk that long-run investors can achieve if inflation-indexed bonds are unavailable. Once inflation-indexed bonds become available, the minimum long-run risk portfolio consists entirely of these bonds and has zero long-run risk. Thus, the difference between the minimized long-run standard deviation of the GMV portfolio and zero measures the risk reduction that inflation-indexed bonds make possible.[9]

We constructed a ten-year GMV portfolio consisting of U.S. stocks, nominal five-year Treasury bonds, and three-month Treasury bills. To derive the composition of this portfolio and its volatility at each horizon, we used the long-horizon mean-variance approach described in Campbell and Viceira (2005) and its companion technical guide (Campbell and Viceira 2004). We estimated a VAR(1) system for the ex post real return on Treasury bills and the excess log return on stocks and nominal bonds. The system also includes variables known to forecast bond and equity risk premiums: the log dividend-price ratio, the yield on Treasury bills, and the spread between that yield and the five-year Treasury bond yield. From this system we extracted the conditional variance-covariance of

ten-year returns using the formulas in Campbell and Viceira (2004) and found the portfolio that minimizes this variance.

Instead of estimating a single VAR system for our entire quarterly sample, 1953Q1–2008Q4, we estimated two VAR systems, one for 1953Q1–1972Q4 and another for 1973Q1–2008Q4. We split the sample this way because we are concerned that the process for inflation and the real interest rate might have changed during the period as a whole. The conditional long-horizon moments of returns also depend on the quarterly variance-covariance matrix of innovations, which we estimated using three-year windows of quarterly data. Within each window and VAR sample period, we combined the variance-covariance matrix with the full-sample estimate of the slope coefficients to compute the ten-year GMV portfolio and its annualized volatility.

Figure 3.11 compares the estimated standard deviation of the GMV portfolio with the annualized daily standard deviations of TIPS and inflation-indexed gilts over the period where these bonds exist. Figure 3.12 compares the same GMV standard deviation with the estimated standard deviation of hypothetical TIPS returns, constructed from the VAR system using the method of Campbell and Shiller (1997) and section 3.2 of this chapter, which assumes the log expectations hypothesis for inflation-indexed bonds. The annualized ten-year standard deviation of

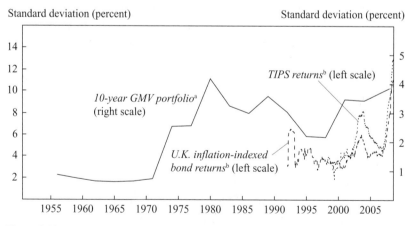

Figure 3.11
Volatility of returns on the global minimum variance portfolio and on inflation-indexed government bonds. *Notes:* a. Annualized ten-year standard deviation of the ten-year global minimum variance portfolio of U.S. stocks, nominal five-year Treasury bonds, and three-month Treasury bills, computed from a VAR model as described in the text. b. Annualized standard deviation of daily returns. *Source:* Authors' calculations from Bloomberg and Center for Research on Security Prices data.

Standard deviation (percent)

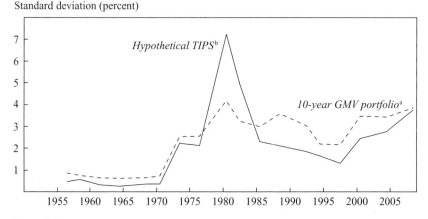

Figure 3.12
Volatility of returns on the global minimum variance portfolio and of hypothetical quarterly TIPS returns. *Notes:* a. Annualized ten-year standard deviation of the ten-year global minimum variance portfolio of U.S. stocks, nominal five-year Treasury bonds, and three-month Treasury bills, computed from a VAR model as described in the text. b. Annualized standard deviation of quarterly returns. *Source:* Authors' calculations from Bloomberg and Center for Research on Security Prices data.

the ten-year GMV portfolio is fairly low in the 1960s, at around 1 percent a year. This is the period that led Fama (1975) to assert that the ex ante real interest rate is constant over time. Starting in the 1970s, however, persistent movements in the real interest rate cause the standard deviation to rise rapidly to about 4 percent a year. The standard deviation drops back to about 2 percent in the mid-1990s, but by 2008 it is once again at a historical high of 4 percent. These numbers imply that inflation-indexed bonds substantially reduce risk for long-term investors.

Both comparisons show that, historically, the minimum long-run risk that can be achieved using other assets has been high when short-term TIPS returns have been volatile. In other words, inflation-indexed bonds are particularly good at reducing long-run risk whenever their short-run risk is high. Such a result may seem paradoxical, but it follows directly from the fact that the need for inflation-indexed bonds for long-term safety is greater when real interest rates vary persistently over time.[10]

Inflation-indexed bonds also play an important role for institutional investors who need to hedge long-term real liabilities. Pension funds and insurance companies with multiyear commitments should use inflation-indexed bonds to neutralize the swings in the present value of their long-dated liabilities due to changes in long-term real interest rates. Of course, these swings become apparent to institutional investors only

when they discount real liabilities using market real interest rates, as the UK has required in recent years. The resulting institutional demand for inflation-indexed gilts seems to have been an important factor driving down their yields (Viceira and Mitsui 2003; Vayanos and Vila 2007).

The total demand of long-term investors for inflation-indexed bonds will depend not only on their risk properties but also on their expected returns relative to other available investments and on the risk tolerance of the investors. An aggressive long-term investor might wish to short inflation-indexed bonds and invest the proceeds in equities, since stocks have only very rarely underperformed bonds over three or more decades in U.S. and UK data. In 2008 it was reported that Clare College, University of Cambridge, was planning to undertake such a strategy (Turner 2008). However, Campbell, Chan, and Viceira (2003) estimated positive long-term demand for inflation-indexed bonds by long-term investors who also have the ability to borrow short term or to issue long-term nominal bonds.

Long-term inflation-indexed bonds may be of interest to some short-term investors. Given their high short-run volatility, however, short-term investors will wish to hold these bonds only if they expect to receive high excess returns over Treasury bills (as might reasonably have been the case in 1999–2000 or during the yield spike of the fall of 2008), or if they hold other assets, such as stocks, whose returns can be hedged by an inflation-indexed bond position. We have shown evidence that TIPS and inflation-indexed gilts did hedge stock returns during the downturns of the early 2000s and the late 2000s, and this should make them attractive to short-term equity investors.

The illiquidity of inflation-indexed bonds is often mentioned as a disadvantage. But in developed countries these bonds are illiquid only relative to the same countries' nominal government bonds, which, along with foreign exchange, are the most liquid financial assets. Compared with almost any other long-term investment vehicle, inflation-indexed government bonds are extremely cheap to trade. In addition, long-term buy-and-hold investors should care very little about transaction costs since they will rarely need to turn over their bond positions.

3.5.2 Implications for Policy Makers

In managing the public debt, the Treasury seeks to minimize the average cost of debt issuance while paying due regard to risk, including refinancing risk. It is commonly thought that short-term Treasury bills are less expen-

sive than long-term debt but that exclusive reliance on bills would impose an unacceptable refinancing risk, as bills must frequently be rolled over.

In the period since TIPS were introduced in 1997, they have proved to be an expensive form of debt ex post, because of the unexpected decline in real interest rates from the 1990s through early 2008. However, our analysis implies that the cost of TIPS should be lower than that of Treasury bills ex ante, because TIPS offer investors desirable insurance against future variation in real interest rates. This is the relevant consideration going forward, as Jennifer Roush, William Dudley, and Michelle Steinberg Ezer (2008) emphasize, and therefore governments should not be deterred from issuing inflation-indexed bonds by the high realized returns on their past issues.

In the current environment, with inflation positively correlated with stock prices, the inflation risk premium in nominal Treasury bonds is likely negative. This implies that long-term nominal debt should be even cheaper for the Treasury than TIPS. However, the correlation between inflation and stock prices has changed sign in the past (Campbell, Sunderam, and Viceira 2009), and it may easily do so again in the future.

Several other considerations also suggest that inflation-indexed bonds are a valuable form of public debt. First, to the extent that particular forms of debt have different investment clienteles, all with downward-sloping demand curves for bonds, it is desirable to diversify across different forms so as to tap the largest possible market for government debt (Greenwood and Vayanos 2008; Vayanos and Vila 2007).

Second, inflation-indexed bonds can be used to draw inferences about bond investors' inflation expectations, and such information is extremely valuable for monetary policy makers.[11] It is true that market disruptions, such as those that occurred in the fall of 2008, complicate the measurement of inflation expectations, but our analysis shows that it is possible to derive meaningful information even in these extreme conditions.

Finally, inflation-indexed bonds provide a safe real asset for long-term investors and promote public understanding of inflation. Fiscal authorities should take these public benefits into account as part of their broader mission to improve the functioning of their economies.

Acknowledgments

Reprinted from John Y. Campbell, Robert J. Shiller, and Luis M. Viceira, "Understanding Inflation-Indexed Bond Markets," *Brookings Papers on*

Economic Activity, Spring 2009, with permission from the Brookings Institution Press.

Campbell and Viceira's research was supported by the Division of Research at the Harvard Business School and by the U.S. Social Security Administration (SSA) through grant no. 10-M-98363–1-01 to the National Bureau of Economic Research (NBER) as part of the SSA Retirement Research Consortium. The findings and conclusions expressed are solely those of the authors and do not represent the views of SSA, any agency of the federal government, or the NBER. We are grateful to Carolin Pflueger for exceptionally able research assistance, to Mihir Worah and Gang Hu of PIMCO, Derek Kaufman of Citadel, and Albert Brondolo, Michael Pond, and Ralph Segreti of Barclays Capital for their help in understanding TIPS and inflation derivatives markets and the unusual market conditions of the fall of 2008, and to Barclays Capital for providing data. We acknowledge the helpful comments of Brookings Panel participants and our discussants Frederic Mishkin and Jonathan Wright.

Notes

1. The online appendix can be found at kuznets.fas.harvard.edu/~campbell/papers.html.

2. We calculate the yield for the longest-maturity inflation-indexed bond outstanding at each point in time whose original maturity at issue was ten years. This is the on-the-run TIPS issue. We obtain constant-maturity ten-year yields for nominal Treasury bonds from the Center for Research in Security Prices (CRSP) database. Details of data construction are reported in the online appendix.

3. The duration of a bond is the average time to payment of its cash flows, weighted by the present values of those cash flows. Duration also equals the elasticity of a bond's price with respect to its gross yield (1 plus its yield in natural units). A coupon bond has duration less than its maturity, and its duration increases as its yield falls. Since TIPS yields are lower than nominal bond yields, TIPS have greater duration for the same maturity, and hence a greater volatility of returns for the same yield volatility, but the differences in volatility explained by duration are quite small.

4. A more careful derivation of this expression can be found in Campbell (2003, 841), equation 34.

5. Campbell, Sunderam, and Viceira (2009) consider a much richer term structure model in which σ_m^2 is time varying. They note that in that case, the process for the log real SDF admits an interpretation as a reduced form of structural models such as those of Bekaert, Engstrom, and Grenadier (2006) and Campbell and Cochrane (1999), in which aggregate risk aversion is time varying. Campbell, Sunderam, and Viceira find that time-varying risk aversion plays only a limited role in explaining the observed variation in bond risk premiums. For simplicity, we set σ_m^2 constant.

6. The CRSP (Center for Research in Security Prices) data cover all three major U.S. stock exchanges. Gürkaynak, Sack, and Wright (2008) estimate zero-coupon TIPS yields by fitting

a flexible functional form, a generalization of Nelson and Siegel (1987) suggested by Svensson (1994), to the instantaneous forward rates implied by off-the-run TIPS yields. From fitted forward rates it is straightforward to obtain zero-coupon yields.

7. Figure 3.6a illustrates the positive correlation of U.S. inflation and stock returns during the 2000s, and figure 3.6b shows that this correlation has changed sign in the UK since the early 1990s.

8. Strictly speaking, this argument assumes that real yields are described by the expectations hypothesis of the term structure, so that constant short-term real interest rates imply constant long-term real yields. Volatile risk or liquidity premiums on inflation-indexed bonds could make their yields volatile even if short-term real interest rates are constant. However, it is quite unlikely that time variation in risk or liquidity premiums would stabilize the yields on inflation-indexed bonds in an environment of time-varying real interest rates.

9. As an alternative approach, Campbell, Chan, and Viceira (2003) calculate the utility of an infinite-lived investor who has access to stocks, nominal bonds, and bills, and the utility gain when this investor also can hold an inflation-indexed perpetuity. We do not update this more complex calculation here.

10. This point is related to the asset pricing result discussed in section 3.3.1, namely, that when one controls for the stock market covariance of inflation-indexed bonds, the equilibrium risk premium on these bonds for a conservative, infinite-lived, representative investor is declining in their variance.

11. Recent papers extracting information from the inflation-indexed yield curve include Beechey and Wright (2008), Christensen, Lopez, and Rudebusch (2009), D'Amico, Kim, and Wei (2008), Grishchenko and Huang (2008), and Haubrich, Pennacchi, and Ritchken (2008).

References

Backus, David K., and Stanley E. Zin. 1994. Reverse Engineering the Yield Curve. NBER Working Paper 4676, National Bureau of Economic Research, Cambridge, MA.

Bansal, Ravi, and Amir Yaron. 2004. Risks for the Long Run: A Potential Resolution of Asset Pricing Puzzles. *Journal of Finance* 59 (4): 1481–1509.

Bansal, Ravi, Robert Dittmar, and Dana Kiku. 2009. Cointegration and Consumption Risks in Asset Returns. *Review of Financial Studies* 22 (3): 1343–1375.

Bansal, Ravi, Varoujan Khatchatrian, and Amir Yaron. 2005. Interpretable Asset Markets? *European Economic Review* 49 (3): 531–560.

Bansal, Ravi, Dana Kiku, and Amir Yaron. 2007. Risks for the Long Run: Estimation and Inference. Working Paper, Duke University, Durham, NC, and the University of Pennsylvania, Philadelphia.

Barr, David G., and John Y. Campbell. 1997. Inflation, Real Interest Rates, and the Bond Market: A Study of UK Nominal and Index-Linked Government Bond Prices. *Journal of Monetary Economics* 39 (3): 361–383.

Beechey, Meredith J., and Jonathan H. Wright. 2008. The High-Frequency Impact of News on Long-Term Yields and Forward Rates: Is It Real? FEDS Working Paper 2008–39, Board of Governors of the Federal Reserve, Washington, DC.

Bekaert, Geert, Eric Engstrom, and Steven R. Grenadier. 2006. Stock and Bond Returns with Moody Investors. NBER Working Paper 12247, National Bureau of Economic Research, Cambridge, MA.

Bernanke, Ben. 2004. The Great Moderation. Address to the Eastern Economic Association, Washington, DC, February. Available at http://www.federalreserve.gov/boarddocs/speeches/2004/20040220/default.htm.

Blanchard, Olivier, and John Simon. 2001. The Long and Large Decline in U.S. Output Volatility. *Brookings Papers on Economic Activity* (1): 135–164.

Brennan, Michael J., and Yihong Xia. 2002. Dynamic Asset Allocation under Inflation. *Journal of Finance* 57 (3): 1201–1238.

Brière, Marie, and Ombretta Signori. 2009. Do Inflation-Linked Bonds Still Diversify? *European Financial Management* 15 (2): 279.

Campbell, John Y. 1986. Bond and Stock Returns in a Simple Exchange Model. *Quarterly Journal of Economics* 101 (4): 785–804.

Campbell, John Y. 1993. Intertemporal Asset Pricing without Consumption Data. *American Economic Review* 83 (3): 487–512.

Campbell, John Y. 1996. Understanding Risk and Return. *Journal of Political Economy* 104 (2): 298–345.

Campbell, John Y. 2003. Consumption-Based Asset Pricing. In *Handbook of the Economics of Finance,* vol. IB, ed. George M. Constantinides, Milton Harris, and René Stulz, 803–887. Amsterdam: North-Holland.

Campbell, John Y., Yeung Lewis Chan, and Luis M. Viceira. 2003. A Multivariate Model of Strategic Asset Allocation. *Journal of Financial Economics* 67 (1): 41–80.

Campbell, John Y., and John H. Cochrane. 1999. By Force of Habit: A Consumption-Based Explanation of Aggregate Stock Market Behavior. *Journal of Political Economy* 107 (2): 205–251.

Campbell, John Y., and Robert J. Shiller. 1997. A Scorecard for Indexed Government Debt. *NBER Macroeconomics Annual* 1996: 155–197.

Campbell, John Y., Adi Sunderam, and Luis M. Viceira. 2009. Inflation Bets or Deflation Hedges? The Changing Risks of Nominal Bonds. NBER Working Paper 14701, National Bureau of Economic Research, Cambridge, MA.

Campbell, John Y., and Luis M. Viceira. 2001. Who Should Buy Long-Term Bonds? *American Economic Review* 91 (1): 99–127.

Campbell, John Y., and Luis M. Viceira. 2002. *Strategic Asset Allocation: Portfolio Choice for Long-Term Investors.* New York: Oxford University Press.

Campbell, John Y., and Luis M. Viceira. 2004. Long-Horizon Mean-Variance Analysis: A User Guide. Working paper, Harvard University, Cambridge, MA. Available at http://www.globalriskguard.com/resources/assetman/assetall_0015.pdf.

Campbell, John Y. , and Luis M. Viceira. 2005. The Term Structure of the Risk-Return Trade-off. *Financial Analysts Journal* 61 (1): 34–44.

Campbell, John Y., and Tuomo Vuolteenaho. 2004. Bad Beta, Good Beta. *American Economic Review* 94 (5): 1249–1275.

Christensen, Jens H. E., Jose A. Lopez, and Glenn D. Rudebusch. 2009. Inflation Expectations and Risk Premiums in an Arbitrage-Free Model of Nominal and Real Bond Yields. Financial Institutions Center Paper 09-02, Wharton School, University of Pennsylvania, Philadelphia.

D'Amico, Stefania, Don H. Kim, and Min Wei. 2008. Tips from TIPS: The Informational Content of Treasury Inflation-Protected Security Prices. FEDS Working Paper 2008-30, Board of Governors of the Federal Reserve, Washington, DC.

Epstein, Larry G., and Stanley Zin. 1989. Substitution, Risk Aversion, and the Temporal Behavior of Consumption and Asset Returns: A Theoretical Framework. *Econometrica: Journal of the Econometric Society* 57 (4): 937–969.

Epstein, Larry G., and Stanley Zin. 1991. Substitution, Risk Aversion, and the Temporal Behavior of Consumption and Asset Returns: An Empirical Investigation. *Journal of Political Economy* 99 (2): 263–286.

Fama, Eugene F. 1975. Short-Term Interest Rates as Predictors of Inflation. *American Economic Review* 65 (3): 269–282.

Gollier, Christian. 2007. The Consumption-Based Determinants of the Term Structure of Discount Rates. *Mathematics and Financial Economics* 1 (2): 81–101.

Greenwood, Robin, and Dimitri Vayanos. 2008. Bond Supply and Excess Bond Returns. NBER Working Paper 13806, National Bureau of Economic Research, Cambridge, MA.

Grishchenko, Olesya V., and Huang Jing-zhi. 2008. Inflation Risk Premium: Evidence from the TIPS Market. Working paper, Pennsylvania State University, University Park.

Gürkaynak, Refet S., Brian Sack, and Jonathan H. Wright. 2008. The TIPS Yield Curve and Inflation Compensation. FEDS Working Paper 2008-05, Board of Governors of the Federal Reserve, Washington, DC.

Hansen, Lars Peter, John C. Heaton, and Nan Li. 2008. Consumption Strikes Back? Measuring Long-Run Risk. *Journal of Political Economy* 116 (2): 260–302.

Haubrich, Joseph, George Pennacchi, and Peter Ritchken. 2008. Estimating Real and Nominal Term Structures Using Treasury Yields, Inflation, Inflation Forecasts, and Inflation Swap Rates. Working Paper 08-10, Federal Reserve Bank of Cleveland, Cleveland, OH.

Hu, Gang, and Mihir Worah. 2009. Why Tips Real Yields Moved Significantly Higher after the Lehman Bankruptcy. Special report, PIMCO, Newport Beach, CA.

Kim, C.-J., and Charles R. Nelson. 1999. Has the U.S. Economy Become More Stable? A Bayesian Approach Based on a Markov-Switching Model of the Business Cycle. *Review of Economics and Statistics* 81 (4): 608–616.

McConnell, Margaret M., and Gabriel Perez-Quiros. 2000. Output Fluctuations in the United States: What Has Changed Since the Early 1980's? *American Economic Review* 90 (5): 1464–1476.

Merton, Robert C. 1973. An Intertemporal Capital Asset Pricing Model. *Econometrica: Journal of the Econometric Society* 41 (5): 867–887.

Nelson, Charles R., and Andrew F. Siegel. 1987. Parsimonious Modeling of Yield Curves. *Journal of Business* 60 (4): 473–489.

Piazzesi, Monika, and Martin Schneider. 2007. Equilibrium Yield Curves. *NBER Macroeconomics Annual* 2006: 389–472.

Restoy, Fernando, and Philippe Weil. 1998. Approximate Equilibrium Asset Prices. NBER Working Paper 6611, National Bureau of Economic Research, Cambridge, MA.

Roush, Jennifer, William Dudley, and Michelle Steinberg Ezer. 2008. The Case for TIPS: An Examination of the Costs and Benefits. Staff Report 353, Federal Reserve Bank of New York, New York.

Stock, James, and Mark Watson. 2003. Has the Business Cycle Changed and Why? *NBER Macroeconomics Annual* 2002:159–218.

Svensson, Lars E. O. 1994. Estimating and Interpreting Forward Interest Rates: Sweden 1992–1994. NBER Working Paper 4871, National Bureau of Economic Research, Cambridge, MA.

Turner, David. 2008. College to Invest 15m Loan in Shares. *Financial Times,* October 27, 2008.

Vayanos, Dimitri, and Jean-Luc Vila. 2007. *A Preferred-Habitat Model of the Term Structure of Interest Rates.* London: London School of Economics; New York: Merrill Lynch.

Viceira, Luis M., and Akiko M. Mitsui. 2003. Pension Policy at the Boots Company PLC, Case 203-105, Harvard Business School, Cambridge, MA.

Viceira, Luis M., and Akiko M. Mitsui. 2007. Bond Risk, Bond Return Volatility, and the Term Structure of Interest Rates. Working Paper 07-082, Harvard Business School, Cambridge, MA.

Wachter, Jessica A. 2003. Risk Aversion and Allocation to Long-Term Bonds. *Journal of Economic Theory* 112 (2): 325–333.

Wachter, Jessica A. 2006. A Consumption-Based Model of the Term Structure of Interest Rates. *Journal of Financial Economics* 79 (2): 365–399.

4 Crisis and Innovation in the Housing Economy: A Tale of Three Markets

Susan J. Smith

The global financial crisis that emerged between 2006 and 2008 has still to be adequately explained. Most agree that it was triggered by events in the housing economy, and that these in turn were precipitated by a round of financial innovation that failed. The source of the problem is generally located in the loosely regulated integration of housing, mortgage, and financial markets. Analysts refer, in particular, to the indiscriminate securitization of risky home loans; the advent of opaque, mortgage-heavy, collateralized debt obligations; and the failure of credit derivatives to insure overly optimistic investors. A common reaction is to argue that financial innovation went too far: that lending should now be reined in, securitization reviewed, and debt derivatives unwound. And if this were to result in better management and closer regulation of financial services, there would be little to quibble with. This chapter nevertheless takes a complementary position, noting that some elements of the crisis were less a legacy of innovation than a product of conservatism.

My argument, broadly, is this. Most reservations concerning financial innovation currently stem from debates that are dominated by debt. Yet the analysis is incomplete until the equity side of the housing equation is more fully and effectively addressed. The drivers of home price volatility, the risks in housing-centered wealth portfolios, and the financial instruments required to manage these are all underexplored. Reviewing these themes, I conclude that had there been more, not less, engagement with truly innovative financial tools across the whole housing economy, some elements of instability—some part of the wider crisis—might have been averted. Were such innovation still to occur, it could, with adequate monitoring and appropriate checks and balances, assist sustainable recovery.

The discussion is in three sections, drawing examples from the housing systems of the English-speaking world. These jurisdictions—I refer in particular to the United States, the UK, and Australia—are characterized

by reasonably high rates of highly mortgaged owner-occupation. They do not top the global league table for home ownership rates, or indeed for mortgaged home purchase (Scanlon and Whitehead 2004). They do, however, set the trend in some other important ways. These include the extent to which individual home ownership is valorized over renting or co-ownership,[1] the degree to which personal wealth is concentrated in housing, and the use of mortgage product innovations both to expand the market at the margins and to normalize secured borrowing for discretionary expenditures.

The story of home ownership in these societies is, I suggest, a tale of three markets—in housing, mortgages, and financial derivatives—and of the flows of capital, credit, and cash that link them together. It is often asked what social scientists, such as myself, who are not economists can bring to understandings of markets. One answer is that multidisciplinary approaches are an exercise in making connections. As John Kay (2003) so aptly illustrates in his essays in *The Truth about Markets*, storytelling is one vehicle for this. Kay's concern is with the veracity of the many "small stories" embedded in a variety of economic models. Mine is to respect the very specific methodologies that economists routinely employ, and to overlay them with the narrative style preferred by anthropologists and sociologists. That is, I use qualitative insights to fill empirical gaps (MacKenzie and Millo 2003), "close dialog" to revisit stylized facts (Clark 1998), and evidence from the "ordinary" economy to engage in otherwise more formalized debates (Lee 2006).

The first, short section of the chapter makes the point that housing market dynamics—in particular the volatility of home prices and their wealth portfolio implications—are still quite poorly understood. This explains why price instabilities persist and are problematic at both the macro- and microscale (having an impact on the fortunes of home-buying households as well as whole economies). It explains, too, why the operation of housing markets turns on a limited range of traditional financial instruments, and why financial innovations linked to residential property remain embryonic. Greater preoccupation with the measurement, drivers, and trajectories of price might have altered the financial landscape of the new millennium. Equally, an interdisciplinary effort to disentangle the price effects of fundamentals from the influence of an "irrational" emotional economy may be key to housing's financial future.

A much-misrepresented "mortgage finance revolution" is addressed in the second section of the chapter, which is concerned with the almost

complete integration of housing and mortgage markets in the English-speaking world. This degree of integration was enabled (and advanced) by the kind of financial innovation that has recently been frowned on—by the trading of (mortgage) debt-backed bonds and derivatives thereof on financial markets. However, it is the abundance of credit rather than the character of mortgages that these inventions really changed. Financial innovation reduced the costs and increased the availability of housing finance; it did not greatly alter the structure of the standard debt-funding instruments (principally annuity mortgage contracts) that delivered loans to households. Nor did it encourage the development of products to minimize risks overall, or to share capital and credit risks more equitably between lenders and borrowers.

Such innovation as there was in mortgage markets sensu stricto took the form of embellishments of traditional mortgage instruments that, in a deregulated lending regime, opened up the collateral channel between housing wealth and consumption by triggering an unprecedented wave of equity borrowing.[2] There is a great deal still to say about the macroeconomic implications of this—about the way that, as the twenty-first century gathered pace, housing's wealth effects flowed increasingly through the collateral channel (Muellbauer 2008; Muellbauer and Murphy 2008). Nevertheless, this section of the chapter concentrates on a more neglected microeconomic theme, exposing the importance of secured credit in amplifying investment (as well as credit) risks in housing markets. Had the implications of this been fully embraced, policy responses might have been different.

The third and final section of the chapter considers the possibility that financial innovation as much as retrenchment holds the key to sustainable recovery and stability in the housing economy. In the early 2000s, when the pace of change around debt was unprecedented, there was nearly no financial innovation in relation to home prices or housing assets. In the discussion, I consider the economic, social and policy costs of this imbalance. I suggest that, at the very least, investment behaviors may have been different, and the recession less deep, had there been a market for residential property (price) derivatives. That is, I question the eccentric position of housing with respect to otherwise widely used modern financial instruments. I further suggest that the foundations of financial crisis were laid not by the too close integration of housing, mortgage, and financial markets but rather by the unevenness of this process. Were this to be addressed, the future might include more, not less, financial innovation. This could be a solution rather than a problem,

providing that important lessons are learned regarding the regulation and management of the housing economy.

How Housing Markets Work: The Problem of Price

Housing is neither the kind of commodity nor style of investment that naturally occupies the financial frontier. In the home-ownership societies of the English-speaking world, residential property is overwhelmingly the province of small investors, who value their homes as consumption goods, bundles of housing services, and (to varying degrees) styles of wealth holding and sources of capital gain. The professional investment community finds residential property less appealing, not least because as an asset it is idiosyncratic. Housing is physically fixed, indivisible, costly to trade, expensive to hold, and hard to cash in quickly. Perhaps as a consequence of this, the instruments used to trade residential property have changed very little over the years.

Residential property is exchanged primarily in physical form, using simple forward contracts. Methods of price determination vary and are less binding in some markets than in others. Essentially, however, a price is agreed on today for goods that are delivered (made available) on a specified future date. Models of professionalism in such markets are more geared to the exchange of goods and services than to the management of investments (Smith, Munro, and Christie 2006), and even a growing interdisciplinary literature concerned with how housing markets work has inspired little in the way of financial innovation. There are few secondary markets or indirect housing investments,[3] and there is almost no trading of housing (home price) derivatives—a theme I return to later. Yet the stakes are high. Residential property is the world's largest asset class. Small investors (households) hold the majority of their wealth in this form and are overexposed to the price risks of a single residential unit; most major institutional investors have little wealth in property, even though it is an appealing option for diversification.

Some, perhaps most, of this financial conservatism has to do with the problem of price. For housing markets as for any other market, price is the bottom line—a metric critical for understanding the composition of wealth portfolios, measuring the collateral available for lending and borrowing, and benchmarking residential investment risks and rewards. However, home prices are poorly understood: they are hard to measure, awkward to analyze, and difficult to account for formally.

Measurement difficulties reflect the peculiarities of property that are posed, among other things, by the durability, fixity, uniqueness, and heterogeneity of housing units, and by the infrequency with which residential property trades. Not for nothing did Dwonczyck (1992) dub housing "the actuary's last big frontier." Even today, there are many areas of the globe where reliable price runs cannot be derived. Although by 2006, the Bank for International Settlements had recognized that as many as forty countries (a little over 20 percent of the total) regularly publish usable home price series, the practical challenges of securing key data are enormous. Some prices are assembled from a wide range of consistently measured attributes, others contain little information other than location. Many jurisdictions have few collecting points whose values are rarely updated; only a minority have long runs of data that are consistent from beginning to end.

The more these gaps are filled, the more attention turns to the practicalities of capturing (in an index) or discovering (through modeling exercises) the prices of residential property. The more successful these exercises are, the more scope there will be for anticipating volatility and innovating to manage it. It is significant, therefore, that the very earliest work in this vein was completed by a small coterie of economists who had long recognized the possibility of making productive use of financial instruments that harness home prices. Case and Shiller's (1987) pioneering work on a repeat-sales index for the United States is a case in point, as is John Edwards's contemporary if less well-known work on a similar index for Australia. Debates over the accuracy and utility of different methods of house price indexing have now become a hot topic for economists (e.g., Clapman et al. 2005; Deng and Quigley 2008; Hansen 2006; Shiller 1993), but this is just the start.

There is also the challenge of explaining home prices statistically: of understanding what drives them and how far they are predictable. Accounting for price runs in housing markets is complicated by a number of well-rehearsed factors, including the tendency for home prices to deviate substantially and for long periods from predictions based on fundamentals (Hott and Monnin 2008). It is therefore more striking than surprising that, a large and rapidly growing body of research notwithstanding, neoclassical economics has struggled to account for the history and geography of home prices using tried and tested tools. This is true at both the macro- and micro- scales (Leung 2004; Watkins 2009). I present fuller justification for this claim, as well as proper recognition of the substantial progress that *has* been made, elsewhere (Smith 2011). What

follows is a summary of this longer article and therefore, of necessity, a caricature of a complex debate.

At the macroscale, despite a long-standing interest in asset price fluctuations generally, attention to property prices came surprisingly late (Goodhardt and Hofmann 2007). The foundation is an equation in which markets are efficient and prices some function of the variables shaping supply and demand. To capture this balance, econometricians tend to use just one or two basic model specifications (Meen 2012). This broad theoretical consensus has been helpful in accounting for the most recent housing cycle, whose international dimension can be attributed, to a greater or lesser extent, to low interest rates, rising real incomes, cheap credit, and population growth, as well as to constraints on supply (Renaud and Kim 2007; Kim and Renaud 2009). It has helped in specific national settings, too (Meen 2008). It is striking nevertheless that even those drivers of home prices that can reliably be identified as "fundamentals" range widely across time and space in their salience and consistency. Even the most comprehensive modeling exercises leave much to explain (Miles and Pillonca 2008). And, of course, such models are most helpful for describing past trends and identifying the predictors of prices *in the long run*. They say little about the instabilities that are so important for understanding, managing, and benefiting from price risks in housing markets, and for building sustainable recovery (Just and Mayer 2010; Housing Market Task Force and Stephens 2011).[4]

A similar point can be made at the microscale, where a wide array of hedonic modeling exercises, grounded in the common assumption that sellers and buyers are broadly rational,[5] has produced a proliferation of fascinating empirical results. Often, however, such exercises are inconclusive, and their findings tend to be idiosyncratic rather than cumulative. A flurry of refinements—attempts to quantify the monetary value of different combinations of a surprising variety of housing attributes, from age, size, amenities, and location to deed type and traffic noise—has added a great deal of interest to this literature, arguably without substantially improving its explanatory power. Our recent systematic review suggests that despite notable methodological achievements and intriguing substantive results, standard models of home price determination raise as many questions as they resolve.[6]

In short, an elephant in the room of the recent financial crisis is analysts' limited understanding of the behavior, and especially the volatility, of housing asset prices. The problem is compounded by the fact that other disciplines have failed to comment, though arguably they could.

This strange silence is sometimes attributed to an enduring division of intellectual labor established in a "pact" between the sociologist Talcott Parsons and his colleagues in economics at the University of Chicago (Stark 2000). As the disciplines grew, a substantive distinction between the study of economy (the domain of economists, on the one hand) and the analysis of society (the non-economic subject matter for other social researchers, on the other) was apparently agreed on. The story is probably not as simple as the "pact thesis" suggests, but however established, the disciplinary divide is no longer sustainable. Recognizing this, one of the most important intellectual innovations in the past decade has been a paradigm shift at the interface between economics and the rest of the social sciences. This has brought cross-disciplinary alliances to bear on the analysis of key economic themes.

The most notable such collaboration is the alliance between economics and psychology, which inspired the project of behavioral finance. It seems unlikely that key themes in behavioral economics will not be helpful in addressing the formal unpredictability of prices. Home purchase decisions must, for example, be responsive to anchoring, framing, and contextual effects (Camerer and Loewenstein 2004; Simonsohn and Loewenstein 2006). Curiously, however, and in marked contrast to its rapid uptake in cognate areas, behavioral economics is rarely applied to the analysis of residential property prices. The one sustained exception is the work of Robert Shiller. Having first recognized that "irrational exuberance" was inflating the stock market bubble of the late 1990s, Shiller realized—in time for the second edition of his seminal book—that similar emotional drivers were underpinning home price volatility, too (Shiller 2005). This finding encouraged a flurry of new empirical research among housing economists, which is again summarized elsewhere (Smith 2011). However, the debate remains underdeveloped.

Discussions tend to turn on the extent to which housing markets *either* respond to fundamentals, and are therefore rational and efficient (on the one hand), *or* are driven by irrational emotions and unrealistic expectations (on the other). Most modeling exercises adopt a "fundamentals first" approach, assigning "psychological" factors a catch-all or residual role, even where such residuals are large. And while "fundamental" variables tend to be highly differentiated and closely specified, irrational influences are often bundled under one or two broad labels—such as "speculation"—which, even then, are often imputed from data designed for other things. It is therefore probably fair to say that, in relation to housing, there is far more debate over whether price instabilities are

rational or not (whether markets are efficient) than over what those "irrationalities" consist of, or how powerful they might be in determining the peakiness of prices.

Nevertheless, there is something about nonrational price expectations and pricing behaviors—overoptimism, speculation, imitation, and the rest—that economists are increasingly drawn toward when accounting for housing market instability. There is indeed a growing sense that enlarging these debates is where the research frontier lies (Mayer 2010). It is significant, therefore, that in a more general text, Akerlof and Shiller (2009) add greater texture to the variety of behavioral drivers represented by what they call "animal spirits." It may be that house prices, too, are sensitive to the negative emotions that pepper this wider literature. Certainly, it seems reasonable to imagine that home prices bear the imprint of myopia, fear, money illusion, and a host of similar terms.[7]

My own enthusiasm for these now-standard behavioral accounts is dampened, however, by the extent to which the language of behavioral economics so often implies that households' calculative practices are naïve, underdeveloped, uncivilized, or impaired. To be sure, debtors may be deliberately duped by predatory service providers, but in the UK, where predatory lending was relatively constrained, my experience is that home buyers have capabilities and competencies that are often underestimated (e.g., Cook, Smith, and Searle 2009). To enlarge the canvas, therefore, it is worth recognizing that once the Pandora's box of interdisciplinarity is opened up, there are perspectives from subjects other than psychology that might demand attention. A wider disciplinary sweep could indeed prove helpful as the cutting edge of behavioral economics is drawn toward styles of psychology—experimental, clinical, neurobiological—that may not be best placed to illuminate housing market activity. A more sociological oeuvre might, moreover, identify other sensibilities at work in the housing economy.

In fact, the few studies that use the qualitative tools of economic anthropology and sociology to explore housing market behaviors associate a wide spectrum of emotions with home price determination. My own research (with others) in the UK, for example, has drawn attention to the price implications of "feeling rules" that are rooted in a much more positive emotional economy than the behavioral tradition generally allows for. Prices are sensitive to hopes as well as fears, pragmatism as much as overconfidence, affection or attachment alongside hedonism, and social psychology alongside more individual psychological drivers. Details are given in Christie, Smith, and Munro (2008) and Munro and

Smith (2008); see also the essays in Smith and Munro (2009). In these studies, alternatives to rational calculation may be conceptualized as deliberation rather than speculation, and prices paid explained with reference to emotional intelligence as much as irrational exuberance. In short, while there is good evidence that there are passions in housing markets, which have measurable price effects, it may be premature to bundle these into undifferentiated terms like "psychology" or to categorize them a priori with value-laden labels like "animal spirits." The more critical point, however, is that, whatever labels are attached to the behavioral drivers of price, it is unlikely that volatility will be fully understood without more nuanced recovery and measurement of the emotional economy. For this, sociology, anthropology, and geography, as well as psychology, contain important clues.

These alternative approaches to housing assets, whether rooted in animal spirits or emotional intelligence, were, of course, marginal to academic debate, public policy, and financial practice in the early twenty-first century. With home prices hard to account for, property poorly understood, and financial innovations linked to home equity little more than embryonic, professional investors looked to debt-backed bonds and derivatives as proxies for housing market exposure (among other things). In the physical housing market, meanwhile, without a firm grasp of the drivers of home prices, the rule of thumb adopted by lenders and borrowers alike was that prices would rise in the long run, and stagnate rather than decline if the economy were to stall. This, rather than any more balanced suite of innovations, or any more sophisticated analysis of residential property markets, is what drove the integration of housing and mortgage markets into the twenty-first century.

A Mortgage Market Revolution?

Housing and mortgage markets are almost completely integrated in those English-speaking economies that sparked the financial crisis. Although between a third (United States) and around one-half (Australia and the UK) of owner-occupiers in these jurisdictions are unmortgaged at any given time, most outright owners are in the older age groups, and only a small proportion have never serviced a home loan. Indeed, the conventional, twentieth-century story is one in which the steady growth of mortgage markets and the expansion of home ownership proceeded hand in hand, albeit at variable pace (Grebler, Blank, and Winnick 1956; Harris and Rognetti 1998; Scott 2004).

To an extent, this trend continued into the credit-rich 2000s through the innovation of "affordability" products. These entry-level mortgages aimed to grow home ownership at the margins, reducing entry costs through some or all of the following mechanisms: low (or no) deposit requirements, low interest rates, interest-only or other deferred amortization structures, and longer terms. This "affordability" range was taken to its extreme in the United States, where a racialized surge of predatory subprime lending turned previously underserved enclaves into "oversold" markets whose debts were only viable while home prices rose (Wyly et al. 2008).[8] In the UK and Australia, lending was more tightly regulated, and the predatory market was much smaller. Nevertheless, affordability products still exposed borrowers to a range of unanticipated costs and risks (Scanlon, Lunde, and Whitehead 2008). There is, of course, more to say about these contracts. However, even in the United States, where they increased home-ownership rates among visible minorities by almost 20 percent in some urban neighborhoods, the net effect was to extend owner-occupation by just 5 percent in the decade to 2005. In the UK and Australia, such products barely enlarged owner-occupation at all. Expansion at the margins was not the main vehicle by which the flow of secured credit to household borrowers in countries with already high rates of owner-occupation was increased into the millennium. Lending to new buyers is not what doubled the value of mortgage debt in the United States between 2001 and 2007, or produced a steep rise in the ratios of secured debt to GDP throughout the English-speaking world.

Instead, toward the end of the 1990s, in the wake of ongoing deregulation, rising prices, sustained low interest rates, and unprecedented competition among lenders, a new style of borrowing gained momentum. It was driven by a suite of mortgages whose features encouraged the use of in situ equity extraction for nonhousing consumption. That is, the twenty-first-century story of mortgage market expansion centers on new lending to those who already own, or are buying, their homes. Although it has long been possible, perhaps usual in some income groups, to "overborrow" in association with residential relocation or initial home purchase, the advent of mass in situ equity borrowing is a relatively new phenomenon.[9] It was enabled by a round of product innovation achieved less by a sea change in the structure of mortgage contracts than by a stretching or embellishing of the status quo to channel a flood of secured credit (which, as discussed later, *was* generated by the invention of new financial instruments) into households' accounts.

In the United States, equity borrowing occurred mainly through a practice known as "cash-out refinance." The opportunity to refinance not only to reduce housing outlays but also to borrow cheaply, in situ, against rising home prices allowed refinance origins significantly to outpace new purchase loans between 2001 and mid-2004.[10] In the more "complete" mortgage markets of the UK and Australia, refinancing (known as remortgaging) was also common, but in these latter jurisdictions it became standard for mortgage products to enable borrowers routinely to withdraw funds from their homes, without remortgaging, to pre-agreed limits, and with practically no transaction costs (Girouard 2010; Mercer Oliver Wyman 2003; Smith, Ford, and Munro 2002).[11]

If the sums involved in the equity borrowing bonanza are hard to measure, the beliefs and behaviors that inspired it are barely documented at all. Of course, economists have a long-standing interest in the impact of housing versus other asset-generated wealth effects on the macro-economy (Case, Quigley, and Shiller 2005). And although debate has been heated, few now contest the salience of housing's wealth effects or challenge the significance of the collateral channel between home prices and consumption (Iacoviello and Ortalo-Magné 2002; Muellbauer and Murphy 2008). However, the concern in this mainstream literature is with the extent to which the wider economy is (or is not) insulated from the impact of housing market dynamics. The *micro*-economics of equity borrowing have been strangely overlooked. As a result, the risks associated with such practices are underspecified and only partially understood.

My own recent work, with colleagues, is one attempt to address this issue. The studies I summarize are ongoing. They refer to the UK and Australia, where the opportunities for equity borrowing are most varied. They use quantitative evidence to document key themes and qualitative data to tease out motivations and effects. The argument here is necessarily compressed, though I do refer as appropriate to the more substantial articles that inform, and enlarge on, these ideas.

The quantitative analysis is based on two national longitudinal surveys, the British Household Panel Survey (BHPS) and the survey of Housing, Income and Labour Dynamics in Australia (HILDA). Using matched data for 2002–2008, Ong et al. (forthcoming) provide a roundup of all styles of housing equity withdrawal that can be measured in, or imputed from, these surveys. To this end, each year is regarded as one accounting cycle for each household that is an owner in that period.[12] Each cycle is then classified according to whether or not it is associated with an

episode of equity withdrawal. Equity withdrawal can be achieved through selling up (exiting owner-occupation and realizing any profit), trading on (within owner-occupation, releasing cash by downsizing, borrowing up, or a combination of the two), or in situ equity borrowing (measured as the increase from year-end to year-end in the value of outstanding mortgages among nonmovers). This study shows that overall, one in five episodes is an equity extraction cycle, and 90 percent of equity extraction events occur through in situ equity borrowing. Although (as might be expected) the median values of equity extracted are higher per episode for those who sell up or trade on, the greater frequency (and not insubstantial size) of in situ borrowings makes this latter style of mortgage equity withdrawal by far the most significant flow of funds (worth over £50 billion p.a. in the UK alone), and increasingly so across the study period.

A question that few surveys and almost no analysts ask is why these loans are in demand, and what they are used for. This reflects a primary concern in the macroeconomic literature with how much cash is released, and with whether it is spent or saved. From a microeconomic and social perspective, however, it matters what these sums are for. To address this, Smith and Searle (2008) reviewed the evidence contained in all available UK survey resources. The most useful direct survey questions are contained in the BHPS. However, the only direct measure (the follow-up to a question on additional mortgages) may substantially underestimate the rate of in situ equity borrowing. Furthermore, response categories are broad and not exhaustive. By far the most interesting trends they exhibit across seventeen annual survey waves are, first, a decline in the tendency to reinvest borrowings into homes, and second, a growth in the proportion of households that spend some or all of their equity loan on "other" things—not home repairs or improvements, not cars, not other consumer goods (see also Searle and Smith 2010).

To consider what these undocumented expenditures might be, there is another way to identify the triggers for equity borrowing using panel survey data. Such surveys, because they interview the same households in each wave, allow the timing of equity borrowing events to be compared with that of other life events as well as with borrower characteristics. To that end, Parkinson and colleagues (2009) provide an exploratory analysis of matched data sets across HILDA and BHPS for the early years of the millennium (2000–2005).[13] Wood and colleagues (forthcoming) undertook a more formal modeling exercise using the same sample.[14] The findings pertinent to this discussion may be summarized as follows.

First, the analyses confirm that equity borrowing was widespread during the run-up to the financial crisis. Between one-third and two-fifths of homeowners conducted at least one net equity borrowing cycle across a five-year period. Furthermore, the sums involved were not trivial: the mean net annual withdrawal accounted for over 10 percent of a household's unmortgaged home equity in both jurisdictions, with a wide upper range. A surprising finding, given that incomes (and therefore ability to service loans) generally increase with age, is that added years substantially decreased rather than increased the likelihood of in situ equity borrowing. Wood and colleagues (forthcoming) attribute this to the possibility that equity borrowing represented the only way that younger home buyers, with an undiversified housing-centered wealth portfolio, could raise funds to meet pressing spending needs. The growing importance of home prices relative to earned incomes in lending criteria may have compounded this bias.

Second, the correlates of equity borrowing are consistent with its role as a financial buffer, even controlling for debt consolidation and portfolio diversification motivations. In this, our analysis extends the earlier work of Benito (2007, 2009).[15] The indication is that that the odds of equity borrowing increased in association with pressing spending needs, including those arising from *events*, such the onset of unemployment or (in the UK) relationship breakdown; the *ongoing condition* of being separated or divorced (possibly linked to loss of risk sharing and economies of scale in consumption); and the demands of caring for school-aged children. Detachment from the labor market depressed the likelihood of borrowing (relative to households with at least one earner in permanent employment), but those reliant on the temporary job market or in self-employment had similar or only slightly lower likelihoods of borrowing than those with more secure, salaried jobs. It seems possible that equity borrowing for these "near-labor" market groups was being used to bridge incomes across what may be regarded as a temporary loss of more permanent employment.

This is consistent with the findings of our most recent qualitative research among households in receipt of the UKs "support for mortgage interest" benefit (Munro, Smith, and Ford 2010).[16] Where they could, borrowers in this study used payment holidays or accumulated overpayments to prevent arrears during a compulsory waiting period between job loss and benefit payment. More striking still is the finding that many used up their borrowing options before turning to the benefits system, believing they would not be out of work for long. This financial hardship

model of equity borrowing is amplified by Searle (2011), who shows that over the entire period of 1994–2008 in the UK, irrespective of whether in times of expansion or recession, episodes of equity borrowing were around 20 percent more likely to occur among households experiencing financial difficulty than among those that described themselves as financially comfortable.

Third, however, there are some indicators of pressing spending needs that failed to elevate the odds of equity borrowing. These include the onset of adverse health conditions and the state of widowhood. One interpretation of this finding is that such circumstances are "insured" in other ways. Australia and the UK both have well-instituted public health services, for example, which may reduce the likelihood of households having to mobilize precautionary savings to meet the costs of cure and care. In the United States, in contrast, even health needs may have to be met through equity borrowing or other equity withdrawal strategies (Libman, Fields, and Saegert 2012). In a similar vein, widowhood is usually associated with a transfer of assets to the surviving spouse and is less likely to prompt equity borrowing than other transitions into single-person households. Additionally, there are indicators of financial hardship that depress rather than elevate the odds of equity borrowing, such as permanent transitions out of the labor force and continuing detachment from it (withdrawal from job seeking). These events signal a loss of income that is known in advance to be "unbridgeable," and that might therefore prompt—if anything—other styles of home equity withdrawal, such as selling up or trading down.

In sum, building on foundations laid by Skinner (1996) and developed by Hurst and Stafford (2004) for the United States and by Benito (2007, 2009) for the UK, these new analyses suggest that equity borrowing is prompted by economic shocks or biographical disruptions that create potentially bridgeable periods of financial stress. In this context, the facility for equity borrowing has turned housing wealth into a fungible store of precautionary savings, offering protection against the financial scars of otherwise uninsurable events. That is, the integration of housing and mortgage markets in the twenty-first century has enabled a wave of income substitution rather than income-driven consumption, and this in turn has positioned housing wealth as a de facto asset base for welfare (as discussed in Lowe, Searle, and Smith 2011).

This interpretation is encouraged by the findings of what I believe to be the largest single qualitative study of equity borrowing to date (Smith, Searle, and Cook 2007). Drawing on in-depth interviews with a cross

section of British mortgagors, this research points to a shift among home buyers in how housing wealth, in its newly fungible state, is conceptualized. Whether engaged in equity borrowing or not, study participants referred to their unmortgaged home equity with words like "shield," "comfort zone," "lifeline," and "buffer." They made clear reference to the safety net function of equity borrowing while also regarding it as a strategy to approach with caution and use sparingly (Smith, Searle, and Cook 2009). Much of the evidence across a wide range of interview transcripts suggests that UK households have begun to think of housing wealth today much as they thought of the institutions of the welfare state in the past: as a safety net of last resort (Smith 2012).[17] Equity borrowing may thus have a "welfare switching" role, feeding resources into the income gaps opened up by life events and transitions whose financial effects are neither insurable through private means nor (any longer) underwritten by the state (Smith 2010a). Two points follow.

First, equity borrowing in these circumstances—funding subsistence needs as much as consumption wants—carries substantial credit risks for indebted individuals as well as for lending institutions. The systemic risks this implies have been set out by Khandani, Lo, and Merton (2009), who indicate that equity borrowing makes the "refinance ratchet" six times riskier for lenders than it would be in a market without equity extraction. For individuals, Parkinson and colleagues (2009) show that even using an annual accounting period, and tapping into just five annual survey sweeps, equity borrowing in Britain and Australia is often serial. More than one-third of equity borrowers engaged in two extraction cycles over the same short study period, substantially increasing their leverage.[18] The result is that, among mortgagors, the debt-to-income ratios of equity borrowers and injectors have diverged over time. This observation dovetails with growing evidence across the English-speaking jurisdictions that serial reborrowing, like serial refinancing, quickly becomes unsustainable in the face of financial shocks. In the United States, for example, Mian and Sufi (2009, 2010) estimate that equity borrowing against accumulating housing equity accounted for over one-third of new mortgage defaults in 2006–2008. In a similar vein, Ong and colleagues' (forthcoming) analysis of housing equity withdrawal in the UK and Australia hints that, in both countries, the different methods of equity extraction (equity borrowing, trading on, and selling up) are, for those in financial stress, not so much alternatives as sequential strategies on a pathway out of ownership. Qualitative research underlines this observation, showing, for borrowers in receipt of support for mortgage interest, how easily an initially

bridgeable gap between incomes and costs becomes unsustainable as debts accumulate (Munro, Smith, and Ford 2010).

Following the financial events of 2006–2008, this escalation of credit risks was quickly and widely recognized. Most governments took steps to manage an epidemic of arrears and foreclosures by rescheduling debts and rewriting mortgage contracts. The various national schemes are summarized in Smith (2010b): without exception, they are based on reducing housing outlays in the short term by deferring capital repayments, rolling up interest, and reducing payments due in the hope of timely financial recovery. They are all debt management solutions that aim to restore "business as usual" in lending and borrowing. Just as mortgage markets grew in the early twenty-first century by using variants on a financial instrument that has changed little since its invention, so, in a similar vein, mortgage debts were mitigated by embellishing conventional payment protection or deferment, and income support, strategies by enlarging conventional models of insurance (Belsky, Case, and Smith 2008).

Credit and investment risks are closely linked in housing markets (Case and Quigley 2008, 2010) and may be equally damaging to well-being. Significantly, however — and this is my second point — none of the measures described above directly addresses the capital or investment risks to which home occupiers are exposed in an equity borrowing environment. In that sense, debt mitigation, credit withdrawal, and loan rationing address just half the problem. They do not tackle the periodic illiquidity in housing markets that prevents timely sale in the event of mortgage stress; in fact, they make housing wealth less fungible and more costly to realize. They do not address the falling property prices that erode households' asset base, produce debt overhang, and increase the risk of bankruptcy. They do not recognize that housing-centered wealth portfolios fail when either residential property generally, or single-family homes in particular, perform less well than other investments in the long run. They do not readily reverse a process, spanning more than half a century, in which owner-occupation has been positioned as an investment (as well as a bundle of housing services) whose returns are material to households' welfare. Most critically, they do not capitalize on the fact that even households in mortgage stress or negative equity hold the title to an asset whose future value has financial worth.

Investment risks in property markets are not new, but the more housing forms an asset base for welfare, the more such risks are underlined, and the more they threaten social as well as economic stability. In light of that, the sustained lack of attention to housing's investment risks is one

of the more puzzling financial features of the last half-century. Such myopia may have helped limit the scope for more balanced and imaginative styles of financial innovation. It leaves home-owning households overexposed to property prices and powerless to adjust their wealth (and debt) portfolios to a changeable economic environment. There is, then, a housing paradox. The credit markets that drove an unprecedented lending spree in the early twenty-first century were saturated in financial innovation. The residential property assets on whose fortunes this depended were starved of anything similar. This paradox is the subject of the next, final, section of the chapter.

Managing Financial Risks: The Strange Case of Housing

The steady integration of housing, mortgage, and financial markets may be a hallmark of modern economies. In practice, however, most financial innovation around housing has taken the form of complex credit-linked bonds and derivatives, whose popularity channeled an unprecedented flow of funds into mortgage markets. Instruments designed to share the returns and spread the risks associated with residential property investments gained far less traction. So, while mortgage markets and financial markets became very closely linked in the early twenty-first century, housing markets, though well integrated with the former, were practically untouched by the latter. If financial innovation is flawed in principle, as the debt debacle might imply, this may be a state worth preserving. If my broad argument holds water, however, the imbalance should be questioned.

Addressing the matter of principles first, it may be worth revisiting some key points concerning recent dealings in debt. There are many accounts already of the construction and undoing of the world's credit markets, and no space to rehearse them here. It is probably fair to say that most critics subscribe to the "collective failure to recognize risks" thesis, as set out in the British Academy's response to Queen Elizabeth II's question, "Why did no one see it coming?" (Besley and Hennessey 2009). The steer, from this perspective, is to unwind positions and draw back from debt. This is a persuasive argument. However, it is important not to lose sight of the fact that the innovation most associated with the financial crisis — mortgage securitization — was originally designed to boost financial inclusion by raising funds for loans underwritten by government-sponsored enterprises. This same process was expected to increase the liquidity required to make mortgage markets more complete

and, by implication, efficient. Neither goal was met. The reason, I suggest, has less to do with failing to recognize risks than with having insufficient motivation or incentive to minimize or manage them.

I refer elsewhere to this valorization of inaction as testimony to the "institutionalization of carelessness" (Smith, forthcoming)—a state that is deplorable, yet was preventable and is not inherent in the facts of financial innovation. The indignity it implies stems from the surprisingly large appetite investors had for mortgage-heavy debt-backed bonds (see Green and Wachter 2010)[19] in a setting not only devoid of effective regulation but also full of incentives to create, underestimate, and underinsure risk (Immergluck 2009). There is what I would call an ethopolitics of inhumanity in play.[20] To my reading, however, this is not the product of *necessarily* flawed financial instruments but rather a consequence of lax financial architecture, inappropriate models of professionalism, and unaccountable organizational management wound within a cycle of innovation whose institution was imprudent. That is not to argue that returning to a somewhat more principled "business as usual" in lending and borrowing (the dominant postcrisis model) is socially acceptable or adequate for managing the complex mix of credit and investment risks associated with home ownership. Rather, it raises the possibility of exercising a different kind of financial imagination: certainly one that is regulated to be more "care-full"; perhaps, in that context, one that looks less to debts and more to assets when considering the possibilities for financial innovation; conceivably, a round of well-regulated humane inventiveness that enables households to hold their wealth in a more diverse portfolio, hedge their housing risks, and avoid unsustainable mortgage debt.

The most elegant proposition so far has been crafted by Robert Shiller (e.g., 2003, 2008a, 2008b), who has long advocated trading home price–linked instruments (options, futures, and swaps) in financial markets. Home price derivatives effectively split the cost of housing services from the price of the investment vehicles that are indivisibly linked to them in modern housing markets. Using products enabled by this innovation, households could effectively buy the housing services component of a family home without the entirety of its associated investment vehicle. At the same time, other actors (individuals and institutions) could invest incrementally in the wider fortunes of the housing market without owning a property at all. Such instruments also create the possibility for residential property investors to hedge their housing risks—an option that housing, uniquely among the major asset classes, has never had before.

These ideas are well documented. They have early antecedents (LeComte 2007); they inspired a flurry of papers in the 1990s (e.g., Case,

Shiller, and Weiss 1993; Gemmil 1990; Miller, Sklarz, and Stedman 1989; Thomas 1996); and they occupy the entire Part 3 of Wiley-Blackwell's recently published *Blackwell Companion to the Economics of Housing* (Smith and Searle 2010). Housing economists generally agree that there is both an economic logic, and a social argument, in favor of this innovation (e.g., Caplin, Joye, et al. 2003; Quigley 2006). Indeed, derivatives benchmarked by home prices could—if simple, transparent, and effectively regulated—be used to develop products with the potential to realize a wide range of housing and urban policy goals. They could address problems that, currently, are either tackled incrementally or managed with riskier, debt-based instruments. I have detailed these applications elsewhere (Smith 2010b). They can be thought of in two ways.

First, a liquid market in housing derivatives could be (and to an extent has been) used to create home price–linked investment vehicles and savings accounts. If appropriately tax-exempted (i.e., treated in the same way as wealth held as housing), these could form an appealing savings gateway to owner-occupation. Such vehicles would insulate deposits against home price volatility, enabling households to postpone purchase until ownership was both appropriate to needs and affordable (Syz, Vanini, and Salvi 2006; Syz 2010). Such vehicles could also be used to hold, and protect, price premiums gained in one housing market in the case of, say, labor migration to another.

The option to invest in residential property price–linked investment vehicles might also promote financial inclusion. Renters, including those who cannot afford whole-home purchase, could hold their wealth incrementally in property price-linked accounts, with practically frictionless injections and withdrawals. (On the other side, first-time buyers could effectively sell a portion of their likely investment gains in return for lower entry costs.) Investors in the rental or buy-to-let market, on the other hand, whose main returns in the last decade have been in capital gains, could avoid the transactions, holding, and management costs of real property investments by using a price-indexed indirect investment vehicle. To the extent that "absentee purchasers" are drivers of volatility (Mayer 2010), this in itself should have a stabilizing effect. Finally, because such vehicles have the advantage of spreading investments across a basket of properties, they could lay the foundations of a substantial and sustainable shared ownership or equity share market—one that is attractive to institutional investors and thus available in the mainstream, as well as at the margins, of the ownership market.[21]

Second, in what is, if anything, a more radical set of applications, because these instruments can be sold as well as bought, they therefore

have a hedging function (Englund, Hwang, and Quigley 2002). The obvious application is a form of home equity insurance to protect households' asset base, support neighborhood regeneration, and help stem urban decline (Caplin, Goetzmann, et al. 2003; Shiller and Weiss 1994).[22] The same hedging function could be used to underwrite the role of housing in retirement planning. As well as guaranteeing a minimum sale value for downsizing, such vehicles could be used by institutional investors to offset the capital risks associated with reverse mortgages and equity release schemes for older outright owners who do not wish to move. Such schemes might thereby prove more cost-effective all around.

An apposite application for this hedging function in the current environment is to enable mortgagors in arrears to "sell" future capital gains to raise funds to preempt foreclosure and clear debts. This latter tactic is effectively an equity, rather than debt, solution to mortgage arrears. There is growing interest in the possibility of building such instruments into mortgage contracts that truly would be innovative. These contracts would allow for better risk sharing and continuous risk adjustment, not only in relation to debt, but also with respect to home prices (Ambrose and Buttimer, forthcoming; Ebrahim, Shackleton, and Wojakowski 2011; Liu 2006 (and a series of related work); Miles 2012; Miles and Pillonca 2008; Shiller 2009; Shiller et al. 2011; Syz and Vanini 2012). These equity finance models all help create the very real possibility, which I explore elsewhere, that financial innovations around home prices and housing equity could, if handled with sufficient care, transform entire housing systems, erasing tenure inequalities and creating accommodation options that are fairer, more affordable, and more inclusive than before (Smith, forthcoming).

I have hinted already that, had there been a liquid synthetic housing market by the turn of the millennium, it might have tempered or diverted the enthusiasm among institutional investors for buying into mortgage debt. I have also suggested that some risks in credit markets, and certainly their social and economic effects, could have been contained by policy options enabled by housing derivatives. This raises the intriguing possibility that the current financial crisis was prolonged, if not precipitated, less by the too close integration of housing, mortgage, and financial markets than by the unevenness of this encounter—by the fact that housing and financial markets are barely integrated at all when there could be benefits, not least to households, if they were.

If this analysis is correct, the answer seems obvious. However, there are reasons to be skeptical. I refer not so much to the fact that debt-based innovations turned sour (though there are important lessons to take from

this) as to the awkward truth that home equity–linked innovations have been in play for more than twenty years and have never yet gained traction. A market for housing derivatives has been possible in theory since the early 1980s, when the requirement for physical delivery was abolished (Millo 2007). Yet, despite theoretical appeal and a succession of practical efforts by major financial exchanges, and in the over-the-counter (OTC) sector, trading has been slow and sporadic. To conclude, summarizing ideas explored more fully in Smith (2009), I consider why this is, and whether it is insurmountable.

Conventionally, economists approach the question of whether derivatives markets do or do not gain traction empirically and quantitatively (Black 1986). However, most agree that uncertainty is high so that success, in truth, is hard to predict. I therefore report here on a project that has explored the problem empirically and qualitatively, including interviews with key actors and attendance at signature events in the run-up to the latest attempt to bring these markets to life. Space precludes all but a brief overview.

Bringing this paper full circle, part of the difficulty for innovations on the equity side of housing undoubtedly revolves around the quality, quantity, and coverage of tradable home price indexes. The importance of benchmarking to an established, accurate, reliable, frequently published price measure is hard to overstate. The case made by the Chicago Mercantile Exchange to the Commodities Futures Trading Commission prior to launching a new market in housing options and futures in 2006 opened with an eighteen-page account of the quality and merits of its chosen index (the repeat-sales index developed by Case and Shiller [1987]). At the launch of the new market in New York, seventeen of twenty-three questions from the floor focused on the quality and computation of that index. However, a sound price index is just the start. Indeed, scholars are divided on what makes an index tradable (Clapman et al. 2005; Deng and Quigley 2008), and professionals are, too (Blank et al. 2010). The crux, perhaps, is that once a particular quality threshold is passed, the challenge is whether price benchmarks can be used resolve this paradox:

property derivatives need to reflect as much as possible real estate's space-time components but the more they do so, the less likely they are to make it in the world of finance. (LeComte 2007, 351)

If resolving this is key, I suggest that three trends are encouraging. First, technological innovation (the advent of electronic trading platforms) has made it possible—to an extent—to bring the rhythm of exchange

trading more into line with housing market dynamics. Such platforms make it easier to keep trading open through a slow start (traders can monitor more than one market at once), easier to accommodate (even encourage) "buy-and-hold" tactics that are suited to housing market dynamics, and, of course, easier for market makers to "tap into" from remote locations, boosting the size of the trading pool. This technological fix for the mismatch between conventional exchange trading and the physical housing market means that even if housing does not meet the traditional criteria for a successful futures market, financial innovation should be possible.

Second, it might be feasible to develop or depict a price index that brings housing dynamics (which are generally cyclical rather than peaky, over periods of months, not minutes) more into line with the volatility of other index-based derivatives. In 2007, for example, Radar Logic began licensing a measure that represents U.S. residential property prices by recording daily (as well as weekly and monthly) fluctuations of the price per square foot of dwellings. The result is both a volatile index (whose visual signature is immediately more in line with that of other tradable financial indices) and something of an "index war" played out as the new measure vies for business with more traditional formulas. To my reading, the fact of this debate, as much as any resolution to it, serves as an indicator that the market is alive.

Third, there is the possibility that key issues hinge not on index quality, construction, or trading technologies but rather on the design of derivatives contracts. In the UK, where property derivatives trading is best developed, business is conducted almost exclusively over-the-counter (OTC). One reason, aired by some market actors, for the relative success of this OTC market hinges not on index quality[23] but on the possibility that exchange-traded futures, which are key to securing liquidity in derivatives trading, may nevertheless be "the wrong kind of derivative" with which to kick-start a synthetic housing market. Futures are time-limited and standardized. OTC contracts, in contrast, can be tailored to housing dynamics, with swaps extending over years, spanning periods, and containing a degree of customization that is far more in tune with what one broker calls "the heartbeat" of the housing market. This may explain why the UK, which had no exchange-traded housing derivatives for the preceding twenty years, nevertheless built a lively OTC market in the 2000s, whose buoyancy perhaps reflected the sensitivity of its carefully tailored contracts to the material world they represent.

There is more to say about the impact of price index construction, contract design, licensing, and regulation on the success of housing deriv-

atives markets. A well-documented mismatch between the expectations and competencies of housing professionals and of financial market makers remains a constraint, as do issues around the pricing and management of instruments that are still at an early stage of development (Fabozzi, Shiller, and Tunaru 2010). Yet none of the most frequently cited barriers to financial innovation around home equity seems insurmountable. There are four far more pressing concerns.

First, there is the issue of consumer aversion. Is there demand among those households that own the majority of residential real estate for an opportunity to diversity investments or hedge property risk? There is limited evidence here, but what there is hints that home buyers are alert to investment risks, averse to single-property-centered wealth portfolios, and sympathetic to some of the alternatives (Smith et al. 2009). Second, there is the question of consumer protection. Households should not dabble directly in derivatives, and the products they buy will need to be transparent, legible, and carefully regulated. Third, there is the issue of provider avoidance: there may be little institutional interest in engaging with novel products in the wake of the subprime scandal. After all, if the aim is to secure property exposure without acquiring and holding a cumbersome physical asset, the business community can invest in a fledgling market for commercial property derivatives where key actors are financially skilled and providers can conduct business with minimal "reputational risk." Finally, then, it is important to consider whether there is sufficient political imagination to support financial innovation and steer it in socially appropriate directions. Housing derivatives have the potential to change the way credit as well as investment risks are experienced, and to transform the meaning and use of physical housing markets. This could potentially work in the interests of home-occupiers. It is a radical idea whose success, ironically, relies on instruments too closely associated with careless markets, predatory institutions and financial failure. There is, however, no reason in theory why markets cannot be reclaimed for virtuous ends. I have argued for this myself (Smith 2005, forthcoming). In which case, there is equally no reason why simple, transparent, and effectively regulated housing derivatives could not be harnessed by governments to achieve rather different, more public-spirited goals.

Conclusion

The uneven integration of housing, mortgage, and financial markets is risky for individuals and for whole economies. This is clear from the debt

debacle, about which there is more to say, particularly concerning the institutionalization of carelessness at the interface of mortgage and financial markets. There is, however, a great deal to gain by more squarely addressing the asset side of the housing equation. Accordingly, the aim of this chapter has been to profile some ongoing but underdeveloped debates over home price dynamics, housing wealth effects, and residential property derivatives. To achieve this, I have made a case for exploring the microeconomic underpinnings of macroeconomic events, and for adopting multidisciplinary perspectives to that end.

Interdisciplinary alliances cast new light on the beliefs, expectations, and behaviors of economic actors; on the positioning of housing wealth in relation to savings, spending, and debt; and on the character and management of housing's financial risks. Reflecting on key findings, I suggest that better understandings of price volatility, fuller recognition of the determinants of equity borrowing, and a greater appreciation of the risks and rewards of residential property investment set the scene for more, not less, financial innovation. As governments seek to restore "business as usual" in the world of credit and debt, I use these insights to argue for a more imaginative financial future.

In particular, I draw attention to the policy goals that a balanced approached to financial innovation in the housing economy might score. These outcomes are not inevitable, nor are they desirable without the transparency, checks and balances that previous innovations lacked. Whether or not they work in the public interest will, in the end, be determined less by the facts of financial invention than by innovations in regulation and governance. Success will therefore depend as much on the energy and diligence of politics as on the achievements of economics.

Acknowledgments

This chapter was prepared with support from the ESRC's Professorial Fellowship Scheme (RES 051-27-0126). It was originally presented at the Symposium on Financial Innovation and Economic Crisis, convened by the Centre for Financial Studies, Goethe University, on the occasion of the award of the Deutsche Bank Prize in Financial Economics to Robert Shiller (Frankfurt, September 2009). Funded projects whose results are cited in the text also include: ESRC, "Anatomy of a Housing Boom" (R000222902); ESRC/AHRC, "Banking on Housing; Spending the Home" (RES 154-24-0012); and the project "Pathways from Housing Wealth to Wellbeing," funded through the ESRC/Australian Research

Council bilateral agreement (RES 000-22-1985/LX 0775767). I am indebted to many research collaborators, in particular Beverly Searle and Gavin Wood, together with Rachel Ong and Sharon Parkinson for the analyses herein. I also acknowledge the support, through election to an Adjunct Professorship, of RMIT University, Melbourne.

Notes

1. Even in the most recent British Social Attitudes survey, for example, carried out in 2010, only 3 percent of respondents would not advise a newly married couple to enter owner-occupation (Taylor 2011).

2. I use the term "equity borrowing" throughout to refer to the use of mortgages, secured against owned homes, to raise money for discretionary spending (i.e., not only for home purchase).

3. Residential REITS are an obvious exception, but even this market is comparatively small.

4. There are some exceptions; for example, Gyourko, Mayer, and Sinai (2006), Himmelberg, Mayer, and Sinai (2005), and Meen (2008) all argue that even simple supply-and-demand models can generate the appearance of volatility.

5. Hedonic approaches conceptualize dwellings as bundles of generalized and separately priced attributes: a mix of characteristics that buyers identify, seek out in different combinations, compare with the attributes of other dwellings, and choose to pay for or not. The underlying assumption is that there is a more or less consistent link between home prices and specified housing attributes because buyers generally (in aggregate) make rational choices based on expected utility.

6. Thanks to Gareth Powells for assembling this review; the methods are outlined in Smith, Searle, and Powells (2010).

7. Ackert, Church, and Jayaraman (2011) providing an interesting recent example.

8. Mayer and Pence (2008) also show that, even controlling for incomes and credit scores, subprime mortgages vary between neighborhoods according to the proportions of Black and Hispanic residents.

9. Mortgage equity withdrawal is cyclical, closely linked to home price appreciation, and has occurred before. It is generally measured in the aggregate, and for previous housing cycles it is hard to disentangle in situ equity borrowing from other styles of mortgage equity withdrawal. However, it is only in the current cycle that the regulatory, institutional, and cultural factors enabling widespread in situ equity extraction have come together.

10. Between 2003 and 2006, the proportion of refinance loans that had a cash-out component increased from 38 percent to 63 percent, and accounted for almost a third of the value of the refinance market.

11. Across the early 2000s in the UK, such borrowing may have accounted for between 6 and 8 percent per year of post-tax incomes (Smith, Searle, and Powells 2010).

12. Over the eight-year reference period, there are 34,000 cycles for the UK and 26,000 for Australia.

13. This paper also sets out the method of sample construction.

14. This analysis uses a random effects logistic regression model to identify the characteristics, events, and circumstances that elevate or depress the likelihood of equity borrowing.

15. Benito's analysis is based on the "additional mortgages" question in the BHPS; he finds that the timing of equity borrowings, based on this measure, is consistent with the use of housing equity as a buffer against shocks.

16. This benefit is available to households that have lost all earned income and have few savings.

17. This "last resort" thesis is supported in Searle's (2011) analysis across fourteen years of the BHPS, which suggests that equity borrowing is a tactic invoked when other borrowing opportunities are exhausted.

18. In contrast to the United States, where the impact of falling property values is felt with every refinance request, in Australia and the UK, equity borrowing can occur to a pre-agreed limit (set with reference to property values when the mortgage was originated) even if the price of the underlying asset subsequently declines.

19. This may, in part, have been because they had no other option for gaining significant exposure to housing markets (Smith 2009); it was also because returns were so high.

20. The concept of ethopolitics (taken from the work of Nikolas Rose and Michel Foucault) refers to acts of governance, contractual arrangements, vocabularies of motivation, and other devices that prescribe and define accepted norms and behaviors in particular political and organizational settings.

21. Shared ownership and shared equity schemes are currently limited by the aversion of institutional partners to the high costs and moral hazard of owning shares of physical property. As a result, they are generally limited to partnerships between low-income households and social or charitable landlords.

22. The idea of home equity insurance predates the interest in using derivatives to deliver it; however, the price-index model avoids the problems of adverse selection and moral hazard. Whether it is, even then, cost-effective is still an open question (Sommervoll and Wood 2009).

23. Most UK residential property derivatives trading has used the Halifax house price index, which has no repeat-sales element and is based on the lending data of a single banking group.

References

Akerlof, G. A., and R. J. Shiller. 2009. *Animal Spirits: How Human Psychology Drives the Economy, and Why It Matters for Global Capitalism*. Princeton, NJ: Princeton University Press.

Ackert, L. F., B. K. Church, and N. Jayaraman. 2011. Is There a Link between Money Illusion and Homeowners' Expectations of Housing Prices? *Real Estate Economics* 39: 251–275.

Ambrose, B., and R. Buttimer. Forthcoming. The Adjustable Balance Mortgage: Reducing the Value of the Put. *Journal of Real Estate Economics*.

Benito, A. 2007. Housing Equity as a Buffer: Evidence from UK Households. Bank of England Working Paper 324, London.

Benito, A. 2009. Who Withdraws Housing Equity and Why? *Economica* 76: 51–70.

Belsky, E., K. Case, and S. J. Smith. 2008. Identifying, Managing and Mitigating Risks to Borrowers in Changing Mortgage and Consumer Credit Markets. Working Paper UCC08-14, Cambridge, Joint Center for Housing Studies, Harvard University, Cambridge, MA.

Besley, T., and P. Hennessey. 2009. Reply from the British Academy to Her Majesty the Queen. London.

Black, D. G. 1986. *Success and Failure of Futures Contracts: Theory and Empirical Evidence.* Monograph Series on Finance and Economics 1986–1. New York: New York University, Salomon Brothers Center for the Study of Financial Institutions.

Blank, J., J. Reiss, P. Sceats, and J. Edwards (in interview with S. J. Smith). 2010. Hedging Housing Risk: A Financial Markets Perspective. In *The Blackwell Companion to the Economics of Housing: The Housing Wealth of Nations*, ed. S. J. Smith and B. A. Searle. Oxford: Wiley-Blackwell.

Camerer, C. F., and G. Loewenstein. 2004. Behavioral Economics: Past, Present, Future. In *Advances in Behavioral Economics*, ed. C. F. Camerer, G. Loewenstein, and M. Rabin, 3–15. Princeton, NJ: Princeton University Press.

Caplin, A., W. Goetzmann, E. Hangen, B. Nalebuff, E. Prentice, J. Rodkin, M. Spiegel, and T. Skinner. 2003. Home Equity Insurance: A Pilot Project. Yale International Center for Finance Working Paper 03-12, Yale University, New Haven, CT.

Caplin, A., C. Joye, P. Butt, E. Glaeser, and M. Kuczynski. 2003. *Innovative Approaches to Reducing the Costs of Home Ownership: A Report Commissioned for the Prime Minister's Home Ownership Task Force.* Canberra: Menzies Research Centre.

Case, K. E., and J. Quigley. 2008. How Housing Booms Unwind: Income Effects, Wealth Effects and Feedback through Financial Markets. *European Journal of Housing Policy* 8: 161–180.

Case, K. E., and J. Quigley. 2010. How Housing Busts End: House Prices, User Costs and Rigidities during Down Cycles. In *The Blackwell Companion to the Economics of Housing: The Housing Wealth of Nations*, ed. S. J. Smith and B. A. Searle. Oxford: Wiley-Blackwell.

Case, K. E., Quigley J., and R. J. Shiller. 2005. Comparing Wealth Effects: The Stock Market versus the Housing Market. *Advances in Macroeconomics* 5 (1): art. 1.

Case, K. E., and R. J. Shiller. 1987. Prices of Single Family Homes Since 1970: New Indexes for Four Cities. *New England Economic Review,* September–October, 45–56.

Case, K. E., R. J. Shiller, and A. N. Weiss. 1993. Index-Based Futures and Options in Real Estate. *Journal of Portfolio Management,* Winter, 83–92.

Christie, H., S. J. Smith, and M. Munro. 2008. The Emotional Economy of Housing. *Environment & Planning A* 40: 2296–2312.

Clapman, E., P. Englund, J. Quigley, and C. L. Redfern. 2005. Revisiting the Past and Settling Scores. Institute of Business and Economic Research Working Paper W04-005, University of California, Berkeley.

Clark, G. 1998. Stylized Facts and Close Dialogue: Methodology in Economic Geography. *Annals of the Association of American Geographers* 88: 73–87.

Cook, N., S. J. Smith, and B. A. Searle. 2009. Mortgage Markets and Cultures of Consumption. *Consumption, Markets and Culture* 12: 133–154.

Deng, Y., and J. M. Quigley. 2008. Index Revision, House Price Risk and the Market for House Price Derivatives. Institute of Business and Economic Research Working Paper W07-003, University of California, Berkeley

Dwonczyk, M. D. 1992. Housing: The Actuary's Last Big Frontier. *Transactions of the 24th International Congress of Actuaries* 5: 53–74.

Ebrahim, S., M. B. Shackleton, and R. M. Wojakowski. 2011. Participating Mortgages and the Efficiency of Financial Intermediation. *Journal of Banking & Finance* 35 (11): 3042-3054.

Englund, P., M. Hwang, and J. M. Quigley. 2002. Hedging Housing Risk. *Journal of Real Estate Finance and Economics* 24: 167–200.

Fabozzi, F. J., R. J. Shiller, and R. S. Tunaru. 2010. Property Derivatives for Managing European Real-Estate Risk. *European Financial Management* 16: 8–26.

Gemmil, G. 1990. Futures Trading and Finance in the Housing Market. *Journal of Property Finance* 1: 196–207.

Girouard, N. 2010. Housing and Mortgage Markets: An OECD Perspective. In *Blackwell Companion to the Economics of Housing. The Housing Wealth of Nations*, ed. S. J. Smith and B. A. Searle. Oxford: Wiley-Blackwell.

Goodhart, Charles, and Boris Hofmann. 2007. *House Prices and the Economy: Implications for Banking and Price Stability*. Oxford: Oxford University Press.

Grebler, L., D. M. Blank, and L. Winnick. 1956. The Growth in Residential Mortgage Debt. In *Capital Formation in Residential Real Estate: Trends and Prospects*, ed. L. Grebler, D. Blank, and L. Winnick. Princeton, NJ: Princeton University Press.

Green, R., and S. Wachter. 2010. The Housing Finance Revolution. In *The Blackwell Companion to the Economics of Housing*, ed. S. J. Smith and B. A. Searle. Oxford: Wiley-Blackwell.

Gyourko, J., C. Mayer, and T. Sinai. 2006. Superstar Cities. NBER Working Paper 12355, National Bureau of Economic Research, Cambridge, MA.

Hansen, J. 2006. Australian House Prices: A Comparison of Hedonic and Repeat-sales Measures. Research Discussion Paper RDP 2006-03, Reserve Bank of Australia, Sydney.

Harris, R., and D. Rognetti. 1998. Where Credit Is Due: Residential Mortgage Finance in Canada 1901–1954. *Journal of Real Estate Finance and Economics* 16: 225–238.

Himmelberg, C., C. Mayer, and T. Sinai. 2005. Assessing High House Prices: Bubbles, Fundamentals and Misperceptions. *Journal of Economic Perspectives* 19 (4): 67–92.

Hott, C., and P. Monnin. 2008. Fundamental Real Estate Prices: An Empirical Estimation with International Data. *Journal of Real Estate Finance and Economics* 36: 427–450.

Housing Market Task Force and M. Stephens. 2011. *Tackling Housing Market Volatility in the UK*. York: Joseph Rowntree Foundation.

Hurst, E., and F. Stafford. 2004. Home Is Where the Equity Is: Mortgage Refinancing and Household Consumption. *Journal of Money, Credit and Banking* 36 (6): 985–1014.

Iacoviello, M., and F. Ortalo-Magné. 2002. Hedging Housing Risk in London. *Journal of Real Estate Finance and Economics* 27 (2): 191–209.

Immergluck, D. 2009. *Foreclosed*. Ithaca, NY: Cornell University Press.

Just, T., and T. Mayer. 2010. Housing Markets in OECD Countries. Deutsche Bank Research International Topics, March 3, Frankfurt am Main, Germany.

Kay, J. 2003. *The Truth about Markets*. London: Allen Lane.

Khandani, A. E., A. Lo, and R. C. Merton. 2009. Systematic Risk and the Refinancing Ratchet Effect. NBER Working Paper 15362, National Bureau of Economic Research, Cambridge, MA.

Kim, K.-H., and B. Renaud. 2009. The Global House Price Boom and Its Unwinding: An Analysis and a Commentary. *Housing Studies* 24: 7034.

LeComte, P. 2007. Beyond Index-based Hedging: Can Real Estate Trigger a New Breed of Derivatives Market? *Journal of Real Estate Portfolio Management* 13: 342–378.

Lee, R. 2006. The Ordinary Economy: Tangled Up in Values and Geography. *Transactions of the Institute of British Geographers* 31: 413–432.

Leung, Charles. 2004. Macroeconomics and Housing: A Review of the Literature. *Journal of Housing Economics* 13: 249–267.

Libman, K., Fields, D., and S. Saegert. 2012. Housing and Health: A Social Ecological Perspective on the United States Foreclosure Crisis. *Housing, Theory and Society* 29 (1): 1–24.

Liu, R. 2006. SwapRent (SM). Advanced e-Financial Technologies, San Gabriel, CA.

Lowe, S., B. A. Searle, and S. J. Smith. 2011. From Housing Wealth to Mortgage Debt: The Emergence of Britain's Asset-Shaped Welfare State. *Social Policy and Society* 11: 105–116.

MacKenzie, D., and Y. Millo. 2003. Constructing a Market, Performing Theory: The Historical Sociology of a Financial Derivatives Exchange. *American Journal of Sociology* 109: 107–145.

Mayer, C. 2010. *Housing, Subprime Mortgages and Securitization*. New York: Columbia Business School; Cambridge, MA: National Bureau of Economic Research.

Mayer, C., and K. Pence. 2008. Subprime Mortgages. What, Where and to Whom. Finance and Economics Discussion Series 2008-29, Federal Reserve Board, Divisions of Research & Statistics and Monetary Affairs, Washington, DC. Available at http://www.federalreserve.gov/pubs/feds/2008/200829/200829pap.pdf.

Meen, G. 2008. Ten New Propositions in UK Housing Macroeconomics: An Overview of the First Years of the Century. *Urban Studies* 45: 2758–2781.

Meen, G. 2012. Home Price Determination. In *The International Encyclopedia of Housing and Home*, ed. S. J. Smith, M. Elsinga, L. Fox O'Mahony, S. E. Ong, and S. Wachter, et al. Oxford: Elsevier.

Mercer Oliver Wyman. 2003. *Study on the Financial Integration of European Mortgage Markets*, Brussels: Mercer Oliver Wyman and European Mortgage Federation.

Mian, A., and A. Sufi. 2009. House Prices, Home Equity–Based Borrowing, and the US Household Leverage Crisis. Chicago Booth Research Paper 09-20, University of Chicago, Booth School of Business.

Mian, A., and A. Sufi. 2010. Household Leverage and the Recession of 2007–2009. *IMF Economic Review* 1: 74–117.

Miles, D. 2012. Demographics, House Prices, and Mortgage Design. Discussion Paper No. 35. External MPC Unit, Bank of England, London.

Miles, D., and V. Pillonca. 2008. Financial Innovation and European Housing Markets. *Oxford Review of Economic Policy* 24 (1): 176–179.

Miller, N. G., M. Sklarz, and B. Stedman. 1989. It's Time for Some Options in Real Estate. *Real Estate Securities Journal* 9: 42–53.

Millo, Y. 2007. Making Things Deliverable: The Origins of Index-Based Derivatives. *Sociological Review* 55 (s2): 196–214.

Muellbauer, J. 2008. Housing and Personal Wealth in a Global Context. In *Personal Wealth from a Global Perspective*, ed. J. B. Davies. Oxford: Oxford University Press.

Muellbauer, J., and A. Murphy. 2008. Housing Markets and the Economy: The Assessment. *Oxford Review of Economic Policy* 24: 1–33.

Munro, M., and S. J. Smith. 2008. Calculated Affection? The Complex Economy of Home Purchase. *Housing Studies* 23: 349–367.

Munro, M., S. J. Smith, and J. Ford. 2010. An Evaluation of the January 2009 Arrangements for Support for Mortgage Interest. Department for Work and Pensions Research Report 711, Crown Copyright.

Ong, R., S. Parkinson, B. A. Searle, S. J. Smith, and G. Wood. Forthcoming. Pathways from Housing Wealth to Consumption. Manuscript.

Parkinson, S., B. A. Searle, S. J. Smith, A. Stoakes, and G. Wood. 2009. Mortgage Equity Withdrawal in Australia and Britain: Towards a Wealth-fare State? *European Journal of Housing Policy* 9: 363–387.

Quigley, J. 2006. Real Estate Portfolio Allocation: The European Consumers' Perspective. *Journal of Housing Economics* 15: 169–188.

Renaud, B., and K.-H. Kim. 2007. The Global Housing Price Boom and Its Aftermath. *Housing Finance International* 22 (12): 2–15.

Scanlon, K., J. Lunde, and C. Whitehead. 2008. Mortgage Product Innovation in Advanced Economies. *European Journal of Housing Policy* 8: 1–21.

Scanlon, K., and C. Whitehead. 2004. *International Trends in Housing Tenure and Mortgage Finance*. London: CML.

Scott, P. 2004. Selling Owner-Occupation to the Working-Classes in 1930s Britain. Economics and Management Discussion Paper em-dp 2004-23, Henley Business School, University of Reading.

Searle, B. A. 2011. Recession and Housing Wealth. *Journal of Financial Economic Policy* 3: 33–48.

Searle, B. A., and S. J. Smith. 2010. Housing Wealth as Insurance: Insights from the UK. In *The Blackwell Companion to the Economics of Housing: The Housing Wealth of Nations*, ed. S. J. Smith and B. A. Searle. Oxford: Wiley-Blackwell.

Shiller, R. J. 1993. Measuring Asset Values for Cash Settlement in Derivative Markets: Hedonic Repeated Measures Indices and Perpetual Futures. *Journal of Finance* 68: 911–931.

Shiller, R. J. 2003. *The New Financial Order: Risk in the 21st Century*. Princeton, NJ: Princeton University Press.

Shiller, R. J. 2005. *Irrational Exuberance*. 2nd ed. Princeton, NJ: Princeton University Press.

Shiller, R. J. 2008a. Derivatives Markets for Home Prices. Cowles Foundation Discussion Paper 1648, Cowles Foundation for Research in Economics, Yale University, New Haven, CT.

Shiller, R. J. 2008b. *The Subprime Solution*. Princeton, NJ: Princeton University Press.

Shiller, R. J. 2009. Policies to Deal with the Implosion in the Mortage Market. *B.E. Journal of Economic Analysis and Policy* 8 (3): art. 4.

Shiller, R. J., and A. N. Weiss. 1994. Home Equity Insurance. Cowles Foundation Discussion Paper 1074, Cowles Foundation for Research in Economics, Yale University, New Haven, CT.

Shiller, R. J., R. M. Wojakowski, M. S. Ebrahim, and M. B. Shackleton. 2011. Continuous Workout Mortgages. Cowles Foundation Discussion Paper 1794, Cowles Foundation for Research in Economics, Yale University, New Haven, CT.

Simonsohn, Uri, and George Loewenstein. 2006. Mistake #37: The Effect of Previously Faced Prices on Current Housing Demand. *Economic Journal* 116 (1): 175–199.

Skinner, J. S. 1996. Is Housing Wealth a Side Show? In *Advances in the Economics of Aging*, ed. D. Wise, 241–268. Chicago: University of Chicago Press.

Smith, S. J. 2005 States, Markets and an Ethic of Care. *Political Geography*, 24: 1–20.

Smith, S. J. 2009. Managing Financial Risk: The Strange Case of Housing. In *Managing Financial Risks: From Global to Local*, ed. G. Glark, A. Dixon, and A. H. B. Monk. Oxford: Oxford University Press.

Smith S. J. 2010a The Crisis of Residential Capitalism. Progress in Human Geography Annual Lecture, presented at the Annual Meeting of the RGS-IBG, London, September. Available from the author.

Smith, S. J. 2010b. Housing Futures: A Role for Derivatives? In *The Blackwell Companion to the Economics of Housing: The Housing Wealth of Nations*, ed. S. J. Smith and B. A. Searle. Oxford: Wiley-Blackwell.

Smith, S. J. 2011. Home Price Dynamics: A Behavioural Economy? *Housing, Theory and Society* 11: 235–260.

Smith, S. J. Forthcoming. Care-full Markets: Miracle or Mirage? *Tanner Lectures on Human Values*, Vol. 31. Salt Lake City: University of Utah Press.

Smith, S. J., and M. Munro, eds. 2009. *The Microstructures of Housing Markets*. New York: Routledge.

Smith, S. J., and B. A. Searle. 2008. Dematerializing Money: Observations on the Flow of Wealth from Housing to Other Things. *Housing Studies* 23: 21–43.

Smith, S. J., and B. A. Searle, eds. 2010. *The Blackwell Companion to the Economics of Housing: The Housing Wealth of Nations*. Oxford: Wiley-Blackwell.

Smith, S. J., J. Ford, and M. Munro (with R. Davis). 2002. *A Review of Flexible Mortgages*. London: Council of Mortgage Lenders.

Smith, S. J., M. Munro, and H. Christie. 2006. Performing (Housing) Markets. *Urban Studies* 43: 81–98.

Smith, S. J., B. A. Searle, and N. Cook. 2007. Banking on Housing; Spending the Home. ESRC End of Award Report (RES-154–25–0012).

Smith, S. J., B. A. Searle, and N. Cook. 2009. Rethinking the Risks of Owner Occupation. *Journal of Social Policy* 38: 83–102.

Smith, S. J., B. A. Searle, and G. D. Powells. 2010. Introduction. In *The Blackwell Companion to the Economics of Housing: The Housing Wealth of Nations*, ed. S. J. Smith and B. A. Searle. Oxford: Wiley-Blackwell.

Sommervoll, D., and G. Wood. 2009. Home Equity Insurance. Paper presented at the Conference of the European Network for Housing Research, Prague, July.

Stark, D. 2000. For a Sociology of Worth. Working Paper Series, Center on Organizational Innovation, Columbia University. Available at http://www.coi.columbia.edu/pdf/stark_fsw .pdf.

Syz, J. 2010. Housing Risk and Property Derivatives. In *The Blackwell Companion to the Economics of Housing: The Housing Wealth of Nations*, ed. S. J. Smith and B. A. Searle. Oxford: Wiley-Blackwell.

Syz, J., and P. Vanini. 2012. Property Derivatives and the Subprime Crisis. In *The International Encyclopedia of Housing and Home*, ed. S. J. Smith, M. Elsinga, L. Fox O'Mahony, S. E. Ong, and S. Wachter, et al. Oxford: Elsevier.

Syz, J. Vanini, P., and M. Salvi. 2006. Property Derivatives and Index-Linked Mortgages. Manuscript, Zurich Cantonal Bank, Switzerland.

Taylor, E. 2011. *Public Attitudes to Housing in England: Report Based on the Results from the British Social Attitudes Survey*. London: Department of Communities and Local Government.

Thomas, R. G. 1996. Indemnities for Long-Term Price Risk in the UK Housing Market. *Journal of Property Finance* 7 (3): 38–52.

Watkins, C. 2009. Microeconomic Perspectives on the Structure and Operation of Local Housing Markets. *Housing Studies* 23 (2): 163–178.

Wood, G., S. Parkinson, B. A. Searle, and S. J. Smith. Forthcoming. Motivations for Equity Borrowing: A Welfare Switching Effect. Manuscript.

Wyly, E. K., M. Moos, H. Foxcroft, and E. Kabahizi. 2008. Subprime Mortgage Segmentation in the American Urban System. *Tijdschrift voor Economische en Sociale Geografie* 99: 3–23.

5 Style Investing

Nicholas C. Barberis and Andrei Shleifer

One of the clearest mechanisms of human thought is classification, the grouping of objects into categories based on some similarity among them (Rosch and Lloyd 1978; Wilson and Keil 1999). We group countries into democracies and dictatorships based on features of political systems within each group. We classify occupations as blue collar or white collar based on whether people work primarily with their hands or with their heads. We put foods into categories such as proteins and carbohydrates based on their nutritional characteristics.

The classification of large numbers of objects into categories is also pervasive in financial markets. When making portfolio allocation decisions, many investors first categorize assets into broad classes, such as large-cap stocks, value stocks, government bonds, and venture capital, and then decide how to allocate their funds across these various asset classes (Bernstein 1995; Swensen 2000). The asset classes that investors use in this process are sometimes called "styles," and the process itself, namely, allocating funds among styles rather than among individual securities, is known as "style investing." In this chapter, we analyze financial markets in which many investors pursue style investing.

Assets in a style or class typically share a common characteristic, which can be based in law (e.g., government bonds), in markets (e.g., small-cap stocks), or in fundamentals (e.g., real estate). In some cases, the cash flows of assets in the same style are highly correlated, as with automotive industry stocks, while in other cases, such as closed-end funds, they are largely uncorrelated. Some styles are relatively permanent over the years (e.g., U.S. government bonds), while others come (e.g., small stocks) and go (e.g., railroad bonds). One reason for the appearance of a new style is financial innovation, as when mortgage-backed securities were invented. Another reason is the detection of superior performance in a group of securities with a common characteristic: small stocks became a

more prominent investment style following Banz's (1979) discovery of the small-firm effect. Styles typically disappear after long periods of poor performance, as was the case with railroad bonds.

There are at least two reasons why both institutional and individual investors might pursue style investing. First, categorization simplifies problems of choice and allows us to process vast amounts of information reasonably efficiently (Mullainathan 2000). Allocating money across ten asset styles is far less intimidating than choosing among the thousands of listed securities. Second, the creation of asset categories helps investors evaluate the performance of professional money managers, since a style automatically creates a peer group of managers who pursue that particular style (Sharpe 1992). Money managers are now increasingly evaluated relative to a performance benchmark specific to their style, such as a growth or a value index.

These benefits of style investing are particularly attractive to institutional investors, such as pension plan sponsors, foundations, and endowments, who as fiduciaries must follow systematic rules of portfolio allocation. Perhaps for this reason, interest in style investing has grown over the years, paralleling the growth of institutional investors. Not surprisingly, the financial services industry has responded to this interest. Most pension fund managers, as well as some mutual fund managers catering to the needs of individual investors, now identify themselves as following a particular investment style, such as growth, value, or technology.[1]

The growing importance of style investing points to the usefulness of assessing its effect on financial markets and security valuation. This chapter presents a simple model that allows for such an assessment. The model combines the style-based portfolio selection strategies of investors with a plausible mechanism for how these investors choose among styles. Specifically, we assume that many investors allocate funds based on *relative* past performance, moving into styles that have performed well in the past and financing this shift by withdrawing funds from styles that have performed poorly. We also assume that these fund flows affect prices.

These simple assumptions generate a number of empirical predictions, some already available in the theoretical literature, others entirely new. In our model, style investing generates common factors in the returns of assets that happen to be grouped into the same style. These return factors can be completely unrelated to common factors in cash flows (they exist even if there is *no* common component to underlying cash flows) and can be accompanied by higher *average* returns for reasons that have nothing to do with risk. When an asset is reclassified into a new style, it

comoves more with that style after reclassification than before, even if the cash-flow covariance matrix is unchanged. And while style investing increases the correlation between assets in the same style, it lowers the correlation between assets in different styles.

We also predict a rich structure of style return autocorrelations: positive own-autocorrelations and negative cross-autocorrelations in the short run, and with the opposite signs in the long run. The predictions about own-autocorrelations are shared with earlier models, while those about cross-autocorrelations are more unique to our framework. Moreover, while asset-level momentum and value strategies are profitable in our model, as in other models, we make the additional prediction that style-level momentum and value strategies can be as profitable as or even more profitable than their asset-level counterparts.

Our predictions about time-series autocorrelations reflect the fact that in our economy, investment styles follow a specific life cycle. The birth of a style is often triggered by good fundamental news about the securities in a style. The style then matures as its good performance recruits new funds, further raising the prices of securities belonging to the style. Finally, the style collapses, either because of arbitrage or because of bad fundamental news. Over time, the style can be reborn.

We use our model to shed light on a number of puzzling empirical facts. Among other phenomena, we address the common factors in small stock and value stock returns that appear unrelated to common factors in cash flows (Fama and French 1995), the performance of the small stock investment style over time, the poor returns of value stocks in 1998 and 1999 despite good earnings (Chan, Karceski, and Lakonishok 2000), and patterns of comovement when stocks are added to indexes such as the S&P 500.

Of the two assumptions underlying our predictions—investors' policy of allocating funds at the style level and their doing so based on relative past performance—neither has received much prior attention in the theoretical literature. The closest papers to our own are De Long et al. (1990a) and Hong and Stein (1999), in which investors allocate more to assets based on *absolute* past performance. Neither of these papers studies the effect of classifying assets into styles, or the effect of relative rather than absolute performance chasing.[2]

In section 5.1, we construct a simple model of style investing. Section 5.2 develops some of the intuition that lies behind the model's predictions. In section 5.3, we lay out the model's implications in a series of formal propositions. Section 5.4 analyzes two specific kinds of styles—indexes and price-dependent styles—in more detail. Section 5.5 concludes.

5.1 A Model of Style Investing

5.1.1 Assets and Styles

We consider an economy with $2n$ risky assets in fixed supply and a riskless asset, cash, in perfectly elastic supply and with zero net return. Following Hong and Stein (1999), we model risky asset i as a claim to a single liquidating dividend $D_{i,T}$ to be paid at some later time T. The eventual dividend equals

$$D_{i,T} = D_{i,0} + \varepsilon_{i,1} + \ldots + \varepsilon_{i,T}, \tag{5.1}$$

where $D_{i,0}$ and $\varepsilon_{i,t}$ are announced at time 0 and time t, respectively, and where

$$\varepsilon_t = (\varepsilon_{1,t}, \ldots, \varepsilon_{2n,t})' \sim N(0, \Sigma_D), \text{ i.i.d. over time.} \tag{5.2}$$

The price of a share of risky asset i at time t is $P_{i,t}$ and the return on the asset between time $t-1$ and time t is[3]

$$\Delta P_{i,t} = P_{i,t} - P_{i,t-1}. \tag{5.3}$$

We assume that, to simplify their decision making, some investors in the economy group the risky assets into a small number of categories, which we refer to as styles, and express their demand for risky assets at the level of these styles. In other words, a style is a group of risky assets that some investors do not distinguish between when formulating their demand.

To test any predictions that emerge from a model of style investing, it is important to have a concrete way of identifying styles. One way of doing this is to look at the products that mutual and pension fund managers offer clients. If money managers are responsive to their clients, they will create products that correspond to the categories those clients like to use. The fact that many money managers offer funds that invest in small-cap stocks suggests that "small stocks" is a style in the minds of many investors. Large-cap stocks, value stocks, growth stocks, and stocks within a particular industry, country, or index are then also all examples of styles.

We build a simple model of style investing. There are two styles, X and Y, and each risky asset in the economy belongs to one, and only one, of these two styles. Risky assets 1 through n are in style X while $n+1$ through $2n$ are in style Y. For now, we assume that this classification is permanent, so that the composition of the two styles is the same in every time period. It may be helpful to think of X and Y as "old economy" stocks and "new economy" stocks, say.[4]

As a measure of the value of style X at time t, we use $P_{X,t}$, the average price of a share across all assets in style X,

$$P_{X,t} = \frac{1}{n}\sum_{l\in X}P_{l,t}.$$ (5.4)

The return on style X between time $t-1$ and time t is

$$\Delta P_{X,t} = P_{X,t} - P_{X,t-1}.$$ (5.5)

Although our model does not require it, we restrict attention to simple cash-flow covariance structures. In particular, we suppose that the cash-flow shock to an asset has three components: a marketwide cash-flow factor, which affects assets in both styles; a style-specific cash-flow factor, which affects assets in one style but not the other; and an idiosyncratic cash-flow shock specific to a single asset. Formally, for $i\in X$,

$$\varepsilon_{i,t} = \psi_M f_{M,t} + \psi_S f_{X,t} + \sqrt{(1-\psi_M^2 - \psi_S^2)}f_{i,t},$$ (5.6)

and for $j\in Y$,

$$\varepsilon_{j,t} = \psi_M f_{M,t} + \psi_S f_{Y,t} + \sqrt{(1-\psi_M^2 - \psi_S^2)}f_{j,t},$$ (5.7)

where $f_{M,t}$ is the marketwide factor, $f_{X,t}$ and $f_{Y,t}$ are the style-specific factors, and $f_{i,t}$ and $f_{j,t}$ are idiosyncratic shocks. The constants ψ_M and ψ_S control the relative importance of the three components. Each factor has unit variance and is orthogonal to the other factors, so that

$$\Sigma_D^{ij} \equiv \mathrm{cov}(\varepsilon_{i,t},\varepsilon_{j,t}) = \begin{cases} 1, i = j \\ \psi_M^2 + \psi_S^2, i,j \text{ in the same style, } i \neq j \\ \psi_M^2, i,j \text{ in different styles.} \end{cases}$$ (5.8)

In words, all assets have a cash-flow news variance of one, the pairwise cash-flow correlation between any two distinct assets in the same style is the same, and the pairwise cash-flow correlation between any two assets in different styles is also the same.

The results we derive later do not require that styles be associated with cash-flow factors. However, if the purpose of styles is to simplify decision making, it is plausible that investors might create them by grouping together assets with similar cash flows.

5.1.2   Switchers

There are two kinds of investors in our model, "switchers" and "fundamental traders." The investment policy of switchers has two distinctive

characteristics. First, they allocate funds at the level of a style. Second, how much they allocate to each style depends on that style's past performance *relative to other styles*. In other words, each period, switchers allocate more funds to styles with better than average performance and finance these additional investments by taking funds away from styles with below-average performance. To capture this, we write their demand for shares of asset i in style X at time t as

$$N_{i,t}^S = \frac{1}{n}\left[A_X + \sum_{k=1}^{t-1}\theta^{k-1}\left(\frac{\Delta P_{X,t-k} - \Delta P_{Y,t-k}}{2}\right)\right] = \frac{N_{X,t}^S}{n}, \qquad (5.9)$$

where A_X and θ are constants with $0 < \theta < 1$. Symmetrically, switcher demand for shares of asset j in style Y at time t is

$$N_{j,t}^S = \frac{1}{n}\left[A_Y + \sum_{k=1}^{t-1}\theta^{k-1}\left(\frac{\Delta P_{Y,t-k} - \Delta P_{X,t-k}}{2}\right)\right] = \frac{N_{Y,t}^S}{n}. \qquad (5.10)$$

In words, when deciding on their time t allocation, switchers compare style X's and style Y's returns between time t–2 and time t–1, between time t–3 and time t–2, and so on, with the most recent past being given the most weight. They then move funds into the style with the better prior record, buying an equal number of shares of each asset in that style and reducing their holdings of the other style. The fact that their demand for all assets within a style is the same underscores our assumption that they allocate funds at the style level and do not distinguish among assets in the same style. The parameter θ determines how far back they look when comparing the past performance of styles and hence, the persistence of their flows. A_X and A_Y can be thought of as their average long-run demand for styles X and Y, respectively, from which they deviate based on the styles' relative performance.[5]

We think of the relative performance feature in equations (5.9) and (5.10) as arising from extrapolative expectations, whereby switchers think that future style returns will be similar to past style returns, combined with switchers' reluctance to let their allocations to the broadest asset classes—cash, bonds, and stocks—deviate from preset target levels. Put differently, this second condition means that while switchers are quite willing to move between different equity styles, they are much less willing to change their *overall* allocation to equities. Institutional investors in particular try to keep their allocations to the three broadest asset classes close to predetermined targets (Swensen 2000).

The intuition for how extrapolative expectations and target allocation levels combine to give the allocations in equations (5.9) and (5.10) is

straightforward. Holding everything else constant, an increase in $\Delta P_{X,t-1}$, the most recent past return for old economy stocks, leads switchers to forecast higher returns on that style in the future and hence to increase their demand for it at time t. However, since they want to keep their overall allocation to equities unchanged, they have to sell shares of new economy stocks, style Y. Therefore, $\Delta P_{X,t-1}$ has an opposite effect on $N^S_{i,t}$ in equation (5.9) and $N^S_{j,t}$ in equation (5.10), making demand a function of relative past performance.[6]

Extrapolative expectations can themselves be motivated by a cognitive bias that leads investors to put more weight on past returns than they should when forecasting future returns. For example, people often estimate the probability that a data set is generated by a certain model by the degree to which the data are *representative* or reflect the essential characteristics of the model (Tversky and Kahneman 1974). A style that has had several periods of high returns is representative of a style with a high true mean return, which may explain why impressive past returns raise some investors' forecasts of future returns.

The same behavior can also stem from agency considerations. An institutional investor, such as the sponsor of a defined benefit plan, may move into styles with good past performance and out of styles with poor performance simply because such strategies are easier to justify ex post to those monitoring their actions.

Although there is still relatively little work analyzing data on institutional fund flows, the available research supports the idea that investors move funds toward styles with strong past performance. Choe, Kho, and Stulz (1999) and Froot, O'Connell, and Seasholes (2001), for example, show that foreign institutional investors tend to buy into countries with good recent stock market performance.

In reality, investors have many styles to choose from, not just two. Even with many styles, though, the two-style formulation in equations (5.9) and (5.10) remains relevant. When an investor pours money into a style he deems attractive, he may finance this by withdrawing funds from just *one* other style, rather than from many others. One reason for this is transaction costs. In terms of withdrawal fees and time spent, it is likely to be less costly to take $10 million away from one money manager than to take $1 million away from ten of them.

Another, potentially more important, reason is that there is often a natural candidate style to withdraw funds from, namely, a style's *twin style*. Many styles come in natural pairs. Stocks with a high value of some characteristic constitute one style, and stocks with a low value of the

same characteristic, the twin. Value stocks and growth stocks are a simple example. When an investor moves into the growth style, the value style is a tempting source of funds. First, because of the way twins are defined, there is no overlap between them. Second, it is easy to succumb to the mistaken belief that since a style and its twin are defined as opposites, their returns will also be "opposite": if prospects for the growth style are good, prospects for the value style must be bad.

5.1.3   Fundamental Traders

The second investor type in our model is the *fundamental trader*. Fundamental traders act as arbitrageurs and try to prevent the price of each asset from deviating too far from its expected final dividend.

We assume that, at the start of each period, fundamental traders have CARA preferences defined over the value of their invested funds one period later. Our justification for giving them a short horizon is drawn from Shleifer and Vishny (1997), who argue that if investors are not sophisticated enough to understand a money manager's strategies, they will use short-term returns as a way of judging his competence and withdraw funds after poor performance. The threat of this happening forces arbitrageurs to take a short-term view.

Fundamental traders therefore solve

$$\max_{N_t} E_t^F \left(-\exp[-\gamma(W_t + N_t'(P_{t+1} - P_t))]\right), \tag{5.11}$$

where

$$N_t = (N_{1,t}, \ldots, N_{2n,t})', \tag{5.12}$$

$$P_t = (P_{1,t}, \ldots, P_{2n,t})', \tag{5.13}$$

and where $N_{i,t}$ is the number of shares allocated to risky asset i, γ governs the degree of risk aversion, E_t^F denotes fundamental trader expectations at time t, and W_t is time t wealth.

If fundamental traders assume a normal distribution for conditional price changes, optimal holdings N_t^F are given by

$$N_t^F = \frac{(V_t^F)^{-1}}{\gamma}(E_t^F(P_{t+1}) - P_t), \tag{5.14}$$

where

$$V_t^F = var_t^F(P_{t+1} - P_t), \tag{5.15}$$

with the F superscript in V_t^F again denoting a forecast made by fundamental traders.

5.1.4 Prices

Given fundamental trader expectations about future prices, which we discuss shortly, prices are set as follows. The fundamental traders serve as market makers and treat the demand from switchers as a supply shock. If the total supply of the $2n$ assets is given by the vector Q, equation (5.14) implies

$$P_t = E_t^F(P_{t+1}) - \gamma V_t^F(Q - N_t^S), \tag{5.16}$$

where $N_t^S = (N_{1,t}^S, \ldots, N_{2n,t}^S)'$. In contrast to switchers, who form expectations of future prices based on past prices, fundamental traders are forward looking and base price forecasts on expectations about the final dividend. One way they may do this is to roll equation (5.16) forward iteratively, setting

$$E_{T-1}^F(P_T) = E_{T-1}^F(D_T) = D_{T-1}, \tag{5.17}$$

where

$$D_t = (D_{1,t}, \ldots, D_{2n,t})'.$$

This leads to

$$P_t = D_t - \gamma V_t^F(Q - N_t^S) - E_t^F \sum_{k=1}^{T-t-1} \gamma V_{t+k}^F(Q - N_{t+k}^S). \tag{5.18}$$

Suppose that fundamental traders set

$$V_\tau^F = V, \ \forall \tau, \tag{5.19}$$

where V has the same structure as the cash-flow covariance matrix Σ_D, so that V^{ij}, its (i,j)th element, is given by

$$V^{ij} = \begin{cases} \sigma^2, \ i = j \\ \sigma^2 \rho_1, \ i, j \text{ in the same style}, \ i \neq j \\ \sigma^2 \rho_2, \ i, j \text{ in different styles} \end{cases} \tag{5.20}$$

and also that they set

$$E_t^F(N_{t+k}^S) = \bar{N}^S. \tag{5.21}$$

Equation (5.21) means that while fundamental traders recognize the existence of a supply shock due to switchers, they are not sophisticated enough to figure out its time-series properties. They simply lean against the shock, preventing it from pushing prices too far away from expected cash flows.

Our assumptions imply

$$P_t = D_t - \gamma V(Q - N_t^S) - (T - t - 1)\gamma V(Q - \bar{N}^S). \tag{5.22}$$

Dropping the nonstochastic terms, we obtain

$$P_t = D_t + \gamma V N_t^S. \tag{5.23}$$

For the particular form of V conjectured by fundamental traders, this simplifies further. Up to a constant, the price of an asset i in style X is

$$P_{i,t} = D_{i,t} + \gamma\sigma^2(1 - \rho_1 + n(\rho_1 - \rho_2))\frac{N_{X,t}^S}{n} \tag{5.24}$$

$$= D_{i,t} + \frac{1}{\phi}\sum_{k=1}^{t-1}\theta^{k-1}\left(\frac{\Delta P_{X,t-k} - \Delta P_{Y,t-k}}{2}\right),$$

where

$$\phi = \frac{n}{\gamma\sigma^2(1 - \rho_1 + n(\rho_1 - \rho_2))}, \tag{5.25}$$

and the price of an asset j in style Y is

$$P_{j,t} = D_{j,t} + \frac{1}{\phi}\sum_{k=1}^{t-1}\theta^{k-1}\left(\frac{\Delta P_{Y,t-k} - \Delta P_{X,t-k}}{2}\right). \tag{5.26}$$

We study equilibria in which fundamental traders' choices of V and $\bar{N}^S$ in equations (5.19) and (5.21) are reasonable in that they lead, through equation (5.22), to prices for which the conditional covariance matrix of returns actually is V, and for which unconditional mean switcher demand actually is $\bar{N}^S$. Such equilibria exist for a wide range of values of the exogenous parameters Σ_D, A_X, A_Y, θ, and γ.

In a world with only fundamental traders,

$$P_t = D_t. \tag{5.27}$$

We refer to this as the fundamental value of the assets and denote it P_t^*.

Equation (5.23) shows that fundamental traders are unable to push prices back to fundamental values. Their short one-period horizon forces

them to worry about shifts in switcher sentiment and makes them less aggressive in combating mispricing, a mechanism originally suggested by De Long et al. (1990b). Their inability to wipe out the influence of noise traders is consistent with the substantial body of empirical evidence indicating that uninformed demand shocks influence security prices (Harris and Gurel 1986; Shleifer 1986; Kaul, Mehrotra, and Morck 2000; Lamont and Thaler 2000). Moreover, if we think of switchers as institutions chasing the best-performing style, our model is consistent with evidence that demand shifts by institutions in particular influence security prices (Gompers and Metrick 2001).

If we included more sophisticated arbitrageurs in our model—arbitrageurs who understood the form of the demand function in equation (5.9)—they might exacerbate rather than counteract the mispricing. This is the finding of De Long et al. (1990a), who consider an economy with positive feedback traders similar to our switchers, as well as arbitrageurs. When an asset's price rises above fundamental value, the arbitrageurs do not sell or short the asset. Rather, they *buy* it, knowing that the price rise will attract more feedback traders next period, leading to still higher prices, at which point the arbitrageurs can exit at a profit. Since sophisticated arbitrageurs may amplify rather than counteract the effect of switchers, we exclude them from our simple model.

5.1.5 Parameter values

In section 5.3, we prove some general propositions about the behavior of asset prices in our economy. To illustrate some of these propositions, we use a numerical implementation of equations (5.24) and (5.26) in which the exogenous parameters $\Sigma_D, A_X, A_Y, \theta$, and γ are assigned specific values.

From equation (5.8), the cash-flow covariance matrix is completely determined by ψ_M and ψ_S. We set $\psi_M = 0.25$ and $\psi_S = 0.5$, which gives

$$\Sigma_D = \begin{pmatrix} \Sigma_0 & \Sigma_1 \\ \Sigma_1 & \Sigma_0 \end{pmatrix}, \tag{5.28}$$

where

$$\Sigma_0 = \begin{pmatrix} 1 & 0.31 & \cdots & 0.31 \\ 0.31 & \ddots & & \vdots \\ \vdots & & \ddots & 0.31 \\ 0.31 & \cdots & 0.31 & 1 \end{pmatrix}, \Sigma_1 = \begin{pmatrix} 0.06 & \cdots & \cdots & 0.06 \\ \vdots & \ddots & & \vdots \\ \vdots & & \ddots & \vdots \\ 0.06 & \cdots & \cdots & 0.06 \end{pmatrix}. \tag{5.29}$$

The remaining parameters are set equal to

$$A_X = A_Y = 0,$$ (5.30)

$$\theta = 0.95,$$ (5.31)

$$\gamma = 0.093.$$ (5.32)

Equation (5.9) shows that θ controls the persistence of switcher flows; a θ close to 1 indicates a high level of persistence. Fundamental trader risk aversion γ is set so that in equilibrium, returns exhibit a level of excess volatility that is reasonable given historical U.S. data. For these parameter values, style returns have a standard deviation 1.3 times the standard deviation of cash-flow shocks.[7] In this equilibrium, the value of ϕ in equation (5.25) is 1.25.[8]

5.2 Competition among Styles

5.2.1 Impulse Response Functions

As a first step toward understanding the effect of switchers on asset prices, we use the formulas for price in equations (5.24) and (5.26) to generate some impulse response functions. We take $n = 50$, so that there are 100 risky assets, the first 50 of which are in style X and the last 50 in style Y. X and Y can again be thought of as old economy and new economy stocks, respectively. The parameters are set equal to the values in equations (5.28) to (5.32). Figure 5.1 shows how the prices $P_{X,t}$ and $P_{Y,t}$ of styles X and Y, defined in equation (5.4), evolve after a one-time cash-flow shock to style X when $t = 1$.

In the notation of our model,

$$\varepsilon_{i,1} = 1, \ \varepsilon_{i,t} = 0, \ t > 1, \ \forall i \in X,$$ (5.33)

$$\varepsilon_{j,t} = 0, \ \forall t, \ \forall j \in Y.$$ (5.34)

We assume $D_{i,0} = 50, \forall i$.

The solid line in the top half of the graph tracks $P_{X,t}$, the value of style X in the presence of switchers. The dashed line in the top half is the fundamental value of style X, $P^*_{X,t}$, defined through equations (5.27) and (5.4) as the value of style X when there are only fundamental traders in the economy and no switchers.

The figure shows that in the presence of switchers, a cash-flow shock to style X leads to a substantial and long-lived deviation of X's price from its fundamental value. The good cash-flow news about X pushes up

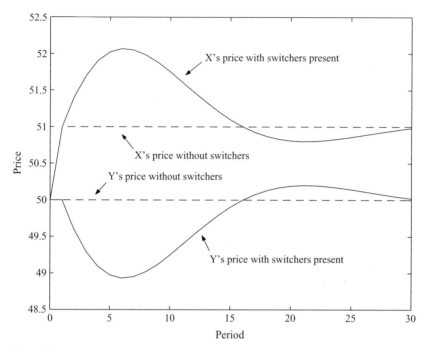

Figure 5.1
Impulse responses to a style-level cash-flow shock. Some investors in the economy, known as switchers, group risky assets into two categories, X and Y, known as styles. The solid lines show how the prices of styles X and Y evolve after a cash-flow shock to style X in period 1. The prices of both X and Y are initially 50. For comparison, the dashed lines indicate fundamental values, or prices in the absence of switchers.

its price. This outperformance catches the attention of switchers, who then increase their demand for X in the following period, pushing X's price still higher and drawing in more switchers. In the absence of any more good cash-flow news, switchers' interest in style X eventually fades and prices return to fundamental value.

The fact that switchers' investment decisions are based on *relative* rather than absolute past performance leads to a more novel prediction, which we refer to as an *externality*. Figure 5.1 shows that the cash-flow shock to X affects not only X's price but also Y's, even though there has been no news about Y. The good news about X draws funds into that style. However, since switchers want to maintain a constant overall allocation to equities, they finance the extra investment in X by taking money out of Y. This pushes Y's price down, making it look even worse relative to X and leading to still more redemptions by switchers.

In practice, the quantitative magnitude of the externality depends heavily on how investors finance their style shifts. If they finance a shift into a particular style by withdrawing small amounts of money from all other styles, the externality is dispersed and therefore hard to detect. However, if as we argue in section 5.1.2, investors finance shifts into a style by withdrawing funds from the style's twin alone, the externality is concentrated and more easily detectable.[9]

We can also look at impulse responses to *asset-specific* cash-flow news. Suppose that asset 1, a member of style X, experiences a one-time cash-flow shock at time 1. In our notation,

$$\varepsilon_{i,1} = 1, \varepsilon_{i,t} = 0, \ t > 1, \text{ for } i = 1, \tag{5.35}$$

$$\varepsilon_{i,t} = 0, \ \forall t, \text{ for } i = 2,\ldots,2n. \tag{5.36}$$

Figure 5.2 plots prices $P_{i,t}$ and fundamental values $P_{i,t}^*$ for $i = 1, 2$, and 100. Recall that assets 1 and 2 are in style X while asset 100 is in style Y.

Figure 5.2 helps bring out the differences between our model and the related positive feedback trading models of De Long et al. (1990a) and Hong and Stein (1999), in which the feedback occurs at the level of an individual asset, so that noise traders increase their demand for an asset if it had a good return in the previous period. In these earlier models, a cash-flow shock to asset 1 only pushes asset 1's price away from fundamental value. Asset 1's outperformance attracts the attention of positive feedback traders, who then buy the asset in the next period, pushing its price up too high. Assets 2 and 100, on the other hand, are unaffected.

Figure 5.2 shows that in our model, *all three* assets deviate from fundamental value after the initial cash-flow shock to asset 1. The fact that assets 2 and 100, which received no cash-flow news at all, also move away from fundamental value is the result of the two new features of our model: a demand function that is defined at the style level and a focus on relative, rather than absolute, performance. The time 1 cash-flow shock to asset 1 boosts not only asset 1's return but also style X's return, attracting attention from switchers, who then allocate more funds to style X at time 2, pushing both assets 1 and 2 away from fundamental value. Since the inflows to X are financed by withdrawing funds from Y, the price of asset 100 is pushed below fundamental value.

5.2.2 Discussion

The impulse response functions show that, in our model, styles go through cycles. A style X is set in motion by good fundamental news about itself or, alternatively, by bad news about another style, Y, which affects it through

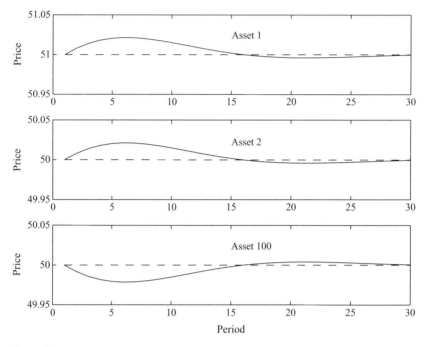

Figure 5.2
Impulse responses to an asset-level cash-flow shock. Some investors in the economy, known as switchers, group risky assets into two categories, X and Y, known as styles. The solid lines show how the prices of assets 1, 2, and 100 evolve after a cash-flow shock to asset 1 in period 1. Assets 1 and 2 are in style X while asset 100 is in style Y. All assets have an initial price of 50 at time 0. For comparison, the dashed lines indicate fundamental values, or prices in the absence of switchers.

the externality. The style then swings away from fundamental value for a prolonged period, powered by fund flows attracted by its superior past performance. Finally, the style returns to fundamental value because of selling by fundamental traders, because of bad news about its own fundamentals, or, most interestingly, because of good news in a competing style Y, which draws attention and investment dollars away from X.

In some cases, the cycles we describe may be reinforced by academic work analyzing the historical performance of a style. It is noteworthy that Banz's (1979) study on the outperformance of small-cap stocks was followed by several years of strikingly good returns on that style. Our model explains this by saying that Banz's study attracted the attention of switchers, who diverted funds to small-cap stocks, pushing them higher, thus drawing in yet more switchers and generating a long period of superior performance. Of course, our model also predicts that these good returns should eventually be reversed, and it is interesting that after 1983, small-cap stocks experienced

two decades of lackluster returns. Indeed, the poor returns of small-cap stocks after 1983 are crucial for distinguishing the style investing story from other explanations of the 1975 to 1983 outperformance, for example that investors were simply pushing small stocks up to their correct values after learning that they had been underpriced for many years.

More radically, cycles may be set in motion by data mining, as analysts looking through historical data identify abnormal returns. When analysts succeed in convincing investors that they have found strategies earning true superior returns, they will recruit new resources to the strategies, thereby confirming the anomaly for a period of time. Perhaps the discovery of the size effect in the 1970s is an example of such creation of a style out of what might have been a fluke in the data.

The externality from style switching is helpful in interpreting other recent evidence. During 1998 and 1999, value stocks performed extremely poorly by historical standards, lagging both growth stocks and the broad index by a significant margin. As Chan, Karceski, and Lakonishok (2000) show, this poor performance occurred even though the earnings growth and sales growth of value stocks over this period were as high as those of growth stocks and unusually good by historical standards. In other words, the poor performance of value portfolios cannot be easily linked to their fundamentals. A more natural explanation comes from our theory. The poor performance of value stocks in 1998 and 1999 could have been due to the spectacular performance of large growth stocks, which generated large flows of funds—unrelated to fundamentals—into these stocks and out of value stocks, the obvious competing style.

Another example comes, once again, from the historical performance of small-cap stocks. Siegel (1999) argues that one reason for the vastly superior performance of small stocks relative to large-cap stocks during 1975 to 1983 was the dismal performance of the "Nifty Fifty" large-cap growth stocks in 1973 and 1974. The demise of these high-profile large-cap stocks left investors disenchanted with the large-cap stock style and generated a flow of funds into the competing style, small-cap stocks, triggering a small-cap stock cycle.[10] A competing increase in the relative demand for large stocks, prompted by the rise of indexation and institutional investing more generally, may have arrested this wave of high small-cap stock returns. According to Gompers and Metrick (2001), institutional investors prefer large-cap stocks, and their ownership of these stocks has increased rapidly in the last twenty years. This increase in demand for the competing style could be one reason for the poor relative performance of small-cap stocks after 1983.

5.3 The Behavior of Asset Prices

We now present a systematic analysis of the effect of switcher flows on asset prices. We summarize the predictions of our model in a series of propositions, focusing on predictions that are largely unique to our framework.

To illustrate the propositions, we use simulated data. As in section 5.2, we take $n = 50$, so that there are 100 risky assets, the first 50 of which are in style X and the last 50 in style Y. For the parameter values in equations (5.28) to (5.32), we use the price formulas in equations (5.24) and (5.26) to simulate long time series of prices for the 100 assets.

5.3.1 Comovement within Styles

Since switcher demand for securities is expressed at the level of a style, the prices of assets that are in the same style comove more than the assets' cash flows do. If style X has had superior past performance, switchers invest more in *all* securities in style X, pushing their prices up together. This coordinated demand generates comovement over and above that induced by cash-flow news. More formally, we can prove[11]

Proposition 5.1 *If two assets i and j, i ≠ j, belong to the same style, then*

$$\text{corr}(\Delta P_{i,t} - \Delta P_{M,t}, \Delta P_{j,t} - \Delta P_{M,t}) > \text{corr}(\varepsilon_{i,t} - \varepsilon_{M,t}, \varepsilon_{j,t} - \varepsilon_{M,t}), \tag{5.37}$$

where

$$\Delta P_{M,t} = \frac{1}{2n}\sum_{l=1}^{2n}\Delta P_{l,t}, \quad \varepsilon_{M,t} = \frac{1}{2n}\sum_{l=1}^{2n}\varepsilon_{l,t}. \tag{5.38}$$

In our simulated data, the correlation matrix of market-adjusted returns is

$$\text{corr}([\Delta P_{1,t} - \Delta P_{M,t},\ldots,\Delta P_{2n,t} - \Delta P_{M,t}]) = \begin{pmatrix} R_0 & R_1 \\ R_1 & R_0 \end{pmatrix}, \tag{5.39}$$

where

$$R_0 = \begin{pmatrix} 1 & 0.34 & \cdots & 0.34 \\ 0.34 & \ddots & \ddots & \vdots \\ \vdots & \ddots & \ddots & 0.34 \\ 0.34 & \cdots & 0.34 & 1 \end{pmatrix}, R_1 = \begin{pmatrix} -0.35 & \cdots & \cdots & -0.35 \\ \vdots & \ddots & & \vdots \\ \vdots & & \ddots & \vdots \\ -0.35 & \cdots & \cdots & -0.35 \end{pmatrix}. \tag{5.40}$$

In the presence of switchers, the correlation between the market-adjusted returns of distinct assets in the *same* style is 0.34. This is indeed higher than the assets' market-adjusted cash-flow news correlation of 0.14.

The proposition is stated in terms of market-adjusted returns and cash-flow news because in general, two assets in the same style may comove more than their cash flows simply because of a market-level return factor induced by changes in interest rates or risk aversion. Controlling for market-level effects allows us to focus on style-level factors, although the proposition also holds for raw returns and cash-flow news.

Proposition 5.1 suggests a novel way of understanding common factors in the returns of groups of assets. Such common factors are usually interpreted as reflecting common factors in the assets' cash-flow news. In our framework, they arise simply because the assets in question form a natural style and are therefore subject to style-level switcher flows that make them comove more than their cash flows. In particular, proposition 5.1 implies that there can be a common factor in the returns of a group of assets even if the assets' cash-flow news are completely uncorrelated.

If there *is* a common factor in the cash flows of assets within a style, not only will the common factor in returns be more pronounced, as per proposition 5.1, but it need not be strongly related to the common factor in cash flows. Since this period's style return is in part driven by switcher flows and hence by *past* returns, it need not line up with this period's cash-flow news.

The idea that style investing generates comovement in returns unrelated to comovement in cash flows has significant implications for the interpretation of security returns. Fama and French (1993) find a striking common factor in the returns of small-cap stocks as well as a clear common component in value stock returns. The simplest rational pricing view of this comovement holds that it must result from common factors in the underlying earnings of small-cap stocks and value stocks. Fama and French (1995) test this explanation and obtain surprising results. Although they do find common factors in the cash-flow news of small-cap stocks and value stocks, they uncover little evidence that the return factors are driven by the cash-flow factors.

These results do not sit well with the view that return comovement is driven by cash-flow comovement, but they emerge very naturally from a style investing perspective. This view holds that, to the extent that small firms belong to a style (because size is a characteristic defining a style), they move together by virtue of fund flows in and out of that style. Even if there is a common component in the earnings of small firms, it need not be related to the common component in their returns. This is exactly Fama and French's (1995) finding.

A common factor in the returns of value stocks unrelated to a common factor in their earnings can arise in two distinct ways in our framework. The more obvious mechanism relies on "value stocks" being a style unto themselves. An alternative story holds that industries are the most important styles and therefore that *they* have common factors in returns only weakly related to cash flows. Since value stocks belong to industries that have fallen out of favor among switchers, they exhibit a common factor in returns unrelated to cash flows simply by inheriting that property from industry styles. Either mechanism explains Fama and French's results for value stocks.[12]

Other evidence is also consistent with this analysis. Pindyck and Rotemberg (1990) find comovement in the prices of different commodities over and above what can be explained by economic fundamentals. Lee, Shleifer, and Thaler (1991) find that the prices of closed-end mutual funds move together even when the net asset values of the funds are only weakly correlated. In the language of the present model, if investors classify all commodities into a "commodity" style and all closed-end funds into a "closed-end fund" style, and then move money in and out of these styles, the coordinated demand induces a common component in returns even when the assets' fundamentals have little in common.

Also relevant are the findings of Froot and Dabora (1999), who study "twin" stocks such as Royal Dutch and Shell. These stocks are claims to the same cash-flow stream but are primarily traded in different locations. Royal Dutch is traded most heavily in the United States and Shell in the UK. In a frictionless market, these stocks should move together. Froot and Dabora show, however, that Royal Dutch is more sensitive to movements in the U.S. market, while Shell comoves more with the UK market. A style-based perspective provides a natural explanation. Royal Dutch, a member of the S&P 500 index, is buffeted by the flows of investors for whom the S&P 500 is a style, and therefore comoves more with this index. For the same reason, Shell, a member of the FTSE index, comoves more with that index.[13]

Proposition 5.1 is driven by our assumption that investors classify assets into styles and then allocate funds at the style level. Traditional models of positive feedback trading in which the feedback occurs at the individual asset level cannot easily deliver proposition 5.1. In these models, asset returns are typically only as correlated as the underlying cash flows.

Another important class of models assumes that investors are uncertain about the growth rate of an asset's cash flows and are forced to learn

it by observing cash-flow realizations. After several periods of impressive cash-flow growth, for example, investors raise their estimate of the rate (Veronesi 1999; Brennan and Xia 2001; Lewellen and Shanken 2002). If learning occurs at the level of individual assets, these models also have trouble delivering proposition 5.1, as asset returns are again only as correlated as cash flows.

In models that combine learning with bounded processing ability (Peng and Xiong 2006), investors simplify the allocation problem by creating categories of assets with correlated cash flows and then learning about cash flows at the category level. In other words, there is information pooling (Shiller 1989). Since investors allocate some of their funds by category, such models can explain why a group of stocks with a strong common factor in cash flows might have an even stronger common factor in returns. However, they are hard-pressed to explain why there would be a common factor in the returns of assets whose cash flows are largely uncorrelated, such as closed-end funds, since investors would be unlikely to create a category out of such assets in the first place.

Some existing models *can* explain why assets with uncorrelated cash flows might move together. Kyle and Xiong (2001) propose a theory of comovement based on the idea that financial intermediaries experience wealth effects. When intermediaries suffer trading losses, their risk-bearing capacity is reduced, leading them to sell assets across the board and inducing correlation in fundamentally unrelated securities. This model seems appropriate for understanding why apparently unrelated assets trading in different countries comove strongly in times of financial crisis, such as August 1998. It is less plausible an explanation for why small-cap stocks move together, regardless of economic conditions.

Finally, in their study of closed-end funds, Lee, Shleifer, and Thaler (1991) propose another view of comovement. Their view is related to our own, in that they assume that shifts in uninformed demand affect prices, but it is nevertheless distinct. They argue that some groups of securities may only be held by a particular subset of all investors, such as individual investors. As these investors' risk aversion or sentiment changes, they change their exposure to the risky assets that they hold, inducing a common factor in the returns to these securities. In other words, this theory predicts that there will be a common factor in the returns of securities that are held primarily by a specific class of investors. This is distinct from our own theory, which predicts a common factor in the returns of securities that many investors classify as a style, even if these securities are in *all* investors' portfolios.

Lee, Shleifer, and Thaler's (1991) theory is well-suited to explaining why small-cap stocks and closed-end funds comove, as both of these asset classes are held almost entirely by individual investors. Indeed, style investing is a less plausible explanation, since small-cap stocks and closed-end funds do not form a natural single style. On the other hand, style investing may be a better way of thinking about the common factor in value stocks, since there is no evidence that these securities are held primarily by a particular investor class.

The style investing view of comovement has other predictions and implications for the interpretation of empirical facts. Not only should stocks within a style comove more than their cash flows do, but stocks that *enter* a style should comove more with the style after they are added to it than before. For example, a stock that is added to an index such as the S&P 500 should comove more with the index after it is added than before. Changes in comovement after a security is added to a style provide one of the more unique empirical predictions of our theory. More formally, we can prove:

Proposition 5.2 *Suppose that asset j, not previously a member of style X, is reclassified as belonging to X. Then* $cov(\Delta P_{j,t}, \Delta P_{X,t})$ *increases after j is added to style X.*

In our analysis so far, we have taken assets 1 through n to be in style X and assets $n+1$ through $2n$ to be in style Y. In our simulated data for this economy, we find that for any asset j not in style X, in other words, for $j = n+1,\ldots,2n$,

$$cov(\Delta P_{j,t}, \Delta P_{X,t}) = -0.17. \tag{5.41}$$

Suppose that asset 1 is reclassified into style Y and asset $n+1$ is reclassified into style X. We now recompute asset $n+1$'s covariance with style X. More specifically, we keep the cash-flow covariance matrix fixed, and use equations (5.24) and (5.26) to simulate prices as before, the only difference being the new composition of styles X and Y. We find that[14]

$$cov(\Delta P_{n+1,t}, \Delta P_{X,t}) = 0.30, \tag{5.42}$$

showing that stock $n+1$'s covariance with style X does indeed increase after it is added to that style.

Proposition 5.2 may also help us differentiate the two views of value stock comovement suggested earlier. If it arises because "value" is itself a style, the proposition predicts that stocks that become value stocks will comove more after entering that category than before. If it arises because

industries are styles, there will be no increased comovement after an industry enters the value category. Daniel and Titman's (1997) evidence is more supportive of the latter view. They find that stocks in the value category today comove roughly as much as they did five years earlier.

5.3.2   Comovement across Styles

Two assets in the *same* style, then, will be more correlated than their underlying cash flows. The opposite is true of two assets in *different* styles, asset i in style X, say, and asset j in style Y. Such assets will be *less* correlated than their underlying cash flows. The reason for this is the externality generated by switchers. A good return for style X leads to a flow out of Y and into X, driving the styles in opposite directions and lowering the correlation between them. More formally, we can prove:

Proposition 5.3   *If assets i and j are in different styles, then*

$$\mathrm{corr}(\Delta P_{i,t} - \Delta P_{M,t}, \Delta P_{j,t} - \Delta P_{M,t}) < \mathrm{corr}(\varepsilon_{i,t} - \varepsilon_{M,t}, \varepsilon_{j,t} - \varepsilon_{M,t}). \qquad (5.43)$$

The prediction is stated in terms of market-adjusted returns, not raw returns. It is tempting to think that the externality makes returns on small stocks and large stocks and returns on value stocks and growth stocks pairwise less correlated than their cash flows. However, reality may be more complicated because of overlap between styles. Competition between value and growth suggests that their returns should be less correlated than their fundamentals, but value stocks and growth stocks are both part of the overall U.S. stock market, itself a style. By proposition 5.1, this would tend to make value and growth stocks *more* correlated than their cash flows. In view of this complication, we make our prediction in terms of market-adjusted returns. In other words, we predict that the market-adjusted returns on value and growth stocks are less correlated than the cash flows of value and growth stocks, in turn adjusted for market cash flows.

Equation (5.39) shows that for any assets i in X and j in Y,

$$\mathrm{corr}(\Delta P_{i,t} - \Delta P_{M,t}, \Delta P_{j,t} - \Delta P_{M,t}) = -0.35, \qquad (5.44)$$

while in our simulated data,

$$\mathrm{corr}(\varepsilon_{i,t} - \varepsilon_{M,t}, \varepsilon_{j,t} - \varepsilon_{M,t}) = -0.16, \qquad (5.45)$$

confirming that market-adjusted returns are indeed less correlated than market-adjusted cash flows. Figure 5.3, which plots the prices of styles X and Y over a 100-period segment of the simulated data, provides another

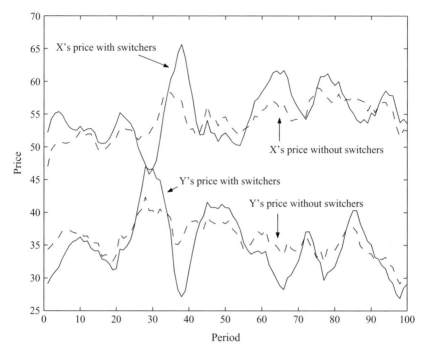

Figure 5.3
Price paths for two styles, X and Y. Some investors in the economy, known as switchers, group risky assets into two categories, X and Y, known as styles. The solid lines show the prices of styles X and Y over a 100-period segment of simulated data. For comparison, the dashed lines indicate fundamental values, or prices in the absence of switchers.

view of the same phenomenon. The price paths of styles X and Y tend to move in opposite directions.

5.3.3 Own- and Cross-Autocorrelations

The presence of switchers in the economy makes style returns positively autocorrelated in the short run and negatively autocorrelated in the long run. A good return for style X draws in switchers, who push its price up again next period, inducing positive autocorrelation. The price swing is eventually reversed, generating long-run reversion to the mean.

Our model's predictions about own-autocorrelations are not unique to our framework. They can also arise in traditional positive feedback trading models or conventional learning models so long as the assets in a style share a common cash-flow factor. However, the relative performance rule driving switcher flows, and the externality that it creates, lead to more unique predictions about *cross*-autocorrelations across styles,

namely, that they should be negative in the short run and positive in the long run. A good return on style X at time t generates outflows from Y into X, pushing Y's price down at time $t+1$. In the long run, Y's price recovers, generating positive cross-autocorrelations at longer lags. In summary, we can show:

Proposition 5.4   *For some* $K \geq 1$,

(i) $\operatorname{corr}(\Delta P_{X,t}, \Delta P_{X,t-k}) < 0$, $1 \leq k \leq K$,

   $\operatorname{corr}(\Delta P_{X,t}, \Delta P_{X,t-k}) < 0$, $k = K + 1$,

and

(ii) $\operatorname{corr}(\Delta P_{X,t}, \Delta P_{Y,t-k}) < 0$, $1 \leq k \leq K$,

   $\operatorname{corr}(\Delta P_{X,t}, \Delta P_{Y,t-k}) > 0$, $k = K + 1$.   (5.46)

Table 5.1 shows the magnitude of these own- and cross-autocorrelations for our particular numerical example. The first-order own-autocorrelation is 0.5, while the correlation of returns nine lags apart is –0.18. It is

Table 5.1
Own- and Cross-Autocorrelations

	$\operatorname{corr}(\Delta P_{X,t}, \Delta P_{X,t-k})$	$\operatorname{corr}(\Delta P_{X,t}, \Delta P_{Y,t-k})$
$k = 1$	0.50	–0.50
$k = 2$	0.36	–0.36
$k = 3$	0.23	–0.23
$k = 4$	0.12	–0.12
$k = 5$	0.02	–0.02
$k = 6$	–0.06	0.06
$k = 7$	–0.11	0.11
$k = 8$	–0.15	0.15
$k = 9$	–0.18	0.18
	$\operatorname{corr}(\Delta P_{X,t} - \Delta P_{M,t}, \Delta P_{X,t-k} - \Delta P_{M,t-k})$	$\operatorname{corr}(\Delta P_{X,t} - \Delta P_{M,t}, \Delta P_{Y,t-k} - \Delta P_{M,t-k})$
$k = 1$	0.78	–0.78
$k = 2$	0.56	–0.56
$k = 3$	0.36	–0.36
$k = 4$	0.18	–0.18
$k = 5$	0.02	–0.02
$k = 6$	–0.10	0.10
$k = 7$	–0.19	0.19
$k = 8$	–0.24	0.24
$k = 9$	–0.28	0.28

Note: Some investors in the economy, known as switchers, group risky assets into two categories, X and Y, known as styles. For a particular set of model parameter values, the table reports the own- and cross-autocorrelations of raw and market-adjusted returns on styles X and Y.

easy to show that corr$(\Delta P_{X,t}, \Delta P_{X,t-k}) = -\text{corr}(\Delta P_{X,t}, \Delta P_{Y,t-k})$ for $k \geq 1$, a pattern that is clearly visible in the table.

The available evidence on own-autocorrelations is generally supportive of part (i) of proposition 5.4. Lo and MacKinlay (1988) and Poterba and Summers (1988) find U.S. monthly stock returns to be positively autocorrelated at the first lag and negatively autocorrelated thereafter. Cutler, Poterba, and Summers (1991) show that monthly returns of international stock and bond indexes, as well as of real estate and commodity markets, are positively autocorrelated at lags of up to a year, and negatively autocorrelated thereafter. Finally, Lewellen (2002) finds that monthly returns on industry- and size-sorted portfolios are positively autocorrelated at a one-month lag and negatively autocorrelated after that.

Testing part (ii) is again complicated by style overlaps: in general, stocks will be affected both by flows into the U.S. stock market as a whole and by intra-stock market flows between styles. A more robust version of proposition 5.4 would therefore be in terms of market adjusted returns:

Proposition 5.5 *For some $K \geq 1$,*

(i) corr$(\Delta P_{X,t} - \Delta P_{M,t}, \Delta P_{X,t-k} - \Delta P_{M,t-k}) > 0, \quad 1 \leq k \leq K,$

$\quad$ corr$(\Delta P_{X,t} - \Delta P_{M,t}, \Delta P_{X,t-k} - \Delta P_{M,t-k}) < 0, \; k = K+1,$

and

(ii) corr$(\Delta P_{X,t} - \Delta P_{M,t}, \Delta P_{Y,t-k} - \Delta P_{M,t-k}) > 0, 1 \leq k \leq K,$

$\quad$ corr$(\Delta P_{X,t} - \Delta P_{M,t}, \Delta P_{Y,t-k} - \Delta P_{M,t-k}) < 0, \; k = K+1.$ $\qquad$ (5.47)

Table 5.1 presents the magnitudes of own- and cross-autocorrelations of market-adjusted returns in simulated data.

5.3.4   Asset-Level Momentum and Value Strategies

We now analyze the profitability of momentum and value strategies that are implemented at the level of individual securities. An asset-level momentum strategy ranks all assets on their return in the previous period, then buys those assets that did better than average and sells those that did worse. It can be implemented through

$$N_{i,t} = \frac{1}{2n}[\Delta P_{i,t} - \Delta P_{M,t}], \; i = 1, \ldots, 2n, \qquad (5.48)$$

where $N_{i,t}$ is the share position in asset i. An asset-level value strategy buys (sells) those assets trading below (above) fundamental value:

$$N_{i,t} = \frac{1}{2n}[P_{i,t}^* - P_{i,t}], \ i = 1,\dots,2n. \tag{5.49}$$

In the presence of switchers, we expect both asset-level momentum and asset-level value strategies to be profitable. If an asset performed well last period, there is good chance that the outperformance was due to the asset's being a member of a "hot" style enjoying inflows from switchers. If so, the style is likely to keep attracting inflows from switchers next period, making it likely that the asset itself also does well next period.

Similarly, an asset trading below fundamental value may be in this predicament because it is a member of a style that is currently unpopular with switchers and is suffering fund outflows. If so, we expect the style and all the assets in it to eventually correct back up to fundamental value, bringing high returns to a value strategy. Specifically, we can prove:

Proposition 5.6 *The asset-level momentum strategy in equation (5.48) and the asset-level value strategy in equation (5.49) have strictly positive expected returns in the presence of switchers.*

Table 5.2 shows that, in our simulated data, these strategies offer attractive Sharpe ratios. The Sharpe ratio we compute is the mean one-period change in wealth from implementing the strategy divided by the standard deviation of the one-period change in wealth.

Together with our earlier results on comovement, proposition 5.6 suggests that our simulated data can match the regression evidence on value stock returns and earnings very closely. Fama and French (1992, 1993, 1995) document a three-part puzzle. First, value stocks earn a premium not captured by the CAPM; second, value stocks comove, and loadings on a specific factor, christened the HML factor, can capture the value premium; and finally, shocks to the common factor in value stock returns are only weakly correlated with shocks to the common factor in value stock earnings news.

To see if our simulated data can replicate this evidence, we run the following three regressions. As usual, we think of X and Y as two fixed styles, such as old economy and new economy stocks:

$$\Delta P_{\text{Val},t} = 0.044 + 1.06\Delta P_{M,t} + u_{\text{Val},t}, \tag{5.50}$$

$$\Delta P_{\text{Val},t} = -0.009 + 1.00\Delta P_{M,t} + 0.48\Delta P_{S,t} + u_{\text{Val},t}, \ R^2 = 92\%, \tag{5.51}$$

$$\Delta P_{\text{Val},t} = 0.033 + 1.00\varepsilon_{M,t} + 0.48\varepsilon_{S,t} + u_{\text{Val},t}, \ R^2 = 50\%. \tag{5.52}$$

Table 5.2
Sharpe Ratios of Various Stock-Picking Strategies

Strategy	Sharpe Ratio
Momentum	
Asset-level	0.61
Style-level	0.61
Within-style	0
Value	
Asset-level	0.12
Style-level	0.12
Within-style	0
Optimal	0.62

Note: Some investors in the economy, known as switchers, group risky assets into two categories, X and Y, known as styles. The table reports Sharpe ratios of certain strategies in this economy, where Sharpe ratio is taken to be the mean one-period change in wealth from implementing the strategy divided by the standard deviation of the one-period change in wealth. An asset-level momentum strategy buys assets that performed better than average last period, a style-level momentum strategy buys styles that did better than average last period, and a within-style momentum strategy buys assets that did better than their style last period. An asset-level value strategy buys assets trading below fundamental value, a style-level value strategy buys styles trading below fundamental value, and a within-style value strategy buys assets trading at a bigger discount to fundamental value than their style. The optimal strategy is the one that would be chosen by an arbitrageur who knows the correct process followed by prices in the economy.

The regression variables are constructed in the following way. Each period, we rank all risky assets on the difference between their prices and fundamental values, $P_{i,t} - P_{i,t}^*$. The 50 percent of stocks with lower such values we call value stocks and split them randomly into two equal-sized groups, $VAL_{A,t}$ and $VAL_{B,t}$. The remaining stocks we call growth stocks and also split them randomly into $GWT_{A,t}$ and $GWT_{B,t}$. We then define

$$\Delta P_{\text{Val},t+1} = \frac{1}{n/2} \sum_{l_t \in VAL_{A,t}} \Delta P_{l_t,t+1}, \tag{5.53}$$

$$\Delta P_{S,t+1} = \frac{1}{n/2} \sum_{l_t \in VAL_{B,t}} \Delta P_{l_t,t+1} - \frac{1}{n/2} \sum_{l_t \in GWT_{B,t}} \Delta P_{l_t,t+1}, \tag{5.54}$$

$$\varepsilon_{S,t+1} = \frac{1}{n/2} \sum_{l_t \in VAL_{B,t}} \varepsilon_{l_t,t+1} - \frac{1}{n/2} \sum_{l_t \in GWT_{B,t}} \varepsilon_{l_t,t+1}. \tag{5.55}$$

In words, $\Delta P_{\text{Val},t}$ is the return on a portfolio consisting of half the available universe of n value stocks; $\Delta P_{S,t}$ is a style factor in returns, analogous to the HML factor, constructed as the return on a portfolio of the remaining value stocks minus the return on half the available growth stocks; and $\varepsilon_{M,t}$ and $\Delta P_{M,t}$ are as defined in proposition 5.1. By splitting value stocks

and growth stocks into two random groups, we ensure that $\Delta P_{\text{Val},t}$ and $\Delta P_{S,t}$ are constructed using different stocks and hence that spurious correlation is avoided.

The intercept in equation (5.50) confirms that the value portfolio $\Delta P_{\text{Val},t}$ earns an anomalously high average return, as judged by the CAPM. The positive slope on $\Delta P_{S,t}$ in equation (5.51) shows that there is a common factor in the returns of value stocks, while the tiny intercept shows that loadings on this factor can help capture the value premium. Finally, the drop in R^2 between equations (5.51) and (5.52) shows that the common factor in fundamentals lines up poorly with the common factor in returns. Note that (5.50) and (5.51) on their own demonstrate that in our model, common factors in returns can be associated with high *average* returns for reasons unrelated to risk.

5.3.5   Style-Level Momentum and Value Strategies

The superior performance of asset-level momentum and value strategies documented in proposition 5.6 can also be explained by the feedback models of De Long et al. (1990a) and Hong and Stein (1999), by the more psychological models of Barberis, Shleifer, and Vishny (1998) and Daniel, Hirshleifer, and Subrahmanyam (2001), as well as by the learning model of Lewellen and Shanken (2002). Moreover, the mechanism used in this chapter—an excessively negative reaction on the part of some investors to poor prior performance—is similar to that used by De Long et al. (1990a) and Hong and Stein (1999).

In order to make predictions that distinguish our framework, we introduce some additional investment strategies. First, we consider style-level versions of the strategies in equations (5.48) and (5.49). A style-level momentum strategy buys into *styles* with good recent performance and avoids styles that have done poorly:

$$N_{i,t} = \frac{1}{2n} \left[\frac{\Delta P_{X,t} - \Delta P_{Y,t}}{2} \right], \ i \in X, \tag{5.56}$$

$$N_{j,t} = \frac{1}{2n} \left[\frac{\Delta P_{Y,t} - \Delta P_{X,t}}{2} \right], \ j \in Y. \tag{5.57}$$

A style-level value strategy buys into styles trading below fundamental value and shorts the remaining styles:

$$N_{i,t} = \frac{1}{2n} \left[P^*_{X,t} - P_{X,t} \right], \ i \in X, \tag{5.58}$$

$$N_{j,t} = \frac{1}{2n}[P^*_{Y,t} - P_{Y,t}], \, j \in Y. \tag{5.59}$$

Finally, we also consider "within-style" versions of the strategies in equations (5.48) and (5.49). In a within-style momentum strategy, the investor buys those assets that outperformed their style last period and sells those that underperformed their style. It can be implemented through

$$N_{i,t} = \frac{1}{2n}[\Delta P_{i,t} - \Delta P_{X,t}], \, i \in X, \tag{5.60}$$

$$N_{j,t} = \frac{1}{2n}[\Delta P_{j,t} - \Delta P_{Y,t}], \, j \in Y. \tag{5.61}$$

Correspondingly, a within-style value strategy buys (sells) assets trading at a larger discount (premium) of price to fundamental value than their style:

$$N_{i,t} = \frac{1}{2n}([P^*_{i,t} - P_{i,t}] - [P^*_{X,t} - P_{X,t}]), \, i \in X, \tag{5.62}$$

$$N_{j,t} = \frac{1}{2n}([P^*_{j,t} - P_{j,t}] - [P^*_{Y,t} - P_{Y,t}]), \, j \in Y. \tag{5.63}$$

These new strategies allow us to make predictions that are unique to our framework. In particular, we can prove:

Proposition 5.7 *(i) Style-level momentum and value strategies offer Sharpe ratios that are greater than or equal to those of their asset-level counterparts; and (ii) within-style momentum and value strategies are unprofitable, offering an expected return of zero.*

Table 5.2 reports the Sharpe ratios of both style-level and within-style momentum and value strategies, illustrating the proposition for one particular set of parameter values.

The intuition behind proposition 5.7 is straightforward. Since mispricing occurs at the level of a style in our model, a strategy designed to exploit this mispricing must be at least as effective when implemented at the style level as it is when implemented at the individual asset level. Moreover, precisely because mispricing is a style-level phenomenon, style-neutral strategies like the within-style strategies will not be able to exploit any mispricing and will remain unprofitable.

Proposition 5.7 does not hold in traditional positive feedback trading models where the feedback occurs at the individual asset level. In this

case, the most effective momentum strategy will buy individual stocks that outperformed last period, in anticipation of further purchases by positive feedback traders. A strategy that simply buys outperforming styles is a less efficient way of picking out future winners and hence offers lower Sharpe ratios. On the other hand, since mispricing occurs at the individual asset level in these models, even style-neutral momentum strategies can be profitable, in contrast to proposition 5.7.

In taking proposition 5.7 to the data, it is worth keeping in mind that it relies on our simplifying but strong assumption that all noise trading occurs at the style level. In practice, at least some noise trading is likely to be an asset-level phenomenon. In this case, we still expect style-level strategies to do well, although not necessarily better than asset-level strategies; and we expect within-style strategies to do less well, although their average return need not be as low as zero.

What evidence there is on style momentum strategies provides some support for style investing. In line with part (i) of proposition 5.7, a number of papers find that certain style-level momentum strategies have earned average returns as impressive as those of individual stock-level momentum. Moskowitz and Grinblatt (1999) show that a momentum strategy based on industry portfolios is profitable.[15] Lewellen (2002) investigates momentum strategies using size-sorted and book-to-market-sorted portfolios, and claims them both to be at least as profitable as individual-stock momentum. Also consistent with our model, Haugen and Baker (1996) track returns on a large number of investment styles and show that a strategy which tilts toward styles with good prior performance earns high risk-adjusted returns—higher than the returns on any one style. They successfully replicate their findings in out-of-sample tests in a number of international markets.

There is little existing work on style-based value strategies, but Asness, Liew, and Stevens (1997) show that a value strategy applied to country portfolios works well. Evidence on part (ii) of proposition 5.7 is also hard to come by. However, some support comes from Moskowitz and Grinblatt (1999), who find that within-industry momentum strategies are unprofitable.

It is also possible to relate the style momentum and style value strategies to the optimal strategy followed by an arbitrageur clever enough to figure out the correct process for asset prices in our economy.

Proposition 5.8 *The optimal strategy for an arbitrageur who knows that prices follow equations (5.24) and (5.26) is given by the following share demands:*

$$N_{i,t}^A = \frac{c}{n}\left[\frac{\Delta P_{X,t} - \Delta P_{Y,t}}{2} - (1-\theta)\sum_{k=1}^{t-1}\theta^{k-1}\left(\frac{\Delta P_{X,t-k} - \Delta P_{Y,t-k}}{2}\right)\right], \ i \in X, \quad (5.64)$$

$$N_{j,t}^A = \frac{c}{n}\left[\frac{\Delta P_{Y,t} - \Delta P_{X,t}}{2} - (1-\theta)\sum_{k=1}^{t-1}\theta^{k-1}\left(\frac{\Delta P_{Y,t-k} - \Delta P_{X,t-k}}{2}\right)\right], \ j \in Y, \quad (5.65)$$

where c is a positive constant.[16]

If we use $N_{i,t}^{\mathrm{mom}}$ and $N_{i,t}^{\mathrm{val}}$ to denote the share demands of the style-level momentum and value strategies in equations (5.56) and (5.58), respectively, then equation (5.64) together with equations (5.24) and (5.26) imply that

$$N_{i,t}^A = 2c[N_{i,t}^{\mathrm{mom}} + \phi(1-\theta)N_{i,t}^{\mathrm{val}}], \ \forall i. \quad (5.66)$$

In words, the optimal strategy is a constant combination of style momentum and style value.

Equation (5.66) shows that when θ is close to 1, as in our parameterized example, the optimal strategy is very similar to style-level momentum. This makes intuitive sense. When switcher flows are very persistent and mispricings take a long time to correct, it makes more sense for an arbitrageur to ride with the switchers than to bet against them. It is also consistent with table 5.2, which shows that the style momentum and optimal strategies have very similar Sharpe ratios. For lower values of θ, switcher flows are less persistent and prices revert to fundamental value more quickly. This suggests that for low θ, the value strategy should be relatively more attractive. Equation (5.66) confirms that as θ falls, value becomes more attractive relative to momentum in the sense that the optimal strategy places relatively more weight on value.[17]

5.4 Special Styles

An important style that deserves further discussion is indexation. In section 5.3, we informally applied some of our propositions to the case where one of the styles is an index, but it may be helpful to restate our predictions about this style more explicitly. Setting $X = I$ and $Y = NI$, where I and NI represent assets within a certain index and assets outside that index, respectively, gives:

Proposition 5.9 *(i) Suppose that asset j, not previously a member of an index I, is reclassified as belonging to I. Then* $\mathrm{cov}(\Delta P_{j,t}, \Delta P_{I,t})$ *increases after j is added to I; (ii) If asset i is in an index I while asset j is not, then*

$$\text{corr}(\Delta P_{i,t} - \Delta P_{M,t}, \Delta P_{j,t} - \Delta P_{M,t}) < \text{corr}(\varepsilon_{i,t} - \varepsilon_{M,t}, \varepsilon_{j,t} - \varepsilon_{M,t}); \tag{5.67}$$

(iii) For some $K \geq 1$,

$$\text{corr}(\Delta P_{I,t}, \Delta P_{I,t-k}) > 0, \ 1 \leq k \leq K,$$

$$\text{corr}(\Delta P_{I,t}, \Delta P_{I,t-k}) < 0, \ k = K + 1,$$

$$\text{corr}(\Delta P_{I,t}, \Delta P_{NI,t-k}) < 0, \ 1 \leq k \leq K,$$

$$\text{corr}(\Delta P_{I,t}, \Delta P_{NI,t-k}) > 0, \ k = K + 1. \tag{5.68}$$

In words, a stock that is added to an index should comove more with the index after inclusion than before; the returns on a stock in an index should comove with the returns on a stock not in the index less than their fundamentals do; indexes should have positive (negative) own-autocorrelations at short (long) horizons; and they should be negatively (positively) cross-autocorrelated with stocks outside the index at short (long) horizons. Moreover, since the importance of indexing has grown over time, these phenomena should be stronger in more recent data samples. Vijh (1994) and Barberis, Shleifer, and Wurgler (2005) examine some of these predictions empirically using data for the S&P 500 index and find supportive evidence.

Another interesting issue arises with *price-dependent* styles, where the characteristic defining the style depends on price. Many common styles such as "small-cap stocks" or "value stocks" fall into this category. When a style is price dependent, its composition changes. Suppose that switchers have kicked off a long upswing in the price of small stocks relative to their fundamentals. They buy small stocks, pushing up their price, which attracts more switchers, and so on. After a while, some of the small-cap stocks experience price increases so large that they cannot be considered small any more and are no longer part of the small-cap stock style.

This change in composition need not brake the evolution of the small-cap stock style itself. However, it may mean that the degree of misvaluation experienced by any individual asset is *lower* than in the case where the style characteristic is not price dependent. If a small-cap stock becomes too highly valued relative to its fundamentals, it ceases to be a small-cap stock, and the buying pressure from switchers following the small-cap stock style eases off, halting its ascent. This argument depends on the correlation between characteristic and price

being negative, so that the higher a stock's price, the less likely it is to be a small stock. When this correlation is positive, misvaluation of individual stocks is more severe when the style is price dependent than when it is not.

5.5 Conclusion

The model of financial markets discussed in this paper is in many ways similar to that proposed by Black (1986). On the one hand, financial markets in our economy are not efficient. Prices deviate substantially from fundamental values as styles become popular or unpopular. For an arbitrageur with a good model of prices, there are substantial profits to be made from a combination of contrarian and momentum trading. On the other hand, despite the fact that markets are inefficient, prices are very noisy. Patterns in security prices are complex and change significantly over time. Without knowing which style or model is favored, arbitrage is risky and consistent profits hard to come by. To some people, such markets might even appear efficient.

In this chapter, we have tried to show that these markets are not entirely anarchic. They do exhibit long run pressures toward fundamentals and there are empirical predictions one can make about them, such as excess comovement within styles and nontrivial autocorrelation patterns in style returns. Further exploration of style investing is likely to generate many more predictions, and may offer new ways of looking at existing empirical facts.

Acknowledgments

We have benefited from the comments of two anonymous referees and from discussions with John Campbell, Doug Diamond, Eugene Fama, Edward Glaeser, Will Goetzmann, Sanford Grossman, Rafael La Porta, David Laibson, Sendhil Mullainathan, Geert Rouwenhorst, Lawrence Summers, Jeffrey Wurgler, and seminar participants at the University of Chicago, Harvard University, London Business School, Princeton University, the University of Iowa, Wharton, the AFA, and the NBER. Reprinted from Nicholas Barberis and Andrei Shleifer, "Style Investing," *Journal of Financial Economics* 68 (2): 161–199, © 2003, with permission from Elsevier.

Appendix

Proof of Proposition 5.1   From equation (5.24), for any $i \in X$,

$$\Delta P_{i,t+1} = \varepsilon_{i,t+1} + \frac{\Delta N_{X,t+1}^{S}}{\phi}, \tag{5A.1}$$

where

$$\Delta N_{X,t+1}^{S} = \frac{\Delta P_{X,t} - \Delta P_{Y,t}}{2} - (1-\theta)\sum_{k=1}^{t-1}\theta^{k-1}\left(\frac{\Delta P_{X,t-k} - \Delta P_{Y,t-k}}{2}\right) \tag{5A.2}$$

is known at time t. Since

$$\Delta P_{M,t+1} = \varepsilon_{M,t+1} = \frac{1}{2n}\sum_{l=1}^{2n}\varepsilon_{l,t+1}, \tag{5A.3}$$

we have, for any distinct $i, j \in X$,

$$\Delta P_{i,t+1} - \Delta P_{M,t+1} = \varepsilon_{i,t+1} - \varepsilon_{M,t+1} + \frac{\Delta N_{X,t+1}^{S}}{\phi}, \tag{5A.4}$$

$$\Delta P_{j,t+1} - \Delta P_{M,t+1} = \varepsilon_{j,t+1} - \varepsilon_{M,t+1} + \frac{\Delta N_{X,t+1}^{S}}{\phi}. \tag{5A.5}$$

This implies

$$\mathrm{cov}(\Delta P_{i,t+1} - \Delta P_{M,t+1}, \Delta P_{j,t+1} - \Delta P_{M,t+1}) = \mathrm{cov}(\varepsilon_{i,t+1} - \varepsilon_{M,t+1}, \varepsilon_{j,t+1} - \varepsilon_{M,t+1})$$
$$+ \frac{1}{\phi^{2}}\mathrm{var}(\Delta N_{X,t+1}^{S}), \tag{5A.6}$$

$$\mathrm{var}(\Delta P_{l,t+1} - \Delta P_{M,t+1}) = \mathrm{var}(\varepsilon_{l,t+1} - \varepsilon_{M,t+1}) + \frac{1}{\phi^{2}}\mathrm{var}(\Delta N_{X,t+1}^{S}), \quad l \in \{i,j\}. \tag{5A.7}$$

The proposition therefore follows if

$$\mathrm{cov}(\varepsilon_{i,t+1} - \varepsilon_{M,t+1}, \varepsilon_{j,t+1} - \varepsilon_{M,t+1}) < \mathrm{var}(\varepsilon_{i,t+1} - \varepsilon_{M,t+1}). \tag{5A.8}$$

Using

$$\varepsilon_{i,t+1} - \varepsilon_{M,t+1} = \frac{\psi_S f_{X,t+1} - \psi_S f_{Y,t+1}}{2} + \sqrt{1-\psi_M^2 - \psi_S^2}\left(f_{i,t+1} - \frac{1}{2n}\sum_{l=1}^{2n}f_{l,t+1}\right), \tag{5A.9}$$

it is easily checked that

$$\mathrm{cov}(\varepsilon_{i,t+1} - \varepsilon_{M,t+1}, \varepsilon_{j,t+1} - \varepsilon_{M,t+1}) = \frac{\psi_S^2}{2} - \frac{1-\psi_M^2 - \psi_S^2}{2n}, \tag{5A.10}$$

$$\text{var}(\varepsilon_{i,t+1} - \varepsilon_{M,t+1}) = \frac{\psi_S^2}{2} + \frac{2n-1}{2n}(1 - \psi_M^2 - \psi_S^2), \tag{5A.11}$$

which means that inequality (5A.8) does indeed hold. ∎

Proof of Proposition 5.2 Suppose that asset $n + 1$ is reclassified from style Y into style X, and that at the same time, asset 1 is reclassified from style X into style Y. Before reclassification, we have

$$\Delta P_{X,t+1} = \varepsilon_{X,t+1} + \frac{\Delta N_{X,t+1}^S}{\phi}, \tag{5A.12}$$

$$\Delta P_{n+1,t+1} = \varepsilon_{n+1,t+1} - \frac{\Delta N_{X,t+1}^S}{\phi}, \tag{5A.13}$$

where

$$\varepsilon_{X,t+1} = \frac{1}{n}\sum_{l \in X}\varepsilon_{l,t+1}. \tag{5A.14}$$

This implies that before reclassification,

$$\text{cov}(\Delta P_{n+1,t}, \Delta P_{X,t}) = \psi_M^2 - \frac{1}{\phi^2}\text{var}(\Delta N_{X,t}^S). \tag{5A.15}$$

After reclassification, we have

$$\Delta P_{X,t+1} = \varepsilon_{X,t+1} + \frac{\Delta N_{X,t+1}^S}{\phi}, \tag{5A.16}$$

$$\Delta P_{n+1,t+1} = \varepsilon_{n+1,t+1} + \frac{\Delta N_{X,t+1}^S}{\phi}, \tag{5A.17}$$

which implies

$$\text{cov}(\Delta P_{n+1,t}, \Delta P_{X,t}) = \psi_M^2 + \frac{1 - \psi_M^2}{n} + \frac{1}{\phi^2}\text{var}(\Delta N_{X,t+1}^S). \tag{5A.18}$$

Therefore, $\text{cov}(\Delta P_{n+1,t}, \Delta P_{X,t})$ does indeed increase after addition. ∎

Proof of Proposition 5.3 For $i \in X$ and $j \in Y$,

$$\Delta P_{i,t+1} - \Delta P_{M,t+1} = \varepsilon_{i,t+1} - \varepsilon_{M,t+1} + \frac{\Delta N_{X,t+1}^S}{\phi}, \tag{5A.19}$$

$$\Delta P_{j,t+1} - \Delta P_{M,t+1} = \varepsilon_{j,t+1} - \varepsilon_{M,t+1} - \frac{\Delta N_{X,t+1}^S}{\phi}. \tag{5A.20}$$

This implies

$$\text{cov}(\Delta P_{i,t+1} - \Delta P_{M,t+1}, \Delta P_{j,t+1} - \Delta P_{M,t+1}) = \text{cov}(\varepsilon_{i,t+1} - \varepsilon_{M,t+1}, \varepsilon_{j,t+1} - \varepsilon_{M,t+1})$$
$$- \frac{1}{\phi^2}\text{var}(\Delta N_{X,t+1}^S), \qquad (5A.21)$$

$$\text{var}(\Delta P_{l,t+1} - \Delta P_{M,t+1}) = \text{var}(\varepsilon_{i,t+1} - \varepsilon_{M,t+1}) + \frac{1}{\phi^2}\text{var}(\Delta N_{X,t+1}^S), \qquad l \in \{i, j\}. \qquad (5A.22)$$

The proposition therefore follows if

$$-\text{cov}(\varepsilon_{i,t+1} - \varepsilon_{M,t+1}, \varepsilon_{j,t+1} - \varepsilon_{M,t+1}) < \text{var}(\varepsilon_{i,t+1} - \varepsilon_{M,t+1}). \qquad (5A.23)$$

Using equation (5A.9) and

$$\varepsilon_{j,t+1} - \varepsilon_{M,t+1} = \frac{\psi_S f_{Y,t+1} - \psi_S f_{X,t+1}}{2} + \sqrt{1 - \psi_M^2 - \psi_S^2}(f_{j,t+1} - \frac{1}{2n}\sum_{l=1}^{2n} f_{l,t+1}), \qquad (5A.24)$$

it is easily checked that

$$\text{cov}(\varepsilon_{i,t+1} - \varepsilon_{M,t+1}, \varepsilon_{j,t+1} - \varepsilon_{M,t+1}) = -(\frac{\psi_S^2}{2} + \frac{1 - \psi_M^2 - \psi_S^2}{2n}), \qquad (5A.25)$$

$$\text{var}(\varepsilon_{i,t+1} - \varepsilon_{M,t+1}) = \frac{\psi_S^2}{2} + \frac{2n-1}{2n}(1 - \psi_M^2 - \psi_S^2), \qquad (5A.26)$$

which means that inequality (5A.23) does indeed hold. ∎

We now prove the following lemma, which will be useful in the remaining proofs.

Lemma *In any stationary equilibrium with $\theta > 0$, it must be true that $0 < \theta < 1$ and $\phi > 1$.*

Proof of Lemma It is easily checked using equations (5.24) and (5.26) that $\rho_1 > \rho_2$, where ρ_1 and ρ_2 are defined in equation (5.20). Equation (5.25) then immediately implies that $\phi > 0$ in any stationary equilibrium.

From equation (5.24), we can write

$$\Delta P_{X,t+1} - \Delta P_{Y,t+1} = (\varepsilon_{X,t+1} - \varepsilon_{Y,t+1}) + \frac{\Delta P_{X,t} - \Delta P_{Y,t}}{\phi}$$
$$- \frac{(1-\theta)}{\phi}\sum_{k=1}^{t-1}\theta^{k-1}(\Delta P_{X,t-k} - \Delta P_{Y,t-k}), \qquad (5A.27)$$

which then implies

$$\Delta P_{X,t+1} - \Delta P_{Y,t+1} = \left(\theta + \frac{1}{\phi}\right)(\Delta P_{X,t} - \Delta P_{Y,t}) - \frac{1}{\phi}(\Delta P_{X,t-1} - \Delta P_{Y,t-1})$$
$$+ (\varepsilon_{X,t+1} - \varepsilon_{Y,t+1}) - \theta(\varepsilon_{X,t} - \varepsilon_{Y,t}). \tag{5A.28}$$

Using standard theory (see Hamilton 1994), $\Delta P_{X,t} - \Delta P_{Y,t}$ will be a stable process so long as the roots of

$$\lambda^2 - \lambda(\theta + \frac{1}{\phi}) + \frac{1}{\phi} = 0 \tag{5A.29}$$

are all less than one in absolute magnitude. Within the range $\theta > 0$, $\phi > 0$, this will be true so long as

$$0 < \theta < 1, \phi > 1. \tag{5A.30}$$

∎

Proof of Propositions 5.4 and 5.5 We use the notation

$$\hat{\Gamma}_k = \mathrm{cov}(\Delta P_{X,t} - \Delta P_{Y,t}, \Delta P_{X,t+k} - \Delta P_{Y,t+k}), \ k \geq 0, \tag{5A.31}$$

$$\Gamma_k = \mathrm{cov}(\Delta P_{X,t}, \Delta P_{X,t+k}), \ k \geq 0, \tag{5A.32}$$

$$\gamma_k = \mathrm{corr}(\Delta P_{X,t}, \Delta P_{X,t+k}), \ k \geq 0. \tag{5A.33}$$

Note that since

$$\mathrm{cov}(\Delta P_{X,t}, \Delta P_{X,t+k}) = -\mathrm{cov}(\Delta P_{X,t}, \Delta P_{Y,t+k}), \ k \geq 1, \tag{5A.34}$$

it follows that

$$\hat{\Gamma}_k = 4\Gamma_k, \ k \geq 1. \tag{5A.35}$$

To prove the first part of the proposition, it suffices to show that $\gamma_1 > 0$ and that $\gamma_{K+1} < 0$ for some $K \geq 1$. Part (ii) of the proposition then follows immediately from equation (5A.34).

First, we show that $\gamma_1 > 0$. Computing the covariance of equation (5A.28) with $\Delta P_{X,t+1} - \Delta P_{Y,t+1}$, $\Delta P_{X,t} - \Delta P_{Y,t}$ and $\Delta P_{X,t-1} - \Delta P_{Y,t-1}$ in turn, gives

$$\hat{\Gamma}_0 = (\theta + \frac{1}{\phi})\hat{\Gamma}_1 - \frac{1}{\phi}\hat{\Gamma}_2 + (1 - \frac{\theta}{\phi})(2\psi_s^2 + k_0), \tag{5A.36}$$

$$\hat{\Gamma}_1(1 + \frac{1}{\phi}) = (\theta + \frac{1}{\phi})\hat{\Gamma}_0 - \theta(2\psi_s^2 + k_0), \tag{5A.37}$$

$$\hat{\Gamma}_2 = \left(\theta + \frac{1}{\phi}\right)\hat{\Gamma}_1 - \frac{1}{\phi}\hat{\Gamma}_0, \tag{5A.38}$$

where

$$k_0 = \frac{2}{n}(1 - \psi_S^2 - \psi_M^2).$$ (5A.39)

This gives us three equations in three unknowns, and after some algebra, we obtain

$$\hat{\Gamma}_1 = \frac{(2\psi_S^2 + k_0)(1 + \theta)}{(\phi - 1)(1 + \theta + 2/\phi)},$$ (5A.40)

which is positive under the restrictions $0 < \theta < 1$ and $\phi > 1$ that we derived in the preceding lemma. Therefore, $\gamma_1 > 0$.

To show that $\gamma_{K+1} < 0$ for some $K \geq 1$, it is sufficient to show that

$$\pi = \hat{\Gamma}_2 + \theta\hat{\Gamma}_3 + \theta^2\hat{\Gamma}_4 + \ldots < 0.$$ (5A.41)

Taking the covariance of equation (5A.27) with $\Delta P_{X,t+1} - \Delta P_{Y,t+1}$, we obtain

$$\hat{\Gamma}_0 = 2\psi_S^2 + k_0 + \frac{\hat{\Gamma}_1}{\phi} - \frac{1 - \theta}{\phi}\pi.$$ (5A.42)

Substituting in $\hat{\Gamma}_1$ from equation (5A.40) and the implied reduced form for $\hat{\Gamma}_0$ from (5A.37) gives

$$\pi = -\left(\frac{\phi}{1 - \theta}\right)\left(\hat{\Gamma}_0 - (2\psi_S^2 + k_0) - \frac{\hat{\Gamma}_1}{\phi}\right)$$

$$= \frac{-(2\psi_S^2 + k_0)}{(\phi - 1)(1 + \theta + 2/\phi)},$$ (5A.43)

which is indeed negative under the restrictions $0 < \theta < 1$ and $\phi > 1$ derived in the lemma. This concludes the proof of proposition 5.4. The proof of proposition 5.5 is identical in structure. ∎

Proof of Proposition 5.6   Define

$$\Lambda_k = \text{cov}(\Delta P_{i,t}, \Delta P_{i,t+k}).$$ (5A.44)

Then, using equation (5A.1), it is simple to show that for $k \geq 1$,

$$\text{cov}(\Delta P_{i,t}, \Delta P_{j,t+k}) = \Lambda_k, \text{ for all } i, j \text{ in the same style,}$$ (5A.45)

$$\text{cov}(\Delta P_{i,t}, \Delta P_{j,t+k}) = -\Lambda_k, \text{ for all } i, j \text{ in different styles}$$ (5A.46)

and

$$\Lambda_k = \Gamma_k. \tag{5A.47}$$

The expected return of the asset-level momentum strategy is given by

$$
E\left(\sum_{i=1}^{2n} N_{i,t}\Delta P_{i,t+1}\right) = \frac{1}{2n}E\sum_{i=1}^{2n}(\Delta P_{i,t} - \Delta P_{M,t})\Delta P_{i,t+1}
$$

$$
= \frac{1}{2n}\sum_{i=1}^{2n}E(\Delta P_{i,t}\Delta P_{i,t+1}) - \frac{1}{4n^2}\sum_{i,j=1}^{2n}E(\Delta P_{i,t}\Delta P_{j,t+1})
$$

$$
= \frac{1}{2n}\sum_{i=1}^{2n}\text{cov}(\Delta P_{i,t}\Delta P_{i,t+1}) - \frac{1}{4n^2}\sum_{i,j=1}^{2n}\text{cov}(\Delta P_{i,t}\Delta P_{j,t+1})
$$

$$
+ \frac{1}{2n}\sum_{i=1}^{2n}(\mu_i - \mu_M)^2
$$

$$
= \Lambda_1 + 0 + \frac{1}{2n}\sum_{i=1}^{2n}(\mu_i - \mu_M)^2 = \Gamma_1, \tag{5A.48}
$$

where μ_i is the mean return of asset i and μ_M is the mean return of the market portfolio of all risky assets. The last equality follows because in our simple economy, all assets have the same mean return μ_i. In the proof of proposition 5.4, we showed that $\Gamma_1 > 0$, which means that the expected return is indeed positive.

The expected return of the asset-level value strategy is given by

$$
E\left(\Sigma_{i=1}^{2n}N_{i,t}\Delta P_{i,t+1}\right) = \frac{1}{2n}E\left(\Sigma_{i=1}^{n}\left(-\frac{1}{\phi}\Sigma_{k=1}^{t-1}\theta^{k-1}\frac{\Delta P_{X,t-k} - \Delta P_{Y,t-k}}{2}\right)\Delta P_{i,t+1}\right)
$$

$$
- \frac{1}{2n}E\left(\Sigma_{i=n+1}^{2n}\left(-\frac{1}{\phi}\Sigma_{k=1}^{t-1}\theta^{k-1}\frac{\Delta P_{X,t-k} - \Delta P_{Y,t-k}}{2}\right)\Delta P_{i,t+1}\right)
$$

$$
= \frac{1}{2}E\left[\left(-\frac{1}{\phi}\Sigma_{k=1}^{t-1}\theta^{k-1}\frac{\Delta P_{X,t-k} - \Delta P_{Y,t-k}}{2}\right)(\Delta P_{X,t+1} - \Delta P_{Y,t+1})\right]
$$

$$
= -\frac{1}{4\phi}(\hat{\Gamma}_2 + \theta\hat{\Gamma}_3 + \theta^2\hat{\Gamma}_4 + \ldots) - \frac{1-\theta}{4\phi}(\mu_X - \mu_Y)^2
$$

$$
= -\frac{\pi}{4\phi}, \tag{5A.49}
$$

where μ_X and μ_Y are the mean returns of styles X and Y, respectively. The last equality follows because all securities have the same expected return in our economy. In the proof of proposition 5.4, we showed that $\pi < 0$, which implies that the expected return of the asset-level value strategy is indeed positive.   ■

Proof of Proposition 5.7, part (i) This part of the proposition is trivially true for value strategies since the share demands of a style-level value strategy are identical to the share demands of an asset-level value strategy.

We now show that the Sharpe ratio of a style-level momentum strategy is strictly greater than that of the asset-level momentum strategy. We do this by showing that both strategies have the same expected return, but that the style-level strategy has a lower expected *squared* return, and hence a lower variance.

The expected return of a style-level momentum strategy is

$$
\mathrm{E}\left(\Sigma_{i=1}^{n} \frac{1}{2n} \left(\frac{\Delta P_{X,t} - \Delta P_{Y,t}}{2} \right) \Delta P_{i,t+1} + \Sigma_{i=n+1}^{2n} \frac{1}{2n} \left(\frac{\Delta P_{Y,t} - \Delta P_{X,t}}{2} \right) \Delta P_{i,t+1} \right)
$$

$$
= \frac{1}{4} \mathrm{E}[(\Delta P_{X,t} - \Delta P_{Y,t})(\Delta P_{X,t+1} - \Delta P_{Y,t+1})]
$$

$$
= \Gamma_1 + \frac{1}{4}(\mu_X - \mu_Y)^2 = \Gamma_1. \tag{5A.50}
$$

This is indeed equal to the expected return of the asset-level momentum strategy, computed in the proof of proposition 5.6.

The expected *squared* return of a style-level momentum strategy is given by

$$
\frac{1}{16} \mathrm{E}[(\Delta P_{X,t} - \Delta P_{Y,t})^2 (\Delta P_{X,t+1} - \Delta P_{Y,t+1})^2]
$$

$$
= \mathrm{E}[(\Delta P_{X,t} - \Delta P_{M,t})^2 (\Delta P_{X,t+1} - \Delta P_{M,t+1})^2]
$$

$$
= \mathrm{cov}[(\Delta P_{X,t} - \Delta P_{M,t})^2, (\Delta P_{X,t+1} - \Delta P_{M,t+1})^2]
$$

$$
+ \mathrm{E}(\Delta P_{X,t} - \Delta P_{M,t})^2 \, E(\Delta P_{X,t+1} - \Delta P_{M,t+1})^2. \tag{5A.51}
$$

Substituting in

$$
\Delta P_{X,t+1} - \Delta P_{M,t+1} = \varepsilon_{X,t+1} - \varepsilon_{M,t+1} + \frac{\Delta N_{X,t+1}^S}{\phi} \tag{5A.52}
$$

and taking the expectation, expression (5A.51) eventually reduces to

$$
\mathrm{cov}\left(\frac{\Delta N_{X,t+1}^2}{\phi^2}, (\varepsilon_{X,t} - \varepsilon_{M,t})^2 + 2(\varepsilon_{X,t} - \varepsilon_{M,t}) \frac{\Delta N_{X,t}}{\phi} + \frac{\Delta N_{X,t}^2}{\phi^2} \right)
$$

$$
+ \left(\frac{\psi_S^2}{2} + \frac{1}{2n}(1 - \psi_M^2 - \psi_S^2) + \frac{\mathrm{var}(\Delta N_{X,t})}{\phi^2} \right)^2. \tag{5A.53}
$$

The expected squared return of the asset-level momentum strategy is given by

$$\frac{1}{4n^2} E\left(\Sigma_{i,j=1}^{2n}(\Delta P_{i,t} - \Delta P_{M,t})(\Delta P_{j,t} - \Delta P_{M,t})\Delta P_{i,t+1}\Delta P_{j,t+1}\right)$$

$$= \frac{1}{4n^2}\Sigma_{i,j=1}^{2n} \operatorname{cov}[(\Delta P_{i,t} - \Delta P_{M,t})(\Delta P_{j,t} - \Delta P_{M,t}), \Delta P_{i,t+1}\Delta P_{j,t+1}]$$

$$+ \frac{1}{4n^2}\Sigma_{i,j=1}^{2n} E[(\Delta P_{i,t} - \Delta P_{M,t})(\Delta P_{j,t} - \Delta P_{M,t})]E[\Delta P_{i,t+1}\Delta P_{j,t+1}]. \tag{5A.54}$$

Substituting in the expressions for $\Delta P_{i,t} - \Delta P_{M,t}$ and $\Delta P_{i,t+1}$ from equations (5A.1) and (5A.20), the expected squared return reduces to

$$\operatorname{cov}\left(\frac{\Delta N_{X,t+1}^2}{\phi^2}, (\varepsilon_{X,t} - \varepsilon_{M,t})^2 + 2(\varepsilon_{X,t} - \varepsilon_{M,t})\frac{\Delta N_{X,t}}{\phi} + \frac{\Delta N_{X,t}^2}{\phi^2}\right)$$

$$+ \left(\frac{\psi_S^2}{2} + \frac{\operatorname{var}(\Delta N_{X,t})}{\phi^2}\right)$$

$$+ \frac{1 - \psi_M^2 - \psi_S^2}{4n^2}\left(\frac{4n\ \operatorname{var}(\Delta N_{X,t})}{\phi^2} + (2n-1)(1 - \psi_M^2 - \psi_S^2) + 2n\psi_S^2\right). \tag{5A.55}$$

It is now simple to show that expression (5A.55) is strictly greater than expression (5A.53). The style-level momentum strategy does indeed have the lower variance and hence the higher Sharpe ratio.

Proof of Proposition 5.7, part (ii) This part of the proposition is trivially true for value strategies since the share demands of a within-style value strategy are identically zero. The expected return of the within-style momentum strategy is

$$\frac{1}{2n} E\left(\Sigma_{i=1}^{n}(\Delta P_{i,t} - \Delta P_{X,t})\Delta P_{i,t+1} + \Sigma_{i=n+1}^{2n}(\Delta P_{i,t} - \Delta P_{Y,t})\Delta P_{i,t+1}\right)$$

$$= \Sigma_{i=1}^{n}(\mu_i - \mu_X)^2 + \Sigma_{i=n+1}^{2n}(\mu_i - \mu_Y)^2 = 0 \tag{5A.56}$$

in our economy, since all stocks have the same expected return. ∎

Proof of Proposition 5.8 Given wealth of W_t at time t, the arbitrageur solves

$$\max_{N_{i,t}} E_t^A\left(-\exp\left[-\gamma\left(W_t + \Sigma_i N_{i,t}\Delta P_{i,t+1}\right)\right]\right) \tag{5A.57}$$

to obtain

$$N_t^A = \frac{(V_t^A)^{-1}}{\gamma} E_t^A(\Delta P_{t+1}) \tag{5A.58}$$

where N_t^A is the vector of optimal demands, V_t^A is the arbitrageur's estimate of the conditional covariance matrix of price changes, and where the "A" superscript in these expressions stands for arbitrageur.

Since he knows that prices are determined by equation (5.24), he is able to conclude that

$$E_t^A(\Delta P_{t+1}) = \left(\frac{\Delta N_{X,t+1}^S}{\phi}, \ldots, \frac{\Delta N_{X,t+1}^S}{\phi}, -\frac{\Delta N_{X,t+1}^S}{\phi}, \ldots, -\frac{\Delta N_{X,t+1}^S}{\phi} \right), \qquad (5A.59)$$

$$V_t^A = \Sigma_D. \qquad (5A.60)$$

Equation (5A.58) then reduces to

$$N_{i,t}^A = \frac{c}{n} \Delta N_{X,t+1}^S, \; i \in X, \qquad (5A.61)$$

$$N_{j,t}^A = -\frac{c}{n} \Delta N_{X,t+1}^S, \; j \in Y, \qquad (5A.62)$$

where c is a positive constant that depends on ψ_M^2, ψ_S^2, γ, and ϕ. ∎

Proof of Proposition 5.9   This proposition follows directly from propositions 5.2, 5.3, and 5.4, with X taken to be the index I, and Y taken to be the set of stocks outside the index, NI. ∎

Notes

1. As indicated earlier, we use the term "style investor" to refer to investors such as pension plan sponsors who allocate funds at the style level rather than at the individual asset level. The term can also be used in a related but distinct sense to describe money managers who restrict themselves to picking stocks from within a specific asset style. While both uses of the term are common in practice, in this chapter "style investor" refers only to the investors providing the funds, and not to the money managers they hire.

2. Empirical work on styles has advanced more rapidly than theoretical work on the topic. Recent contributions to the empirical literature include Brown and Goetzmann (1997, 2003) and Chan, Chen, and Lakonishok (2002).

3. For simplicity, we refer to the asset's change in price as its return.

4. More generally, a given security may belong to multiple overlapping styles. A small bank stock with a low price-earnings ratio may be part of a small-cap stock style, a financial industry style, and a value style. A model capturing such overlaps can be constructed and would yield similar but less transparent predictions.

5. The strategies in equations (5.9) and (5.10) are not self-financing. Rather, we assume that switchers are endowed with sufficient resources to fund their strategies. This allows us to abstract from issues that are not our main focus here—the long-run survival of switchers,

for example—and to concentrate on understanding the behavior of prices when switchers do play a role in setting them.

6. The appendix in Barberis and Shleifer (2000) shows more formally how extrapolative expectations combined with a constraint on asset class allocations leads to demand functions like those in equations (5.9) and (5.10).

7. For comparison, the standard deviation of aggregate dividend growth from 1926 to 1995 is close to 12 percent, while the standard deviation of aggregate stock returns over the same period is close to 18 percent, 1.5 times higher.

8. The parameter values in equations (5.28) and (5.30) also support other equilibria, including one where returns are only slightly more volatile than cash flows. The intuition is that if fundamental traders think that returns are not very volatile, they will trade against switchers more aggressively, with the result that equilibrium returns will indeed have low volatility. To support the equilibrium described in the main text, we need fundamental traders to expect returns to be substantially more volatile than cash flows. Nevertheless, the results in this chapter remain valid across multiple equilibria.

9. Another kind of externality arises when a sector experiences a positive shock to investment opportunities, drawing in capital and driving up interest rates, which then pushes risky asset prices in other sectors down. Our model makes the distinct prediction that the externality will be concentrated in a style's twin and not be dispersed across all other risky assets.

10. In fact, the large-cap growth style did not perform significantly worse than other styles during 1973 and 1974. Siegel's argument depends on investors mistakenly perceiving the large stock style as a poor performer, perhaps because of the Nifty Fifty's very high visibility.

11. Proofs of all propositions are in the appendix.

12. In principle, rational changes in discount rates can also generate comovement. However, changes in interest rates or risk aversion induce a common factor in the returns to *all* stocks and do not explain why a particular group of stocks comoves. A common factor in news about the risk of the assets in a style may be a source of comovement for those assets, but there is little direct evidence to support such a mechanism in the case of small or value stocks.

13. Another prediction of our model is that keeping the cash-flow covariance matrix constant, an increase in the importance of style investing should increase the fraction of a stock's volatility that is due to common, rather than idiosyncratic, shocks. Campbell et al. (2001) find that over the past three decades, firm-specific volatility has risen relative to total volatility. They argue that this is most likely due to the fact that the cash-flow covariance matrix *has* changed, with firm-specific cash-flow news becoming more volatile.

14. There will be a spurious increase in $\text{cov}(\Delta P_{n+1,t}, \Delta P_{X,t})$ arising from the fact that after reclassification, $\Delta P_{n+1,t}$ enters into the computation of $\Delta P_{X,t}$. The change from –0.17 to 0.30, however, is far in excess of this mechanical effect.

15. Grundy and Martin (2001) emphasize that the results of Moskowitz and Grinblatt (1999) depend heavily on the positive autocorrelation of monthly industry returns at the first lag. If a gap of a month is inserted between the portfolio formation period and the portfolio test period, individual stock–level momentum is profitable, while industry-level momentum is less so. This suggests that momentum in individual stock returns cannot be purely a style effect.

16. The "A" superscript in these expressions stands for arbitrageur.

17. This observation requires some computation, because ϕ is itself a function of θ. We find that ϕ, and therefore $\phi(1-\theta)$, is a decreasing function of θ.

References

Asness, C., J. Liew, and R. Stevens. 1997. Parallels between the Cross-sectional Predictability of Stock Returns and Country Returns. *Journal of Portfolio Management* 23: 79–87.

Banz, R. 1979. The Relationship between Return and Market Value of Common Stocks. *Journal of Financial Economics* 9: 3–18.

Barberis, N., and A. Shleifer. 2000. Style Investing. NBER Working Paper 8039, National Bureau of Economic Research, Cambridge, MA.

Barberis, N., A. Shleifer, and R. Vishny. 1998. A Model of Investor Sentiment. *Journal of Financial Economics* 49: 307–343.

Barberis, N., A. Shleifer, and J. Wurgler. 2005. Comovement. *Journal of Financial Economics* 75: 283–317.

Bernstein, R. 1995. *Style Investing*. New York: Wiley.

Black, F. 1986. Noise. *Journal of Finance* 41: 529–543.

Brennan, M., and Y. Xia. 2001. Stock Price Volatility and the Equity Premium. *Journal of Monetary Economics* 47: 249–283.

Brown, S., and W. Goetzmann. 1997. Mutual Fund Styles. *Journal of Financial Economics* 43: 373–399.

Brown, S., and W. Goetzmann. 2003. Hedge Funds with Style. *Journal of Portfolio Management* 29: 101–112.

Campbell, J. Y., M. Lettau, B. Malkiel, and Y. Xu. 2001. Have Individual Stocks Become More Volatile? An Empirical Exploration of Idiosyncratic Risk. *Journal of Finance* 56: 1–43.

Chan, L., H. Chen, and L. Lakonishok. 2002. On Mutual Fund Investment Styles. *Review of Financial Studies* 15: 1407–1437.

Chan, L., J. Karceski, and J. Lakonishok. 2000. New Paradigm or Same Old Hype in Equity Investing? *Financial Analysts Journal* 56: 23–36.

Choe, H., B. C. Kho, and R. Stulz. 1999. Do Foreign Investors Destabilize Stock Markets? *Journal of Financial Economics* 54: 227–264.

Cutler, D., J. Poterba, and L. Summers. 1991. Speculative Dynamics. *Review of Economic Studies* 58: 529–546.

Daniel, K., D. Hirshleifer, and A. Subrahmanyam. 2001. Overconfidence, Arbitrage, and Equilibrium Asset Pricing. *Journal of Finance* 53: 1839–1885.

Daniel, K., and S. Titman. 1997. Evidence on the Characteristics of Cross Sectional Variation in Stock Returns. *Journal of Finance* 52: 1–33.

De Long, J. B., A. Shleifer, L. Summers, and R. Waldmann. 1990a. Positive Feedback Investment Strategies and Destabilizing Rational Speculation. *Journal of Finance* 45: 375–395.

De Long, J. B., A. Shleifer, L. Summers, and R. Waldmann. 1990b. Noise Trader Risk in Financial Markets. *Journal of Political Economy* 98: 703–738.

Fama, E., and K. French. 1992. The Cross-section of Expected Stock Returns. *Journal of Finance* 47: 427–465.

Fama, E., and K. French. 1993. Common Risk Factors in the Returns on Stocks and Bonds. *Journal of Financial Economics* 33: 3–56.

Fama, E., and K. French. 1995. Size and Book-to-Market Factors in Earnings and Returns. *Journal of Finance* 50: 131–155.

Froot, K., and E. Dabora. 1999. How Are Stock Prices Affected by the Location of Trade? *Journal of Financial Economics* 53: 189–216.

Froot, K., P. O'Connell, and M. Seasholes. 2001. The Portfolio Flows of International Investors. *Journal of Financial Economics* 59: 149–193.

Gompers, P., and A. Metrick. 2001. Institutional Investors and Equity Prices. *Quarterly Journal of Economics* 116: 229–259.

Grundy, B., and J. S. Martin. 2001. Understanding the Nature of the Risks and the Sources of the Rewards to Momentum Investing. *Review of Financial Studies* 14: 29–78.

Hamilton, J. 1994. *Time Series Analysis*. Princeton, NJ: Princeton University Press.

Harris, L., and E. Gurel. 1986. Price and Volume Effects Associated with Changes in the S&P 500: New Evidence for the Existence of Price Pressure. *Journal of Finance* 41: 851–860.

Haugen, R., and N. Baker. 1996. Commonality in the Determinants of Expected Stock Returns. *Journal of Financial Economics* 41: 401–439.

Hong, H., and J. Stein. 1999. A Unified Theory of Underreaction, Momentum Trading and Overreaction in Asset Markets. *Journal of Finance* 54: 2143–2184.

Kaul, A., V. Mehrotra, and R. Morck. 2000. Demand Curves for Stocks Do Slope Down: New Evidence from an Index Weights Adjustment. *Journal of Finance* 55: 893–912.

Kyle, A., and W. Xiong. 2001. Contagion as a Wealth Effect. *Journal of Finance* 56: 1401–1443.

Lamont, O., and R. Thaler. 2003. Can the Market Add and Subtract? Mispricing in Tech Stock Carve-outs. *Journal of Political Economy* 111: 227–268.

Lee, C., A. Shleifer, and R. Thaler. 1991. Investor Sentiment and the Closed-End Fund Puzzle. *Journal of Finance* 46: 75–110.

Lewellen, J. 2002. Momentum and Autocorrelation in Stock Returns. *Review of Financial Studies* 15: 533–563.

Lewellen, J., and J. Shanken. 2002. Learning, Asset-Pricing Tests, and Market Efficiency. *Journal of Finance* 57: 1113–1145.

Lo, A., and A. C. MacKinlay. 1988. Stock Market Prices Do Not Follow Random Walks: Evidence from a Simple Specification Test. *Review of Financial Studies* 1: 41–66.

Moskowitz, T., and M. Grinblatt. 1999. Do Industries Explain Momentum? *Journal of Finance* 54: 1249–1290.

Mullainathan, S. 2000. Thinking through Categories. Working paper, MIT.

Peng, L., and W. Xiong. 2006. Investor Attention, Overconfidence, and Category Learning. *Journal of Financial Economics* 80: 563–602.

Pindyck, R., and J. Rotemberg. 1990. The Excess Comovement of Commodity Prices. *Economic Journal* 100: 1173–1189.

Poterba, J., and L. Summers. 1988. Mean Reversion in Stock Returns: Evidence and Implications. *Journal of Financial Economics* 22: 27–59.

Rosch, E., and B. Lloyd. 1978. *Cognition and Categorization*. Mahwah, NJ: Lawrence Erlbaum Associates.

Sharpe, W. 1992. Asset Allocation: Management Style and Performance Measurement. *Journal of Portfolio Management* 18: 7–19.

Shiller, R. 1989. Comovements in Stock Prices and Comovements in Dividends. *Journal of Finance* 44: 719–729.

Shleifer, A. 1986. Do Demand Curves for Stocks Slope Down? *Journal of Finance* 41: 579–590.

Shleifer, A., and R. Vishny. 1997. The Limits of Arbitrage. *Journal of Finance* 52: 35–55.

Siegel, J. 1999. *Stocks for the Long Run*. New York: McGraw-Hill.

Swensen, D. 2000. *Pioneering Portfolio Management*. New York: Free Press.

Tversky, A., and D. Kahneman. 1974. Judgment under Uncertainty: Heuristics and Biases. *Science* 185: 1124–1131.

Veronesi, P. 1999. Stock Market Overreaction to Bad News in Good Times: A Rational Expectations Equilibrium Model. *Review of Financial Studies* 12: 975–1007.

Vijh, A. 1994. S&P Trading Strategies and Stock Betas. *Review of Financial Studies* 7: 215–251.

Wilson, R., and F. Keil. 1999. *The MIT Encyclopedia of the Cognitive Sciences*. Cambridge, MA: MIT Press.

6 MacroMarkets and the Practice of Financial Innovation

Robin Greenwood and Luis M. Viceira

MacroMarkets LLC was founded in 2001 by Yale University economist Robert J. Shiller and Samuel Masucci III with the aim of opening markets for illiquid assets around the world, with a particular emphasis on residential housing.[1] The founders believed that financial markets lacked risk-sharing products designed for some of consumers' biggest risks, such as falling housing prices for existing home owners. According to Shiller, every home owner was required to have fire insurance, yet "fires were a big problem hundreds of years ago. Houses were burning down all the time. Now we've developed a different problem—the residential housing market has gotten much more volatile."[2]

MacroMarkets' main innovation, for which it had eleven patents, was the MacroShare. A MacroShare structure allowed investors to take long or short, levered or unlevered, positions based on the value of *any* index, whether that index was traded or not. The structure was fully collateralized by U.S. Treasuries and cash, was not exposed to counterparty risk, had intraday pricing and liquidity, and allowed for the continuous creation and redemption of units. Both Shiller and Masucci were hopeful that MacroShares could help investors hedge all kinds of macroeconomic risks, a theme that Shiller had advocated for many years through his research. And they believed that MacroShares were well positioned to succeed exchange-traded funds (ETFs) and exchange-traded notes (ETNs) as the next predominant technology for index trading.[3]

Early versions of MacroShares had already been "battled-tested" in the markets. MacroShares Oil, a set of "up" and "down" shares that tracked the performance (or inverse performance, in the case of the down shares) of oil prices, had gathered almost $1.6 billion in assets before being liquidated in early July 2008. However, MacroShares Housing, which tracked the performance of national residential housing prices, had attracted more limited interest, eventually being shut down because of illiquidity.

In early April 2010, Masucci and Shiller felt that MacroMarkets could benefit from a strategic partner willing to provide capital and help with distribution. Such a partner could potentially help the MacroShare become the preferred instrument in exchange-traded products. The financial and economic turmoil of the last two years had put the financing of Macro-Markets on hold. However, as optimism returned to the markets, Masucci and Shiller were confident that MacroMarkets offered a rapid, profitable growth potential that would attract investors' interest.

Origins of MacroMarkets LLC

Housing Derivatives in the 1980s and 1990s

A derivatives specialist, Masucci worked at Merrill Lynch's fixed income derivative trading desk during the 1990s. Through conversations with clients, Masucci had discovered that institutional investors were interested in buying exposure to owner-occupied real estate, yet lacked financial instruments to do so. He explained, "In the U.S. and in most developed countries, residential homes are the largest asset class in that particular area. Yet, those who would like to get exposure can't get access." Prompted by client demand, Masucci and his colleagues developed an option product that would allow home owners to write covered call options on the future price appreciation of their homes. The options were to be sold through Merrill Lynch's retail brokerage operation under the acronym EARN, which stood for "Equity Appreciation Right Now." Home owners who bought this instrument would receive a monthly payment in exchange for a portion of the future appreciation of the value of their home. EARN could then be aggregated into a pool, with the proceeds packaged into securities and sold to institutional investors.

Robert J. Shiller, a financial economist at Yale University, and a company that he cofounded, Case Shiller Weiss, Inc., were brought in by Masucci as outside experts on historical home price returns. Masucci had been trying to value the exposures that Merrill Lynch would accumulate in the EARN program, based on historical measures of real estate price volatility. Disappointed in the off-the-shelf measures of housing prices available, Masucci turned to Shiller, who had been developing his own index of housing prices in collaboration with economist Karl Case from Wellesley College. Case and Shiller's index appealed to Masucci, and Masucci eventually hired Case and Shiller's firm to produce a real estate index for him.

As a developer of new financial market derivatives, Masucci spent a large part of his time on tax and regulatory issues. In the case of the EARN securities, tax issues were a source of frustration. Option-like premiums would be paid out to the home owner for every year of a thirty-year mortgage, but the tax treatment of these payments was uncertain. After failing to get definitive answers on the tax treatment, Masucci felt that the ultimate launch of the EARN security was unlikely. Seeing little prospect for the EARN product at Merrill Lynch, Masucci moved to investment bank SBC Warburg, with the goal of developing real estate derivatives for global housing markets, starting with the United Kingdom.

At SBC Warburg, Masucci refined the concept of a "shared appreciation mortgage," known as a "SAM." SAMs were mortgages in which the lender agreed to receive a lower interest rate in exchange for a percentage of the appreciation of the house at the time of sale. The mortgages were structured such that the fraction of appreciation the home owner would share was equal to the loan-to-value ratio.[4] Masucci also devised and sold a product for retirees called the "zero-SAM," which paid the home owner no interest until the property was sold, at which point the lender would recover the principal and a share of any price appreciation. While SAMs had been originated in limited numbers before, a significant program had never been supported by investors. In addition, SAMs had never been securitized, and thus no capital market existed for SAMs. Masucci and his team at SBC Warburg would pioneer these efforts, allowing institutional investors their first access to home price–linked securities.

As with the EARN, Masucci needed to figure out how to hedge the housing exposure that SBC Warburg accumulated through its sales of SAMs. If housing prices fell, for example, the bank's option on mortgage appreciation would expire worthless. Some of this risk was eliminated because the bank held a diversified pool of mortgages, but SBC Warburg still maintained exposure to *aggregate* housing prices. To limit the risk, Masucci had found that he could short stocks of construction companies, building suppliers, and other companies that would be hurt if housing prices declined. Still, this hedging was imperfect, as Masucci would have preferred to short the housing exposure directly. Masucci felt frustrated by the lack of financial instruments available to buy or sell exposure to housing.

SAMs caught on quickly in the UK, which Masucci attributed in part to fortuitous timing. Following several years of housing price declines in the early 1990s in the UK, home owners were willing to share potential price appreciation, which they believed, by extrapolation, to be unlikely in light of recent price declines. Instead, between 1996 and 1999, UK

home prices rose by an average of 5.6 percent annually, making SAMs extremely profitable for SBC Warburg.[5]

Following the success of the UK SAMs, Masucci worked on designing a similar shared appreciation program to be implemented in the U.S. markets. However, when SBC Warburg merged with Union Bank of Switzerland (UBS) in 1998, the company exited its mortgage businesses on both continents, leaving Masucci to look elsewhere.

Masucci moved to Bear Stearns with the intention of launching another SAM program. By this time, the housing market in the United States was in the early stages of a boom: In 1999, housing prices increased by 11 percent nationwide, and they continued to rise in 2000 and 2001 (see figure 6.1). Booming housing markets made it difficult to sell home price insurance, and the SAM program never caught on with consumers, who were not worried about price declines. Masucci believed that home owners had started to extrapolate the recent gains in property prices: "Buyers just wanted more home than they could afford. People started tapping their home equity and putting all available cash into enhancing their homes with the expectation that no matter what they invested into the home, they would get it back two or threefold." He added, "One of the frustrating pieces of trying to innovate financially is that sometimes financial products don't work because the timing is not right . . . because the market's not there."

While Masucci was at Bear Stearns, Shiller and Weiss approached him with the idea for a security that could securitize any index, as long as one could find two-sided interest — that is, as long as one could find investors who wanted to be long the security and investors who wanted to be short the security. The idea had instant appeal to Masucci, who had faced frequent frustrations in finding instruments to hedge housing exposure.[6] Shiller and Weiss had already received a patent for the security, which they called a "proxy asset data processor" and which would later become known as a MacroShare. Masucci's contract with Bear Stearns was due to expire at the end of the year, and he was keen to pursue financial innovation outside the red tape of the Wall Street banks. After further discussion, Shiller, Masucci, and Weiss cofounded MacroMarkets in 2002 as a limited liability corporation (LLC), with a fully owned subsidiary broker-dealer called Macro Financial.

Innovation in Housing Markets

Yale University professor Robert Shiller (who had earned a PhD from MIT in 1972) was known for his pioneering research in behavioral

finance. Shiller's early research had studied whether volatility in stock prices could be attributed to changes in firms' fundamental values. Starting in 1989, Shiller began survey research to gauge investor sentiment. These surveys were the first formal attempts to measure investors' expectations about the future performance of the stock market. During the late 1990s, Shiller became a household name when his book, *Irrational Exuberance*, questioned the basis for the high valuations of technology companies during the Internet bubble.

During the early 1980s, Shiller collaborated with Wellesley College professor Karl Case on research to measure home price appreciation in U.S. cities. Shiller and Case had noticed that the prevailing measures of local and national home prices were based on simple aggregates, such as the average or median. One problem with such measures was that they could be shaped as much by the composition of houses being sold as by changes in the housing prices of existing properties. For example, if the number of lower-priced houses were to increase in a quarter relative to the number of higher-priced houses, this would result in a lower average sales price, even though the price of any given house might be unchanged. Case and Shiller set out to fix this problem by studying repeat sales of single-family homes. Under their methodology, whenever a home was *re*sold, the new sale was matched to the home's first sale price, forming a "sales pair." All such pairs in a geographic area were then aggregated into one index number.[7] This methodology could be adjusted to deal with factors such as home remodeling or foreclosure sales. Case and Shiller first showcased the methodology in an academic paper, but joined with Allan Weiss in 1991 to form Case Shiller Weiss, Inc., which would calculate and disseminate the Case-Shiller indexes. The company produced and reported a national home price index, ten- and twenty-city composite indexes, indexes for twenty metropolitan areas, and thousands of indexes based on individual Zip Codes and counties. The indexes were published quarterly based on data from the sale of single-family homes, and use of the indexes was licensed to financial services companies. Fiserv, an information management company, bought Case Shiller Weiss in 2002 and continued to publish the Case-Shiller indexes thereafter. Figure 6.1 shows the performance of the Case-Shiller Composite-10 index, which tracked real estate in ten of the largest urban areas in the United States.

Shiller's 1993 book, *Macro Markets*, was devoted to understanding how financial markets could help individuals better manage risk. Shiller felt that sharing economic risk was one of society's "deepest concerns,"

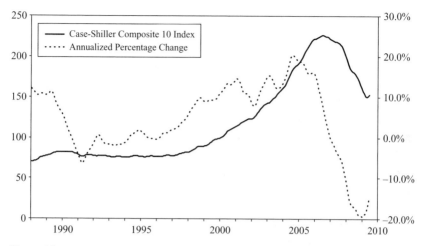

Figure 6.1
Case-Shiller Composite-10 index. The Composite-10 index tracks home prices in Boston, Chicago, Denver, Las Vegas, Los Angeles, Miami, New York, San Diego, San Francisco, and Washington, DC. *Source:* Adapted from S&P/Case-Shiller Home Price Indexes, at http://www.standardandpoors.com/indices/sp-case-shiller-home-price-indices/en/us/?indexId=spusa-cashpidff--p-us----.

because people's standards of living were determined largely "by a game of chance." Shiller viewed the market for insurance very broadly, arguing the potential benefits from hedging "everything from the rising costs of health care and education to national income risk and oil crises" (Benner 2009). Housing was of particular interest to Shiller, however, in part because of his previous work developing indexes for real estate prices. In the United States alone, the aggregate residential housing stock was valued at over $21 trillion in 2008, which was greater than the capitalization of U.S.-listed equities and three to four times larger than the value of commercial real estate. In Shiller's opinion, the majority of the fifty-eight million home owners in the United States were overexposed to local real estate prices. Shiller's view, which Masucci echoed, was that on average, home owners had between 70 and 90 percent of their portfolio in real estate, not by choice but "because they want that utility component, which means that you buy a house in Madison, New Jersey because you want a particular school system, you want five bedrooms." This high exposure to home prices resulted in a high risk of default should a consumer have to move, but few home owners hedged against this risk. In Shiller's view, it was a puzzle that home owners had fire and flood insurance

to protect themselves against disasters but no similar insurance against the more likely event of defaulting on a mortgage owing to fluctuations in prices. Shiller and Masucci both believed that it should be easy to find investors to take the other side of these insurance contracts because historically, real estate had exhibited very low correlation with other asset classes (table 6.1).

The insurance contracts envisioned by Shiller were long-dated, based on perpetual claims linked to an index. A perpetual contract on the stock market, for example, might pay a quarterly dividend proportional to the level of the S&P 500 index. Such contracts had two attractive features. First, they could be used as the basis for developing and pricing shorter-dated contracts. Second, Shiller believed *demand* for insurance was inherently long term. For example, a consumer buying insurance on the price of oil would presumably be doing so to hedge energy consumption over the course of that person's life span.

Shiller and Masucci formed MacroMarkets to bring liquidity to major asset classes, with a focus on oil, real estate, and national income. That same year, Shiller and Weiss sold Case Shiller Weiss (which had developed and disseminated the Case-Shiller index) to Fiserv, which allowed them to be fully committed to MacroMarkets. As part of the sale, MacroMarkets was spun off from Case Shiller Weiss, and the new firm obtained exclusive trading rights to Case-Shiller products. MacroMarkets also brought in Case Shiller Weiss managing director Terry Loebs, who had expertise marketing the indexes.

Soon thereafter, Masucci initiated discussions with the Securities and Exchange Commission (SEC) to foster trading markets around the Case-Shiller index. Futures linked to the Case-Shiller index started trading on the Chicago Mercantile Exchange in 2006. MacroMarkets eventually sold the trading rights to Standard and Poor's in 2008. MacroMarkets licensed rights from S&P starting that year, and Masucci and Shiller used the proceeds from the sale to fund the housing-based MacroShares.

Up and Down Shares

"MacroShares" were a set of paired securities that allowed investors to express a view on any index. The index determined the underlying fundamental value of the shares. Up securities were designed to increase in value when the index went up, and Down securities would decrease in value by a corresponding amount. Figure 6.2 shows the basic structure

Table 6.1
Historical Returns of Real Estate and Other Asset Classes

Year	S&P/Case-Shiller Index	S&P/Case-Shiller Return
1988	71.22	0.076
1989	75.37	0.058
1990	74.59	−0.010
1991	74.65	0.001
1992	74.74	0.001
1993	75.91	0.016
1994	77.89	0.026
1995	79.51	0.021
1996	81.18	0.021
1997	84.80	0.045
1998	90.81	0.071
1999	98.29	0.082
2000	107.90	0.098
2001	116.23	0.077
2002	128.58	0.106
2003	142.29	0.107
2004	163.06	0.146
2005	186.97	0.147
2006	186.44	−0.003
2007	170.75	−0.084
2008	139.43	−0.183
2009	136.22	−0.023
Correlation with Housing		1.000

and agreements between the Up and Down shares, and figure 6.3 shows an example of changes in the value of the Up and Down securities based on a reference index with a starting value of 50. Box 6.1 excerpts portions of the prospectus for Up and Down shares based on the Case-Shiller residential housing index.

Up and Down MacroShares were always issued and redeemed in pairs. At issuance, the proceeds from selling the pair of securities ($100) would be deposited in Up and Down trusts, which invested in Treasury securities. Interest on the Treasuries could be used to pay dividends based on the current level of the reference index, and to pay MacroMarkets a management fee. MacroMarkets adjusted the assets of the Up and Down trusts based on index movements. If the value of the reference index rose, assets (Treasury bonds and swaps) moved from the Down trust to the Up trust. Assets were pledged to the Up or Down MacroShare at the conclusion of each day, but the assets were not transferred until the end of the quarter.

Figure 6.3 shows the dynamics of asset value for a pair of Macro securities, issued at $50 each, with reference index of starting value 50. If the

Table 6.1
(continued)

Year	S&P 500	Bonds	Commodities	NAREIT
1988	0.166	0.070	0.122	0.114
1990	0.317	0.178	0.124	–0.018
1990	–0.031	0.079	0.061	–0.173
1991	0.305	0.188	–0.196	0.357
1992	0.076	0.074	0.023	0.122
1993	0.101	0.130	–0.096	0.185
1994	0.013	–0.073	0.105	0.008
1995	0.376	0.259	0.126	0.183
1996	0.230	0.001	0.058	0.358
1997	0.334	0.120	–0.184	0.189
1998	0.286	0.145	–0.243	–0.188
1999	0.210	–0.075	0.462	–0.065
2000	–0.091	0.172	0.269	0.259
2001	–0.119	0.055	–0.315	0.155
2002	–0.221	0.154	0.390	0.052
2003	0.287	0.005	0.108	0.385
2004	0.109	0.046	0.192	0.304
2005	0.049	0.031	0.391	0.083
2006	0.158	0.022	0.005	0.344
2007	0.055	0.105	0.406	–0.178
2008	-0.370	0.202	–0.428	–0.373
2009	0.265	–0.095	0.503	0.274
Correlation with Housing	0.253	–0.196	0.342	0.442

Source: Compiled by case writers using data from Standard & Poor's (http://www.standardandpoors.com/indices/sp-case-shiller-home-price-indices/en/us/?indexId=spusa-cashpidff--p-us----) and Global Financial Data. S&P/Case-Shiller index refers to the U.S. National Home Price Index.

value of the reference index were to increase to $75, the assets in the Up trust would increase to $75, while the assets in the Down trust would fall to $25. If the reference index fell, assets would be transferred from the Up trust to the Down trust instead. Thus, by buying the Up MacroShare, the investor would earn $1 for each one-unit increase in the index value, and vice versa for the Down MacroShare.

One consequence of the fully collateralized structure was that the MacroShares could reflect the performance of the index only within a specific range: in the example above, once the reference index reached 100, assets in the Down trust would be completely depleted, having been pledged entirely to the Up trust. Similarly, once the reference index reached 0, assets in the Up trust would be completely depleted. In the event this happened, the trusts would be liquidated and the securities redeemed, according to prespecified rules (see box 6.1).

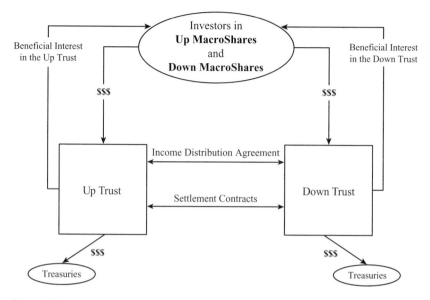

Figure 6.2
Relationships between the Up Trust and the Down Trust. *Notes:* Under the income distribution agreement, as of any distribution date, the Up Trust will either be required to pay a portion of its available income to the Down Trust or be entitled to receive a portion of the Down Trust's available income, based in each case on the reference value of the index. Under the settlement contract, the Up Trust will either be required to make a termination payment to the Down Trust or be entitled to receive a termination from the Down Trust, in each case based on the reference value of the index on the day prior to termination. Treasuries include bills, bonds, notes, and repurchase agreements collateralized by U.S. Treasuries. *Source:* Adapted from Macromarkets and Housing and Oil Macroshares prospectuses, at http://www.macromarkets.com.

It was straightforward to incorporate leverage in the MacroShare structure by simply adjusting the dollar amount that would be transferred between the Down trust and the Up trust when the reference index fluctuated. For example, the reference index could be leveraged 2-to-1 by stipulating that every one-unit change in the index would trigger a transfer of $2 from the Down trust to the Up trust.[8] Leverage was fixed in dollar terms, which implied that the percentage leverage could vary.[9] Both Masucci and Shiller thought this was an attractive feature, however, because constant dollar leverage was more appropriate for buy-and-hold investors. In contrast, levered ETFs rebalance daily to achieve constant percentage leverage.

While the net asset value (NAV) of the Up and Down shares was pinned down by the reference index, the market price of these securities could fluctuate significantly from NAV. These fluctuations reflected supply and

At inception MacroShares Up and MacroShares Down Trust are
equally priced and equally collateralized.

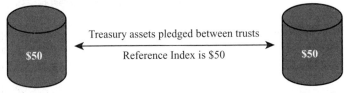

Treasury assets pledged between trusts

Reference Index is $50

MacroShares Up   MacroShares Down

**Example 1: Index Rises to 75: MacroShares Up increases in value and
MacroShares Down decreases in value proportionally.**

Macroshares Up is entitled to
$25 in pledged assets

MacroShares Up   MacroShares Down

**Example 2: Index Falls to 25. MacroShares Down increases in value and
MacroShares Up decreases in value proportionally.**

MacroShares Down is entitled
to $25 in pledged assets

MacroShares Up   MacroShares Down

Figure 6.3
MacroShares mechanics: an illustration for MacroShares at initial trust values of $50.
Source: Case writers' adaptation of MacroMarkets materials.

Box 6.1

Excerpts from MacroShares Major Metro Housing Up Shares Prospectus

Quarterly Distributions
The assets of the Up Trust will consist of an income distribution agreement and settlement contracts entered into with the MacroShares Major Metro Housing Down Trust, referred to as the "Down Trust." The Up Trust will also hold U.S. Treasuries and repurchase agreements on U.S. Treasuries to secure its obligations under the income distribution agreement and the settlement contracts. The Up Trust will make quarterly distributions of net income, if any, on the treasuries and a final distribution of all or a portion of the assets it holds on deposit on the final scheduled termination date, an early termination date or a redemption date. Quarterly distributions of net income, if any, will be declared on distribution dates that are scheduled to occur in March, June, September and December of each year, beginning in September of 2009.

Income Distribution Agreement and Settlement Contracts
The paired trusts will enter into an income distribution agreement under which the trusts make quarterly payments to each other out of the income generated by the treasuries that remain available after each trust has paid its fees and expenses. Under the income distribution agreement, the Up Trust will, on each distribution date, either (1) be required to pay a portion of its available income to the Down Trust or (2) be entitled to receive a portion of the Down Trust's available income, based, in each case, on the level of the Reference Value of the Index during the preceding calculation period. On each distribution payment date, a quarterly distribution of all available income, if any, on deposit in the Up Trust will be made on the Up MacroShares after the Up Trust has made or received a payment under the income distribution agreement.

The Up Trust will also enter into multiple settlement contracts with the Down Trust. In order to facilitate paired issuances and paired optional redemptions, the paired trusts will settle one settlement contract in connection with the paired optional redemption of each existing MacroShares Unit and will enter into a new settlement contract in connection with the paired issuance of each new MacroShares Unit.

A "MacroShares Unit" will consist of 10,000 Up MacroShares and 10,000 Down MacroShares. Under each settlement contract, the Up Trust will either (1) be required to make a termination payment out of its assets to the Down Trust or (2) be entitled to receive a termination payment from the Down Trust out of the assets of the Down Trust. These settlement obligations are based on the change in the level of the Reference Value of the Index from its starting level to its ending level, as measured on the last calendar day preceding the final scheduled termination date, an early termination date or the relevant redemption date. [. . .] The Up Trust will be required to make

Box 6.1
(continued)

a settlement payment to the Down Trust equal to 100% of the assets it holds on deposit in the event that the Reference Value of the Index falls to or below 108.11. The Down Trust will be required to make a settlement payment to the Up Trust equal to 100% of the assets it holds on deposit in the event that the Reference Value of the Index rises to or above 216.23. However, neither trust can ever be required to make a payment under the settlement agreements that exceeds the assets it holds on deposit.

Calculation of Underlying Value
The final distribution made on the Up MacroShares on the final scheduled termination date, an early termination date or a redemption date is based upon the underlying value of the Up Trust on the last calendar day, whether or not such day is a business day, that precedes such final scheduled termination date, early termination date, or redemption date. The underlying value of the Up Trust on each calendar day is calculated by reference to the level of the Reference Value of the Index on that day. The Reference Value of the Index on each day is equal to the level of the S&P/Case-Shiller Composite-10 Home Price Index that was reported on the most recent index publication day.

Final Distribution
The Up Trust will declare a final distribution on all or a portion of the Up MacroShares, as applicable, on the earliest of:

• The "final scheduled termination date";
• An "early termination date," which is the next distribution date that follows the occurrence of a termination trigger; and
• A "redemption order date," which is any business day on which an authorized participant places an order for a paired optional redemption of all or a portion of the paired shares.

The final distribution declared by the Up Trust on the final scheduled termination date, an early termination date or any redemption order date will depend upon the termination payments that it is required to make to, or that it is entitled to receive from, the Down Trust under the settlement contracts being settled in connection with the redemption of shares that will occur on these dates. The termination payment under the settlement contracts will, in turn, be based on the underlying value of the Up Trust on the last calendar day that precedes the final scheduled termination date, the early termination date or the relevant redemption date. On the distribution payment date that follows the final scheduled termination date or early termination date, the trustee will pay the final distribution to each holder of the outstanding Up MacroShares in redemption of its shares. On the relevant redemption date, the trustee will pay the final distribution to

each redeeming authorized participant in redemption of its shares. The purpose of the termination payment under the settlement contracts is to transfer assets between the paired trusts such that each trust has cash and treasuries in an amount equal to its underlying value as of the last calendar day preceding the final scheduled termination date, an early termination date or a redemption date.

Source: MacroMarkets prospectus, available at http://www.macromarkets .com/macroshares/documents/umm_prospectus.pdf.

demand for the securities, and correspondingly, investors' expectations of future values of the reference index. Shiller argued that this was the entire point of the securities, which he called "price discovery." At the same time, an arbitrage relationship governed the relationship *between* the Up and the Down securities because investors could always buy both an Up and a Down security and exchange them for cash (based on the underlying value of the Treasuries held in trust) with MacroMarkets. Symmetrically, qualified investors could also create new MacroShares in pairs.

While there were no direct competitors to the Up and Down Macro security structure, MacroMarkets faced some competition from ETFs and futures markets (table 6.2). Unlike an ETF, MacroShares did not invest in index components, futures, or derivatives. The SEC requires ETFs to purchase such products to replicate the performance of an index. This requirement increases expenses because it forces ETFs to periodically report returns to the SEC. More important, investors in MacroShares bore no credit risk because their money was invested in Treasury bonds. Macro securities also had some advantages relative to futures markets, since the MacroShare could easily be held by a passive investor. In contrast, an investor using futures to get exposure to an index has to "roll" his contracts frequently, trading a series of near-term contracts to achieve long-dated exposure. Such frequent trading incurs transaction costs, and is particularly costly in cases of a "negative roll yield."[10]

Application to Oil Markets

MacroMarkets spent three years and more than $4 million in legal and regulatory fees to obtain approval for the first MacroShare fund, which

Table 6.2
Largest ETFs and ETF Sponsors, December 2009

Fund Name	AUM (U.S. $M)
SPDR S&P 500	85,676
iShares MSCI Emerging Markets Index	39,178
iShares MSCI EAFE Index	35,339
iShares S&P 500 Index	22,025
Vanguard Emerging Markets Stock ETF	19,399
PowerShares QQQ	18,736
iShares Barclays TIPS Bond	18,552
Vanguard Total Stock Market	13,570
iShares Russell 2000 Index	13,115

ETF Sponsor	No. of ETFs	AUM (U.S. $BN)
iShares	413	489
State Street Global Advisors	107	161
Vanguard	47	92
Lyxor Asset Management	125	46
db x-trackers	121	37
PowerShares	125	35
ProShares	78	23
Nomura Asset Management	30	13
Van Eck Associates Corp.	23	13
Bank of New York	1	9

Source: Excerpted from "ETF Landscape Industry Review 2009" from BlackRock, at http://www.blackrock.com.

was launched in November 2006. The MacroShares were planned to terminate twenty years later.[11] MacroMarkets had initially submitted a prospectus to the SEC to create a MacroShare based on housing, but it was rejected. Masucci sensed that MacroMarkets might have more luck if the MacroShare was tied to oil prices. Yet even with oil, the approval process turned out to be more onerous than expected: although Macro-Markets was the first company to file an application with the SEC to launch an oil-based exchange-traded product, regulatory delays resulted in three other competitors releasing oil-linked trading platforms first. By the time MacroShares were issued, the oil futures ETF US Oil had attracted more than $1 billion in assets under management. Masucci blamed the slow approval process to the uniqueness of the offering.

The oil Up and Down securities were listed in November 2006 under the tickers UCR and DCR, and were based on the per-barrel price of crude oil.[12] At inception, UCR and DCR were equally collateralized based on an underlying value of $60 per share and a reference index price of $60 per barrel. For every $1 increase in the price of oil, "Oil Down" (DCR)

pledged $1 of Treasury bills to "Oil Up" (UCR). MacroMarkets partnered with Claymore Securities to design the shares, which became officially known as Claymore MACROshares. MacroMarkets also linked with the specialist firm Bear Wagner, which put up initial capital of $40 million to create the first shares, which were sold to institutional investors. Specialists had a strong incentive to issue shares because they received a large percentage of trading volume. MacroMarkets would earn management fees of 160 basis points (1.60 percent) per annum.

By November 2007, DCR was trading at a substantial premium to net asset value, while UCR was trading at a corresponding discount, which investors attributed to the steep "backwardation" of the oil futures curve.[13] Yet investors still continued to trade the product at higher volumes. In the first quarter of 2008, the assets invested in UCR and DCR rose by 160 percent, and the average daily trading volume was 240,000 shares.

As oil prices increased in 2008, it became increasingly likely that MacroMarkets would be forced to terminate UCR/DCR. Initially, the UCR/DCR MacroShares had launched at $60 each, which meant that the Down shares were worthless if the price of oil reached $120. However, MacroMarkets had built in a forced redemption policy whereby the shares terminated in three months when the closing price of oil reached $111 for three consecutive days, which it did on April 16, 2008.[14] At this point, the redemption period fell from approximately twenty years to three months, as the securities would be liquidated based on oil prices on June 25, 2008. As the likelihood of termination had increased, the *expected* redemption period fell, and trading volume had skyrocketed (figure 6.4). In fact, for several months following the termination trigger, DCR had an NAV of zero, but ten to twenty million shares per day were still trading because investors thought that the price of oil might decline. Trading in the funds peaked in June 2008 after its assets increased from $40 million to $1.6 billion. Masucci attributed this to speculators only being comfortable with short-horizon trades. Shiller found this perplexing, saying, "I have always believed the economic theory that people are long-term maximizers, but sometimes it seems that they are short-term gamblers."

MacroMarkets introduced a second pair of oil MacroShares in July 2008, but they were discontinued in June 2009 after experiencing low volume.

Housing MacroShares

Going into 2009, Masucci and Shiller had high hopes for changing the housing derivatives market, and the time seemed ripe. Despite massive

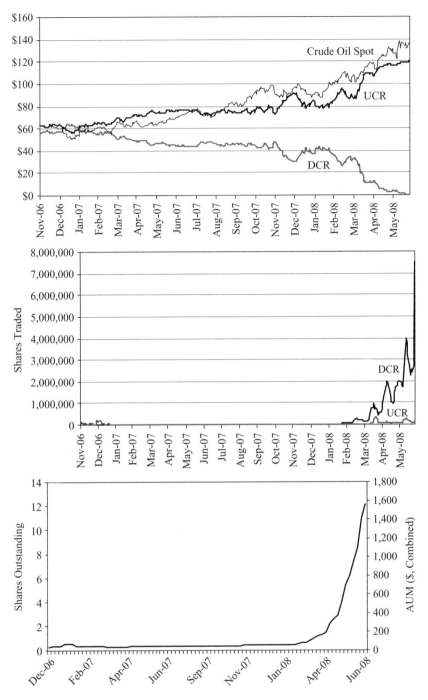

Figure 6.4
a. Up Oil (UCR) and Down Oil (DCR), share price adjusted for stock splits; b. Up Oil (UCR) and Down Oil (DCR), trading volume adjusted for stock splits; c. Up Oil (UCR) and Down Oil (DCR), number of shares outstanding and combined assets under management (AUM). *Source:* Created by case writers using MacroMarkets data, at http://www.macromarkets.com.

declines in all urban markets, at the end of 2008, U.S. residential real estate was valued at $18.3 trillion. It was several years since Masucci had encountered difficulties hedging his exposure to SAMs, yet few housing derivatives existed. Options and futures on the Case-Shiller index were traded on the Chicago Mercantile Exchange starting in 2006, but they had received little interest.

Based on their experience with the oil MacroShares, Masucci and Shiller redesigned several components of the housing MacroShares fund. First, they decided to seed the fund through an initial public offering (IPO) rather than asking the specialist for seed capital. Second, they reduced management fees from 160 basis points to 125 basis points, to be competitive with ETFs. The reduction in management fees was possible because they had reduced the annual cost of running a MacroShares fund from $1.2 million for oil to $400,000, mainly by improving the software that was used to track shareholders, renegotiating vendor fees, and reengineering the security from a four-trust structure to two. Finally, reflecting on investor feedback and MacroMarkets' experience with the oil MacroShares, Masucci and Shiller reduced the maturity of the securities from twenty years to five.

The MacroShares were based on an index returning three times the Case-Shiller Composite-10 housing index. The Up and Down shares, UMM and DMM, respectively, both started with an NAV of $25 per share, based on the Case-Shiller index value of 162.17 on December 31, 2008. The funds were to expire in November 2014, at which point investors would receive a payment equal to 300 percent of the change in the Case-Shiller index between December 31, 2008, and August 31, 2014. As with earlier MacroShares, there were several ways to convert the shares to cash: (1) the securities were designed with specific early termination events, (2) investors were allowed the right to redeem the pair of shares, which involved converting the shares to cash when a shareholder delivered both UMM and DMM at the same time to the Trustee, or (3) shares could be converted to cash at the fund termination in November 2014.

Although no ETF had ever used the open auction model before, MacroMarkets opted to list the initial shares using an auction-based IPO, in collaboration with investment bank WR Hambrecht & Co. The IPO of the housing MacroShares occurred between April 28 and May 5, 2009, during which time MacroMarkets attracted interest in both Up and Down shares. The auction was expected to close when a minimum investment pool of $125 million had been reached. But by the end of the auction, the requirement had not been attained. MacroMarkets extended the auction to generate more interest from institutional investors, who

needed time to understand the product and approval to invest in it. But ultimately, MacroMarkets abandoned the process on May 20, citing an "insufficient demand for an equal number of Down and Up shares."

After the attempted IPO, MacroMarkets approached funds specialist Kellogg and asked them to seed UMM and DMM with a minimum required $10 million each, to which Kellogg agreed. As in the previous launch, UMM and DMM would start with an NAV of $25 per share and would be based on a starting reference index of 162.17, which was the value of the S&P Case-Shiller Composite-10 Home Price Index on February 24, 2009. UMM and DMM started trading on the New York Stock Exchange on June 30, 2009. Figure 6.5 shows the price and volume history of these two securities.

From the beginning, investor interest in trading the housing MacroShares was quite low, with combined daily trading volume of the two shares averaging approximately 25,000 per day in the first month. By December 2009, less than one million UMM and DMM shares were outstanding, following investor redemptions of paired securities. On December 23, MacroMarkets announced that UMM and DMM would be terminated based on an "early termination event" outlined in the prospectus, which stated: "The fund administrator has the right to terminate the fund early when the amount of cash and treasuries on deposit in the Up Trust and/or Down Trust is less than fifty (50) million dollars per trust on any business day and we elect, in our discretion, to terminate the paired trusts." UMM and DMM continued to trade until December 28, the last day of trading, and a final distribution payment was made on January 6, based on shareholders of record on December 31.

The Future of MacroMarkets

Although MacroMarkets had developed an innovative way to securitize the $20 trillion market in residential housing, its main housing product had not taken off in the way that Masucci and Shiller had hoped. It seemed that institutional investors were more interested in trading MacroShares linked to liquid and "arbitragable" assets or indexes. Perhaps MacroMarkets could prosper as an engine of financial innovation, but it would have to move away from the firm's original goal of fostering long-dated insurance markets in illiquid assets—at least until it built a significant MacroShares business around liquid assets.

The whiteboard in Masucci's office was filled with a list of tradable commodities, as well as some items, such as GDP and health care costs, that had never been traded. It was also filled with a table that compared

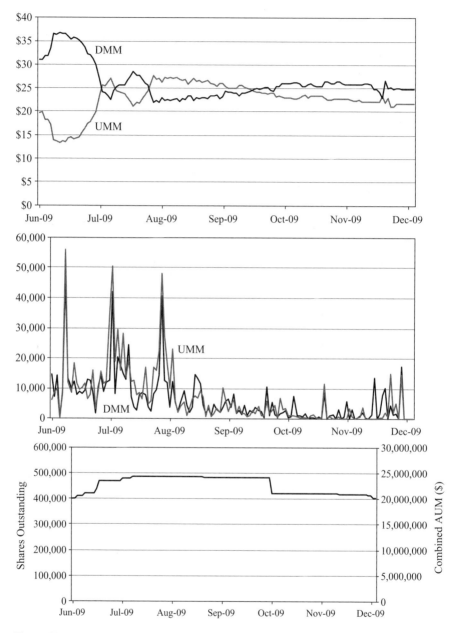

Figure 6.5
a. Major Metro Housing Up (UMM) and Down (DMM), volume (shares). b. Major Metro
Housing UP (UMM) and Down (DMM), volume (shares). c. Major Metro Housing UP
(UMM) and Down (DMM), number of shares outstanding and assets under management
(AUM). *Source:* Created by case writers using MacroMarkets data, at http://www.macromarkets.
com.

the MacroShares' structure to ETFs and ETNs on many dimensions. Masucci and Shiller had thought long and deeply about the design elements that had allowed MacroMarkets' oil MacroShares fund to become one of the largest and most liquid on the market, and at the same time, which factors had caused the Up and Down housing shares to have little liquidity.

If MacroMarkets were eventually to fulfill its long-run objective of fostering long-dated insurance markets in illiquid assets, perhaps the right strategic decision was to take advantage of the potential of the MacroShare structure as a disruptive technology in the exchange-traded product market. Initially, the profitability of the firm could be built on more vanilla asset classes, where MacroMarkets could provide a superior security structure. The profit and success of MacroMarkets' products could be used to fuel more innovative growth, such as housing and inflation MacroShares. These simpler products were a far cry from what Shiller and Masucci originally had in mind when they cofounded the firm, but both men felt that the firm had to face up to the realities of doing radical financial innovation.

Acknowledgments

Reprinted by permission of Harvard Business School. Copyright © 2010 by the President and Fellows of Harvard College. Harvard Business School Case 221-006, "MacroMarkets LLC."

This case was prepared as the basis for class discussion rather than to illustrate either effective or ineffective handling of an administrative situation.

Notes

1. MacroMarkets LLC was originally incorporated as Macro Securities Research LLC on November 1, 1999, but remained largely inactive until late 2001. The name of the company was officially changed to MacroMarkets LLC on February 2, 2006. A third cofounder, Allan N. Weiss, left the firm in 2006, before any products were launched.

2. *Time* magazine, interview with Robert Shiller, May 6, 2009. Available at http://www.time.com/time/business/article/0,8599,1896583,%2000.html (accessed June 12, 2010).

3. ETFs are open-ended funds that track specific indexes and can be traded on an exchange like regular stocks. Their unit creation and redemption mechanism help shares in ETFs to trade at prices that are very close to the NAV of their underlying assets. ETFs based on major indexes are considered attractive investments because of their liquidity, low cost, and tax efficiency. ETNs are similar to ETFs in that they track indexes. However, unlike ETFs,

they typically cannot be redeemed for shares in the underlying index but are backed by the balance sheet of the issuing institution (the underwriting bank). See Harvard Business School Case 208–033, "Barclays Global Investors and Exchange Traded Funds."

4. For example, a borrower with a 75 percent loan-to-value mortgage shared 75 percent of the future appreciation.

5. UK data from Halifax Housing Price Index and U.S. data from Case-Shiller Composite-10 Home Price Index.

6. By this time, the performance of housing could be tracked through the Case-Shiller index, but no instruments existed to get exposure.

7. Case Shiller index factsheet, http://www2.standardandpoors.com/spf/pdf/index/SP_CS _Home_Price_Indices_Factsheet.pdf, accessed June 18, 2010.

8. A consequence of having leverage in the MacroShares structure was that it increased the possibility of early liquidation. For example, with 2-to-1 leverage, if the reference index were to increase from 50 to 75, the Down shares would have to be liquidated. More broadly, higher leverage reduced the index price interval over which a MacroShare could replicate the performance of an index.

9. Consider again the previous example with 2-to-1 leverage. Suppose the reference index increased from 50 to 74, implying that the Up share would have an NAV of $98 and the Down share an NAV of $2. A one-unit change in the index (approximately 1.35% = 1/74) results in a 100 percent change in the value of a Down share and 1.02 percent change in the value of an Up share.

10. Investing in a commodity index using futures involves trading in the liquid near-term (i.e., short maturity) instruments. Thus, for example, a five-year investment horizon might involve "rolling" the underlying futures contracts on a monthly or quarterly basis. When an investor sells an expiring contract to buy the replacement contract, differences in the prices of these contracts constitute the "roll yield." The roll yield is negative if the longer-dated contract is more expensive.

11. Macroshares were designed with the help of Robert Tull of MacroMarkets (formerly vice president of new products at the American Stock Exchange) and Richard Kadlick, a securities lawyer at Skadden Arps.

12. The reference index was the NYMEX front-month light sweet crude oil futures contract.

13. Backwardation refers to a downward-sloping forward curve, such that the difference between the forward price and the spot price is less than the cost of carry.

14. The reference price of oil at inception was $60. When the reference price reached $111, 85 percent of the Down Trust's (DCR) assets had been pledged to the Up Trust (UCR), triggering an early termination event.

Reference

Benner, Katie. 2009. Bob Shiller Didn't Kill the Housing Market. *Fortune Magazine*, July 2009.

7 Robert J. Shiller: Innovator in Financial Markets, Winner of the 2009 Deutsche Bank Prize in Financial Economics

Karl E. Case

Robert Shiller's Place in the History of Economic Ideas

I began graduate school at Harvard in the fall of 1971, and I drew Richard Musgrave as an adviser. Richard was born in Königstein, a few miles west of Frankfurt; he was educated at Heidelberg and Munich; and without doubt he should have been awarded the Nobel Prize in Economics before his death in 2007.

Richard was a member of the Fiscal Policy Seminar at Harvard in the late 1930s and 1940s, run by Alvin Hansen and John Williams. He debated with his contemporaries Paul Samuelson, Seymour Harris, and others the causes of the Great Depression and ways of preventing future catastrophic cycles. In the process, they brought Keynes to America. In the 1970s Professor Musgrave became my mentor and my friend.

Although they did not know each other well and met only a few times, Bob Shiller and Richard Musgrave shared a point of view and a passion. Each has had a major impact on the history of economic ideas and on the course of economic events. Both have stressed the enormous power of the marketplace and the market's ability to guide us toward an efficient allocation of resources. Both believed that the purpose of economic discourse is ultimately to make the world a better place and to make people better off *as they themselves define it*. And they shared a belief that financial markets tend to find and exploit profit opportunities and that "beating the market" is hard, very hard.

But both Richard and Bob also believed that unfettered markets are flawed: that markets are inherently unstable; that participants do not always act rationally; that completely free markets would allocate insufficient resources to the production of public or social goods; and that without regulation, they would see monopolies build market power, raise prices, and block entry to potential competitors. Both believed that in

many circumstances, buyers and sellers do not enjoy full access to information, that externalities often go unaccounted for, and that the market-generated distribution of income may not be fair.

Both agreed that some form of collective action and a significant role for government were required to make the market work better. They both decried those who think of the government as "predator."

The question of the proper role of government lies at the heart of the debate surrounding the efficient markets hypothesis (EMH). Today, in the battle over the proper role of government, much is to be learned from both camps. The EMH has been around for a long time and is included in most texts, including my own, as a key concept in basic economics. But what we are learning as we study individual markets in greater depth is that free agents are not always rational and that decision makers often rely on emotion, psychology, and alternative decision-making processes, with often disastrous results.

Bob and Richard always kept the debate civil. Richard debated James Buchanan for a week in March 1998, at the Center for Economic Studies, the University of Munich, at a forum on the role of the public sector, a meeting I attended. It was an extraordinary event, now published by the MIT Press in book form (Buchanan and Musgrave 1999).

Bob has joined the public debate like the crusader he is. No one in the profession has appeared more frequently in the media worldwide. No one has more articulately explained the causes and the consequences of what has become an economic perfect storm. Bob, like Richard, is a Keynesian. Bob's work takes off directly from Keynes, and his book, *Animal Spirits* (2009), co-authored with George Akerlof, fills a large gap in macroeconomics, a word actually coined by Richard Musgrave. Keynes said in the *General Theory*:

A large portion of our positive activities depend on spontaneous optimism rather than mathematical expectation, whether moral, or hedonistic or economic. Most probably, our decisions to do something positive can only be taken as a result of animal spirits—of a spontaneous urge to action rather than inaction, and not as the outcome of a weighted average of quantitative benefits multiplied by quantitative probabilities. (Keynes 1936, 161)

But Keynes himself just leaves it as an assertion without form. Bob's work has filled that gap. He has explored the relationship between behavior and emotion, rationality and irrationality, and the psychology behind investing and purchase decisions. Most economists have avoided this territory, leaving the realm of preference formation to the theologians. But not Bob.

At the end of 2007, the world economy entered the worst recession since the Great Depression. In the United States, $7.5 million in payroll jobs had been lost since the beginning of the year, and the total number of unemployed reached nearly fifteen million. Almost all the nations in the world experienced falling real GDP, and the world's financial markets came close to total collapse in the fall of 1998. The household balance sheet in the United States lost $15.4 trillion in assets between the end of 2007 and March 2009.[1]

There can be no doubt that this powerful macrovolatility had at its root speculative behavior in the housing, mortgage, and bond markets. Bob knew it was happening, he tried to explain it to a largely indifferent financial world, and he was relentless.

Between 2000 and 2005, the household sector in the United States added $10 trillion in housing assets to its balance sheet (see Case 2007). Of that, $5 trillion was an increase in the value of land and $5 trillion was new capital from the building boom. The boom was fueled by massive liquidity and fierce competition for yield after the credit expansions designed to prevent and ultimately mitigate the recession of 2001.

That expansion of credit in the United States was at first concentrated in refinancing, which accounted for 75 percent of the $5.5 trillion in originations that occurred in five quarters of 2002 and 2003 (see Case and Quigley 2008, 2009). But when mortgage rates spiked in the summer of 2003, attention turned to purchase money: to replace the refinancing volume, the hugely profitable industry turned outward to find new buyers. It is hard to exaggerate the profits. In 2004 alone, $799 billion in gross equity was extracted from houses (see Greenspan and Kennedy 2008). That same year, households netted $599 billion, and the $200 billion dollar difference simply went to the mortgage food chain in fees and charges. Analysts at Fannie Mae and Freddie Mac, at investment banks and rating agencies, as well as underwriters at insurance companies and industry specialists all agreed that with proper pricing, loosening underwriting would produce profitable business.

Why were the models so insensitive to the building tension between loose underwriting standards and a pending disaster? Because of an omitted variable, *house prices*. Between 1975 and 2005, house prices in the United States never fell nationally, not for a single quarter (OFHEO purchase index).[2] The fact that prices never fell meant that the collateral behind mortgages was always there, ready to protect borrowers and lenders.

Bob and I began collaborating almost twenty-five years ago. To date, we have published nine academic papers, a number of op-ed pieces, and

several survey notes that are not yet in print. We have produced an index called the S&P/Case-Shiller Index, founded and sold a company together (of course, Bob founded two others), and we are now both members of the S&P Index Committee.

I want to do two things with the remainder of this chapter. First, I want to describe Bob's absolutely tireless and rigorous pursuit of an understanding of the causes and consequences of extreme asset price volatility, specifically in housing. Second, I want to spend some time discussing and chronicling the practical, hands-on innovations that Bob has worked tirelessly to bring to the field of finance to help the economy function more effectively.

Shiller on the Causes and Consequences of Housing Booms and Busts

Our collaboration began after I wrote a paper, published in the *New England Economic Review* in 1986, titled "The Market for Single Family Homes in Boston, 1979–1985." In that paper, I put together a crude repeat-sales index and then, using data on ten cities, I tried to explain house prices with a simple supply-and-demand model that I was able successfully to identify. The problem for me was that it predicted an increase of 15 percent in Boston from 1984 through 1987, while actual house prices increased by 150 percent. Since I didn't have a story, I called it a bubble, despite knowing little about what that meant.

Paul Krugman said in his column on the *New York Times* website in July 2009, "bubbles drive me nuts." The term is overused and often not very well defined. I was not comfortable using it back then, either.

The intuition is easy to explain. In 1957, Paul Samuelson wrote:

If people think that tulips will appreciate at 10 percent per month, they can be motivated to act so that this will happen. Happen for how long? . . . I have long been struck by the fact, and puzzled by it too, that in all the arsenal of economic theory we have no way of predicting how long such a bubble will last. To say that prices will fall back to earth after reaching ridiculous heights represents a safe but empty prediction. Why do some manias end when prices are ridiculous by 10% while others persist until they are ridiculous to the tune of hundreds of percent? (Samuelson 1957, 216)

But it was Bob who set about adding rigor to the debate with his classic 1981 *American Economic Review* paper, "Do Stock Prices Move Too Much To Be Justified by Subsequent Changes in Dividends?" The paper challenged the EMH directly by hypothesizing reasonable bounds for

the variance of stock prices around total returns and showing that stock market volatility exceeded those bounds by a wide margin.

Turning back to the first paper on Boston: armed with some simple results, I turned to Bob and suggested that we take a look at the issue of bubbles clouding the functioning real estate markets. He was at my dining room table within two days. Clearly, the issue was important. Over $140 billion in housing wealth had been created in Boston alone (see Case 1986). That wealth had the potential to have powerful impacts on spending and on the future path of the regional economy. Indeed, the economy of Massachusetts grew dramatically despite a lag in core export industries. Sharply higher house prices could easily affect consumer spending and regional labor mobility.

As an aside, regional labor mobility is important, and it has come to a grinding halt in the United States today. One of Bob Shiller's grandfathers was a tailor in Chicago and the other worked in a stove shop in Gardner, Massachusetts. In 1914, Henry Ford announced he was raising the pay of assembly-line workers, and both of Bob's grandfathers moved to Detroit, where his parents met. Had there been irrational exuberance in the housing market at the time, his parents would never have met and he would not have been honored with the Deutsche Bank Prize in Financial Economics.

The first step was accurate measurement. In our first co-authored paper, published in 1987, we carefully constructed what we believed to be a clear and accurate measure of home price appreciation (now called the S&P/Case-Shiller Home Price Index). In the second, we set out to define more rigorously a test for weak form inefficiency in the housing market. Here we looked for inertia and found it. House price changes themselves forecasted house price changes.

But that was not enough. We then went looking for strong form efficiency by trying to forecast with more local and regional data. Again, house prices seemed to be forecastable. When a former Harvard professor said to me one day, "the only thing dumber than not owning a house today is not owning two," he was right, and that's not a random walk.

The logical next step was to gather other evidence to confirm the role of expectations. So we did what economists almost never do: we talked to people about what they were thinking. Specifically, we talked to buyers who had bought during the month of June 1988 in Boston, San Francisco, Orange County, California, and Milwaukee. We sent a ten-page questionnaire to two thousand home buyers, five hundred from each area (see Case and Shiller 1988). The results confirmed that home buyers were optimists, that prices were inflexible downward, that home buyers were

buying for investment reasons, and that they were relatively well informed most of the time but ill informed sometimes. After we saw the results of the first survey, in 1988, it was clear that the carefully constructed questionnaires added depth to our understanding of the more rigorous empirical studies of home-buyer behavior. We have conducted the same survey nine times since 1988 and are beginning to build a fairly clear description of how bid prices get formed and how bid and ask spreads have widened in recent years.

We wrote other papers that tried to explain further the causes and consequences of home-buyer behavior. A well-known paper on the wealth effects written by Bob, me, and John Quigley used quarterly state data for the years 1982 through 2001 and found an asymmetric spending effect: Spending seemed to go up when home prices rose but did not go back down when house prices fell (see Case, Quigley, and Shiller 2005). In 2010 we essentially doubled the sample size to include quarterly data from 1975–1982 and 2006–2009. The most recent four years include three years when housing lost nearly 30 percent of its value nationwide and well over 50 percent in some states (Case, Quigley, and Shiller 2011). While the revised paper has not yet been published, it appears that the asymmetry is gone with the new data. That is, housing prices seem to have an effect on spending in both appreciating and depreciating markets. Recall that we added a lot of data specifically in a severe down period, 2007–2009. If an effect doesn't show up in those data it is not likely to show up.

Now, clearly, in normal times, fundamentals in the economy as a whole drive the supply and demand for housing. But on occasion, the tail wags the dog. The decline in GDP, the massive layoffs, and the decline in the economy experienced worldwide began as series of bubbles driven by overly exuberant expectations in the world's housing markets.

Shiller as an Innovator in Financial Markets: More Complete Markets

What comes next is what Bob derives his energy from: what to do about it? In an interview conducted in January 2003 for the Cambridge University Press journal *Macroeconomic Dynamics*, Professor John Campbell of Harvard describes Bob as "both poet and plumber":

Although Bob does not believe that investors use financial markets in a perfectly rational manner, he does believe that these markets offer great possibilities to improve the human condition. His recent work asks how existing financial markets can be improved, and new financial markets can be designed, to improve the sharing of risks across people of different regions, countries and occupations. (see Campbell 2004)

Let me start by describing Bob's efforts to organize more complete markets for housing, including index-based futures and options markets. There can be no doubt that house prices are determined by the basic forces of supply and demand. It is also quite clear that from time to time, booms and busts send prices to very high or low levels relative to any fundamentals. Keep in mind that housing is the sector that normally reacts to monetary policy shifts, and home builders take the brunt of these adjustments.

What makes it worse is that households that own their own houses are generally overleveraged and underdiversified. The degree of risk facing households as a result of the price run-up in the mid-2000s was huge. Bob believes, as do I, that the absence of forward markets or incomplete markets in housing leads to large inefficiencies. A person who bought a house in San Francisco three years ago is finding house prices down as much as 50 percent from a recent peak. Had they been hedged, those households would have been protected on the downside, with the risk transferred to a willing risk taker or speculator. This could take the form of a simple index-based futures trade or a more complex option, allowing home owners to directly hedge. Or it could be built into an easy-to-understand home equity insurance plan, an insurance product that pays off the home owner in cash should housing prices tumble. More than a million homes a year were being sold out of foreclosure, and millions more are "underwater" (see Goodman 2010). As many as seven million properties are in the queue waiting for disposal. Much of this is due to the increasing use of "strategic default": the use of a mortgage as a put option at the time of default exercised at the mortgage amount. With all the sellers in the neighborhood doing short sales, many asked, why not me?

Not only does the absence of complete and well-organized forward markets leave the home owner with potentially overwhelming liabilities, it leaves the value of the implicit, now explicit, guarantees of Fannie Mae, Freddie Mac, and the Federal Housing Administration impossible to accurately mark to market.

From the early days of our partnership, then, Bob has been fighting to create such a market. Establishing a cash-settled, index-based set of financial derivatives that could be used to be the basis of a liquid forward market was the real goal of our collaboration. It was the reason Bob wanted us to start a company in the first place. The now popular S&P/Case-Shiller Indices were originally created to provide a transparent measure of appreciation/depreciation that speculators and hedgers would trust enough to base their contracts on.

Our company, Case Shiller Weiss Inc. (CSW), was founded in October 1991. We had already had extensive talks with the Chicago Board of Trade before its merger with the Chicago Mercantile Exchange. In January of the following year, the board paid CSW $25,000 to develop indexes that could be traded on the exchange. Although the board never traded the indexes, the idea was beginning to take hold.

A number of papers were written and presented as we moved through the 1990s. To everyone involved, it seemed like an open-and-shut case in favor of continuing to push for the establishment of such a market. In 1993, Bob, Allan Weiss, and I published a paper titled "Index-Based Futures and Options Markets in Real Estate" in the *Journal of Portfolio Management* (Case, Shiller, and Weiss 1993). Bob and Allan wrote a separate piece on home equity insurance soon after. In the meantime, CSW was sold to the Milwaukee-based bank software company Fiserv. A number of the former principals, including Bob, kept ownership and the right to use the indexes in a subsidiary called Macro Markets LLC. Ultimately, Standard and Poor's bought the rights to publish and use twenty of the indexes under the name of the S&P/Case-Shiller Indices.

Negotiations with the exchanges continued with a series of talks given at the American Stock Exchange, the Securities and Exchange Commission, the Chicago Board of Trade, and with Standard and Poor's. Finally, on May 22, 2006, the now merged exchanges began listing index-based and cash-settled futures and options, as well as options on futures, for the twenty CSW cities. The first day a total of fifty-two contracts were traded, with a nominal value of $2–3 million. That same year, the S&P/Case-Shiller Home Price Indices won the William F. Sharpe Achievement Award for the Most Innovative Benchmark Index.

Bob's innovative ambitions actually go far beyond real estate. In 1993 he published *Macro Markets: Creating Institutions for Managing Societies Greatest Risks,* which proposed making available instruments that could serve as the basis for hedging or speculating around some of life's other large risks, such as potential changes in the climate. Shiller in fact proposes an index-based market for shares of national income or per capita national income.

But Bob's real ambition was to get the forward housing price contracts to a position of modest liquidity. The listing on the CME did not last long as volumes at first climbed but eventually fell off. Getting a forward housing market actually functioning sounds conceptually easy, but it seems elusive and difficult to achieve. While house prices still seem like

a big risk to most of us, the average home owner had never seen prices fall nationally before the last few years. People did not and still do not believe that house prices actually fall.

Undaunted by the time commitment needed, Bob took Macro Markets Inc. back into the search for a housing futures market, this time using the vehicle of an exchange-traded fund (ETF). After two more years of regulatory review, the ETFs UMM and DMM (Up Major Markets and Down Major Markets) started trading with the ringing of the ceremonial bell that started the trading on the New York Stock Exchange on August 5, 2009. The ETF had a simple structure that let those who wanted to bet that house prices would rise essentially bet with those who thought they were likely to fall. Once again, there was not enough volume for the contract to continue. The last day of trading was December 28, 2010.

The puzzle is, once again, why these efforts have so far failed. Bob remains hopeful; he will never give up. It may be that home owners just don't get it. Even with the crash of home prices nationally, the respondents to our annual home-buyer surveys suggest that home owners and potential buyers are very optimistic that house prices will rise in the next few years. At the same time, potential buyers are still unsure about going long with a new derivative product. Whatever the reasons in the short run, I am convinced that Bob's proposal will eventually get traction and bear fruit.

The Engine That Could

So what has Bob done with his life? He studied economics and found a big gap in our understanding of how the macroeconomy works. He organized what we know about animal spirits, and he worked hard to conceptualize it all into a new theory of behavioral finance. He fought to bring the dangers of excess volatility to the attention of the profession, the public, and the government. He published over 150 scholarly articles and another fifty op-ed pieces, and he wrote six books in recent years. I tried to count how many times he had been on CNN, CNBC, Bloomberg, the BBC, and so forth, and when I figured out that it was easily in the six figures, I gave up. Reaching Bob on the phone has been one of the great challenges of my life. More than anyone in the profession, he saw the recent financial crisis coming. More than anyone else he tried to stop it. Now he will without question continue to work to prevent it from happening again.

Bob is known as a pessimist because he saw the pain that was coming. But he is not. He is really an incredible optimist because he knows we can make things better.

Notes

1. See U.S. Federal Reserve System, Flow of Funds Accounts, available at http://www .federalreserve.gov/releases/z1/current/data.htm.

2. House Price Indices, including the purchase only index, are available at http://www.fhfa. gov/Default.aspx?Page=87.

References

Akerlof, George A., and Robert J. Shiller. 2009. *Animal Spirits: How Human Psychology Drives the Economy, and Why It Matters for Global Capitalism*. Princeton, NJ: Princeton University Press.

Buchanan, James M., and Richard A. Musgrave. 1999. *Public Finance and Public Choice: Two Contrasting Visions of the State*. Cambridge, MA: MIT Press.

Campbell, John, Y. 2004. An Interview with Robert J. Shiller. *Macroeconomic Dynamics* 8: 649–683.

Case, Karl E. 1986. The Market for Single Family Homes in Boston, 1979–1985. *New England Economic Review* (May–June): 38–48.

Case, Karl E. 1990. Regional Economic Cycles: The Massachusetts Downturn in Perspective. In *Bank Regulation, Real Estate and the Massachusetts Economy*. Boston: Massachusetts Bankers Association.

Case, Karl E. 2007. The Value of Land in the United States: 1975-2005. In *Urban Economics and Public Finance*, ed. Gregory K. Ingram. Cambridge, MA: Lincoln Institute of Land Policy.

Case, Karl E. 2008. Musgrave's Vision of the Public Sector: The Complex Relationship between Individual, Society and State in Public Good Theory. *Journal of Economics and Finance* 32 (4): 348–355.

Case, Karl E., and John Quigley. 2008. How Housing Booms Unwind: Income Effects, Wealth Effects and Feedbacks Through Financial Markets. *European Journal of Housing Policy* 8 (2): 161–180.

Case, Karl E., and John Quigley. 2009. How Housing Busts End: Home Prices, User Cost, and Rigidities During Down Cycles. *The Blackwell Companion to the Economics of Housing: The Housing Wealth of Nations*, ed. Susan J. Smith and Beverly A. Searle. Oxford: Wiley-Blackwell.

Case, Karl E., John Quigley, and Robert J. Shiller. 2005. Comparing Wealth Effects: The Stock Market versus the Housing Market. *Advances in Macroeconomics* 5 (1): 1–30.

Case, Karl E., John M. Quigley, and Robert J. Shiller. 2011. Wealth Effects Revisited. NBER Working Paper 16848, National Bureau of Economic Research, Cambridge, MA.

Case, Karl E., and Robert Shiller. 1988. The Behavior of Home Buyers in Boom and Post Boom Markets. November, *New England Economic Review* (November–December): 29–46.

Case, Karl E., and Robert Shiller, and Allan N. Weiss. 1993. Index-Based Futures and Options Markets in Real Estate. *Journal of Portfolio Management* 19 (2): 83–91.

Goodman, Laurie S. 2010. Dimensioning the Housing Crisis. *Financial Analysts Journal* 66 (3): 26–37.

Greenspan, Alan, and James Kennedy. 2008. Sources and Uses of Equity Extracted from Homes. *Oxford Review of Economic Policy* 24 (1): 120–144.

Keynes, John M. 1936. *The General Theory of Employment, Interest and Money*. San Diego: Harcourt Brace.

Samuelson, Paul A. 1957. Intertemporal Price Equilibrium: A Prologue to the Theory of Speculation. *Weltwirtschaftliches Archiv* 79:181–121.

Shiller, Robert J. 1981. Do Stock Prices Move Too Much To Be Justified by Subsequent Changes in Dividends? *American Economic Review* 71 (3): 421–436.

Shiller, Robert J. 1993. *Macro Markets: Creating Institutions for Managing Societies Greatest Risks*. Oxford: Oxford University Press.

FINANCIAL INNOVATION AND CRISIS: PERSPECTIVES FROM POLICY AND PRACTICE

Systemic Risk and the Role of Financial Innovation

Otmar Issing

Challenges from Systemic Risk

It is now more than three years since the world was first confronted with a financial crisis of a dimension that has not been seen since 1929. This is common judgment. However, there is disagreement over whether this crisis is even more severe, and whether it is limited to the financial sector or affects the capitalistic market system as a whole.

Interestingly enough, economics as a science has also suffered in a comparable way. The reputation of economists in general was undermined as they were blamed for not having warned of the situation. The theory of efficient markets in particular is identified as having supported an unfounded belief in the advantages of the financial system and its robustness.

Robert Shiller saw the crisis coming. His verdict on the efficient market hypothesis is devastating: "The efficient market hypothesis is the most remarkable error in the history of economic theory. This is just another nail in its coffin" (quoted in Fox 2009, 232). Shiller put the matter succinctly:

valuations in the stock market have come about for no good reasons. The market level does not, as so many imagine, represent the consensus judgment of experts who have carefully weighed the long-term evidence. The market is high because of the combined effect of indifferent thinking by millions of people, very few of whom feel the need to perform careful research on the long-term investment value of the aggregate stock market, and who are motivated substantially by their own emotions, random attentions, and perceptions of conventional wisdom. Their all-too-human behavior is heavily influenced by news media that are interested in attracting viewers or readers, with limited incentive to discipline their readers with the type of quantitative analysis that might give them a correct impression of the aggregate stock market level. (Shiller 2000, 203)

The fact that you can get a Nobel Prize and the Deutsche Bank Prize in Financial Economics for—at least at first sight—opposite explanations of asset price developments demonstrates how economic theory is in flux.

In this brief chapter, I would like to concentrate on two fundamental aspects of the current financial crisis. The first is related to the problem that many financial institutions had to be bailed out, and the second concerns the role of financial innovation.

There is a great risk that all the interventions by governments around the globe have created the impression that in the future, no major bank will ever be allowed to fail, and that private savers as well, and more generally all bondholders, to a large extent will be bailed out of risky investments. Such a legacy of the crisis and its successful management would be nothing less than a fatal deviation from the principles of a free market system. Risk and uncertainty (in the Knightian sense) are an unavoidable element of life. The welfare of a society depends crucially on the way it handles these challenges. An efficient market system encourages entrepreneurs to take risks by promising rewards, but also by implicating losses for any decisions that turn out to have failed. If the sanctions via potential losses and finally bankruptcy are removed or not credible, moral hazard, gambling, is the consequence. However, there is no justification for keeping the profit in private hands and putting the burden of losses on society, namely, the taxpayers.

Therefore, the challenge stemming from the crisis is to establish a credible order to deal with this problem. It is obvious that this is neither easy nor possible without clear, binding rules that will be perceived as painful from the perspective of some individual players. Those who predict the end of a free society and a market economy as a consequence of such a binding framework have not understood the principles on which it is based and are invited to read Adam Smith, who in *Wealth of Nations* wrote, "But those exertions of the natural liberty of a few individuals, which might endanger the security of the whole society, are, and ought to be, restrained by the laws of all governments; of the most free, as well as of the most despotical. The obligation of building party walls, in order to prevent the communication of fire, is a violation of natural liberty, exactly of the same kind with the regulations of the banking trade which are here proposed" (Smith 1776, vol. 1, bk. 2, chap. 2).

The problem of "too big"—or rather too systemic—"to fail" is a kind of manifestation of this challenge. If this is true for a bank, the government of a country and society as a whole can be taken hostage by the risky activities of such an institution, a fact that by itself is creating moral hazard. Allan Meltzer's dictum is straightforward: "If a bank is too big to fail, it is too big" (Meltzer 2009, 49).

Considering the dimension of the problem, it is more than surprising that for an extended period, authorities did not seem to really care. In the meantime, several proposals have been presented to deal with this problem.[1]

1. A direct approach would set quantitative limits on the size and activities of individual financial institutions. But it would be very difficult to apply this principle in a reasonable way. Relying on the "narrow bank idea" or comparable approaches also do not seem convincing as it would solve the "bank run" problem but leave all risky activities to the rest of the financial system.

2. More convincing is the proposal to impose strict capital and liquidity regulations on systemically relevant financial institutions. An elegant way would be to increase those requirements gradually with the growing size of the relevant institutions.[2]

3. Other proposals go in the direction of making those institutions easier to close, thereby avoiding risks for the whole system. The challenge of any such resolution regime for systematically important banks lies in providing mechanisms that allow banks, even large, complex, and internationally interconnected institutions, to fail, while simultaneously avoiding a systemic credit event.

The required solution, therefore, has to combine an unconditional state guarantee for the bank's new businesses, initiated after the resolution onset, with an orderly unwinding of its old businesses, contracted before the resolution date. The former effectively acquires a senior claim over the earlier business transactions. As an illustration, one could think of creating a resolution scheme that resembles a banking hospital. The hospital would be set up by the state to take over the treasury management of the troubled bank on short notice. An "over-the-weekend bailout drama," as was recently experienced in Germany (e.g., IKB, HRE) and elsewhere (Bear Stearns, Northern Rock), would be replaced by an orderly winding down of the institution, accompanied by a capital restructuring. The hospital would thus support the financial bloodstream of the bank, with liquidity assistance if required, while at the same time allocating losses to capital according to seniority.[3]

The reason for adopting such a resolution regime, using state money only intermittently, is to minimize the risk of a bailout that uses taxpayers' money, thereby diminishing moral hazard. By fighting the abuse of bailout policies (socializing losses while privatizing profits), a resolution regime should be at the heart of any long-term strategy for stabilizing financial markets.

These proposals are not exclusive but should be combined.

In the next section I concentrate on another fundamental aspect of financial reform, the role of financial innovation.

The Role of Financial Innovation

Financial products serve essentially two purposes—the efficient allocation of capital in the economy and the mitigation of risk. However, an increasing share of the financial sector is suspected of conducting a large portion of transactions not with respect to these purposes but for its own sake and without any use for the economy or society. This can lead to financial innovations that render transactions, markets, and agents' behavior less transparent and that do not enhance the (economic) well-being of society—or, worse, are detrimental to it. For example, during the recent crisis financial products like collateralized debt obligations and credit default swaps proved easy to abuse. This does not mean that these instruments are flawed by construction. However, if agents think they cannot be held responsible for their transactions, they will not care about the outcome for other agents. If in addition the other agents' perceptions are blurred by lack of transparency, there is the risk of crisis-laden developments, as seen in the recent period. Nevertheless, one must acknowledge that many financial innovations of the past decades, such as exchange-traded funds and inflation-indexed bonds, are beneficial to the economy and to society. Analyzing the effects of financial innovation, also with respect to their main purposes as outlined above, is closely related to incentive structures and how transparent these products are.

Knowing ex ante whether a financial innovation is good or bad for society is extremely difficult if not impossible. By definition, an innovation is something new and can have unpredictable effects. However, taking the extreme point and suggesting finance should be "boring" again, thus prohibiting financial innovation, cannot be the way forward, as this would be akin to forbidding new medicaments because one may turn out to be detrimental or even fatal in certain circumstances. But because the contribution of several financial innovations to the recent financial crisis cannot be denied, certain issues need to be addressed. A large variety of structured products sold in the run-up to the crisis seemingly embodied low risk and high yield; however, during the crisis they turned out to be quite the opposite (Bank for International Settlements 2009/10, 40). To strike a balance between innovation and safety, the BIS proposed requiring financial product registration analogous to the hierarchy controlling

pharmaceuticals (Bank for International Settlements 2008/09, 126ff.). Nevertheless, it is extremely difficult to assess the tails of the outcome distributions for new financial products without any history. This issue, for example, was of central importance for the innovative products related to the U.S. subprime market (Bank for International Settlements 2008/09, 9). Ultimately, financial innovations—even if there are to be financial product registrations—will always be tested in the market. It is thus important to have rough guidelines for assessing a financial innovation's potential impact on systemic risk. These guidelines should incorporate, inter alia, proper incentive structures and transparency.

It is important to analyze why the financial sector sometimes tends to create financial instruments that yield high profit in the short run but are detrimental to the economy in the medium to long run. Clearly, the capitalistic system is profit-oriented. Still, incentives should be set such that profit is not made in a way that harms society. Hence, there is the need to align incentives in the financial sector with those of the economy and society.[4] One area in which it is crucial to align these incentives is reward schemes, which should be set to longer time horizons for financial managers. Another example, useful for monitoring purposes, is that originators of financial products be obliged to retain part of the risk on their balance sheets.

Furthermore, it is of interest to foster innovations that increase transparency in the financial system and to rein in those that lower it. For example, standardizing financial instruments such as credit default swaps and trading them on central counterparty exchanges would result in greater transparency and lower spreads for market participants. Another example is a regulatory tool proposed by the Issing Commission.[5] The so-called "risk map" is a diagram of the financial system that captures the most important institutions and their mutual interdependencies. To compile such a risk map, the institution charged with macroprudential supervision would require a listing of all (larger) claims and liabilities in connection with other institutions within the financial sector. This device could be used for stress testing the financial sector and measuring systemwide risks, as well as individual institutions' contributions to it.

Designing the foundations and consistent rules to cope with the outlined problems and then implementing them is a tremendous challenge. It is easy to list the obstacles, not least those attached to the imperative of a global level playing field. However, to capitulate to this challenge or just ignore it would lay the ground for the next systemic crisis. This is just not acceptable.

Acknowledgments

I would like to thank Marcel Bluhm for his valuable cooperation.

Notes

1. See the Swiss National Bank, Financial Stability Report 2009, p. 10, and the Bank of England, Financial Stability Report, June 2009, p. 53. Here the problem of "too complex" is also addressed.

2. See, for example, the proposals of the Issing Committee for the G-20 2010 meeting in Toronto: Otmar Issing, Jan Pieter Krahnen, Klaus Regling, and William White, "Criteria for a Workable Approach Toward Bank Levies and Bank Restructuring," CFS White Paper No. 4 (Center for Financial Studies, 2010). The file can be downloaded at https://www .ifk-cfs.de/fileadmin/downloads/publications/white_paper/White_Paper_No_4_2010.pdf.

3. See the proposals of the Issing Committee for the G-20 2010 meeting in Toronto: Issing et al., "Criteria for a Workable Approach Toward Bank Levies and Bank Restructuring."

4. See chapters 6 and 7 in Rajan (2010).

5. Otmar Issing, Jörg Asmussen, Jan Pieter Krahnen, Klaus Regling, Jens Weidmann, and William White, "New Financial Order / Recommendations by the Issing Committee / Preparing G-20—London, April 2, 2009," CFS White Paper No. 2 (Center for Financial Studies, 2009). Available at www.ifk-cfs.de/fileadmin/downloads/publications/white_paper/White _Paper_No_2_2009_Final.pdf.

References

Bank for International Settlements. 2008–2009. Annual Report. Available at http://www .bis.org/publ/arpdf/ar2009e.pdf.

Bank for International Settlements. 2009–2010. *Annual Report.* Available at http://www.bis .org/publ/arpdf/ar2010e.pdf.

Fox, Justin. 2009. *The Myth of the Rational Market: A History of Risk, Reward, and Delusion on Wall Street.* New York: HarperBusiness.

Meltzer, Allan H. 2009. End Too-Big-To-Fail. *International Economy,* Winter, 49.

Rajan, Raghuram G. 2010. *Fault Lines.* Princeton, NJ: Princeton University Press.

Shiller, Robert J. 2000. *Irrational Exuberance.* Princeton, NJ: Princeton University Press.

Smith, Adam. 1776. *An Inquiry into the Nature and Causes of the Wealth of Nations.* London: Strahan and Cadell.

9 Financial Markets: Productivity, Procyclicality, and Policy

Alexander Popov and Frank R. Smets[1]

During the decades-long debate on the link between financial markets and the real economy, academics have tended to side either with Joseph Schumpeter's view of the ability of well-developed financial systems to stimulate economic growth or with Joan Robinson's observation that "where enterprise leads, finance follows" (Robinson 1952). The experience of the past several decades in emerging as well as industrialized countries has mostly confirmed the first claim, namely, that deeper domestic financial markets improve economic efficiency, lead to better allocation of productive capital, and increase long-term economic growth.[2] A similar case has been made for international financial integration, which has been one of the main global phenomena of the past twenty years or so. A host of empirical analyses has demonstrated that integrated financial systems raise long-term economic growth, improve the allocation of productive resources, foster entrepreneurship and innovation, enhance market discipline, and help countries insure against macroeconomic fluctuations (Agenor 2003).

At the same time, the frequent financial shocks associated with more dynamic financial industries and more integrated financial markets—especially in view of the recent global crisis—highlight the contribution of financial markets to macroeconomic risk. Put differently, financial development, broadly speaking, has implications not only for growth but also for the variability of growth. The perception has been strong for quite a while in both academic and policy circles that foreign capital, for example, increases volatility both in the financial markets and in the real economy (Stiglitz 2000). Nevertheless, considerably less attention has been devoted to this link than to the finance-and-growth nexus. One simple explanation for this discrepancy is that the favorite measure of variability is the volatility of the growth process, and while the welfare implications of higher growth are obvious, the welfare benefits of removing

all of the business cycle volatility are much smaller (Lucas 1987). There-fore, while past studies have pointed to a positive relation between finance and volatility (Kose et al. 2003; Levchenko, Rancière, and Thoenig 2009), it has also been customary to include the caveat that the negative effect on welfare from higher growth volatility is fully outweighed by the growth effect. However, recently the literature has moved away from volatility toward higher moments of growth that describe better asymmetric variability, or the probability of rare, abrupt, and large macroeconomic contractions. The argument has been made that changes in consumption uncertainty, which reflect shifts in the probability of economic disaster, can have major implications for welfare. In particular, within a class of models that replicate how asset markets price consumption uncertainty, it is estimated that individuals would be willing to pay very high premiums (of the order of 20 percent of GDP each year) in exchange for eliminating all chances of large macroeconomic contractions (Barro 2006). Therefore, it is essential to understand the contribution of finance not just to volatility but also to tail risk. Recent studies have addressed this point and have found that financial globalization, broadly speaking, increases not just level growth but also the left-skewness of the distribution of output growth, which — to the degree that output risk is not completely insurable — has important welfare implications (Popov 2011).

Presumably, such an effect would come from large contractions of output during recessions resulting from financial crises, when the cost of renting productive capital increases and general demand declines. However, a number of indirect channels exist through which "excessive" financial development could affect growth. To name just one, R&D investment tends to decrease during economic downturns. For a while it was widely believed that it was the other way around: during recessions, unproductive activities are scrapped down and the opportunity cost of production increases, making it more lucrative to allocate idle resources to R&D. However, recent evidence has suggested that in fact, R&D investment is highly procyclical, implying that firms' decisions whether to engage in R&D are dominated by short-term gain arguments rather than by the opportunity cost of production (Barlevy 2007). This not only goes against the Schumpeterian view of the cleansing effect of recessions, it also implies that one channel through which some of the growth effects of finance can be eroded is the disruption of the innovation process as a result of a more volatile business cycle.

This combined evidence implies that there is a trade-off between a highly vibrant financial sector and the overall stability of the financial system. In fact, some scholars have recently gone so far as to claim that eliminating financial instability altogether can only come at the expense of restricting the same productive forces responsible for long-term growth (Rancière, Tornell, and Westermann 2008). The purpose of macroprudential regulation, then, is to alleviate the costs imposed by financial fragility without restricting too much the contribution of deep and interconnected financial markets to long-term economic growth. Ideally, the tools employed would be such as to allow policy makers to forcefully "lean against the wind" during costly booms driven by excessive debt and characterized by no fundamental contribution to long-term growth (as in the mid-2000s) while reacting more cautiously during low-cost booms driven by equity finance and characterized by a wave of new technologies (such as the dot-com bubble). Of course, there are many pitfalls along the way. To take a purely statistical challenge, is it really possible to distinguish the "good" (Industrial Revolution–type) bubbles from the "bad" (real estate–type bubbles), where "good" and "bad" are defined by the contribution of the credit boom to long-term economic growth? Or, to take a challenge from the realm of political economy, even if an unproductive boom associated only with cheap mortgage credit and no investment in new technologies can be diagnosed in real time, is it feasible to act on it? Both consumers and bankers like cheap mortgages, and so governments and regulators, being to a degree captured by their respective interest groups, would be unwilling to act against such bubbles. Finally, a practical challenge is choosing what tool to use, even if the bubble is diagnosed early enough and the political will to act is available. It is unclear whether macroprudential regulators will ever have in their arsenal a policy tool as simple and as effective as the repo rates, which central banks throughout the world have been using so successfully to control inflation. To address all these issues, ideally a sound macroprudential framework would be needed, encompassing an authority with a clear mandate, sufficiently independent, and with a set of simple tools whose usefulness and achievements can be easily communicated to the general public.

Below we discuss the contribution of financial market to both long-term growth and the variability of the growth process, and consider how policy can be used to address the procyclicality of the financial system while maintaining its contribution to long-term growth.

Financial Markets, Growth, and Productivity

In general, deep and efficient financial markets improve economic performance both by raising the level of growth (Rajan and Zingales 1998) and by a more efficient allocation of productive capital (Wurgler 2000), ultimately generating benefits for society as a whole. Evidence from emerging markets suggests that for these effects to be realized, a country needs to have a reasonably large financial sector. Therefore, if in any way financial markets have been associated with "threshold" effects in academic thinking in the past, these have been linked to the inefficiencies associated with "too small" (i.e., underdeveloped) financial markets, when their contribution to economic growth has been found to be seriously limited, and even negative (Demirgüç-Kunt, Beck, and Honohan 2008). For example, in an international context, it is well understood that the positive effects of financial integration accumulate only when the domestic financial system is relatively developed (Kose et al. 2004; Bekaert, Harvey, and Lundblad 2005). Important theoretical contributions have also argued that when economic agents dislike risk and investment projects have a sunk cost, financial underdevelopment will result in lower capital accumulation and lower productivity because entrepreneurs will prefer to invest in low-risk, low-return projects rather than pursue the most profitable opportunities (Acemoglu and Zilibotti 1997).

That larger financial markets are associated with higher economic efficiency is not a feature of emerging markets only. Consider the long-standing point in academic and policy discussions on the differences in average GDP growth between the United States and continental Europe. It has been suggested that deeper financial markets in North America are to a large extent responsible for the larger increases in productivity, the faster pace of industrial innovation, and the generally more dynamic economy that the United States possesses relative to the European continent. For example, deeper credit markets are probably responsible for the higher rate of small business creation in the United States. The divide is especially visible when it comes to the financing of innovative ideas, where the much larger U.S. venture capital industry has been credited over the years with the emergence of whole new industries and such innovative corporate giants as Microsoft, Cisco, and Google. Out of the five hundred largest companies in the world, there are twenty-six U.S. ones that were born after 1975, compared with only three European ones (Philippon and Veron 2008). These two aspects of "creative destruction"— new business creation and innovation—are crucial when we consider

why deeper financial markets can benefit economic growth, and it seems that larger and deeper financial markets stimulate them better.

One financial market that has been singled out recently by economists for its contribution to productivity and growth is the venture capital industry. This particular type of financial intermediation is a good case to emphasize the microeconomic channels through which financial activity affects aggregate growth. In particular, while credit markets are a "prime suspect" to investigate while studying the finance-and-growth nexus, banks are often reluctant to finance small young firms because of high uncertainty, information asymmetries, and agency costs. In comparison, venture capitalists are specialized to overcome these problems through the use of staged financing, private contracting, and active monitoring (Kaplan and Stromberg 2001). The involvement of venture capitalists with microprojects should then result in greater innovation through the higher survival rates of highly innovative but highly risky projects. Empirical investigations into this question have measured an elasticity of up to 0.09 of ultimately successful patent applications to venture capital investment. Alternatively put, while the ratio of venture capital to industrial R&D averaged less than 3 percent between 1983 and 1992, venture capital accounted for 8 percent of industrial innovation over that period (Kortum and Lerner 2000). More recent investigations with data up to 2008 have broadly confirmed this result (Hirukawa and Ueda 2008).

The same pattern—that larger financial markets allow countries to better exploit the benefits of innovation in terms of productivity and growth—is observed when one compares European economies. Econometric estimations indicate that improving certain aspects of corporate governance, the efficiency of legal systems in resolving conflicts in financial transactions, and some structural features of the less developed European banking sectors is likely to enhance the speed with which the financial system helps reallocate capital from declining sectors to sectors with good growth potential (Hartmann et al. 2007). In this respect, pan-European developments such as the introduction of the euro; equity, bond, and retail markets integration; the Second Banking Directive of the European Economic Community; and national initiatives to foster risk capital markets have contributed substantially to deepening financial markets and subsequently narrowing these differences. In addition, recent European Central Bank (ECB) research has pointed to the fact that large differences persist among European countries in terms of new business creation and patenting activity, and has concluded that much of

this difference can be attributed to more developed credit markets, and especially risk capital markets (Popov and Rosenboom 2009).

Another point in order is financial innovation. In principle, financial innovation (in particular, new credit-risk transfer instruments) contributes to economic efficiency by enhancing the diversification of risk. Securitization, for example, allows risk to be transferred from the originators of the loans to financial investors willing to hold the risk, leading to a more efficient allocation of risk both at national and international levels, at least when symmetric distribution of information prevails. As a consequence, the overall amount of credit available to the nonfinancial sector expands, funding productive opportunities that were previously shut out of credit markets. Other examples include different types of financial innovation, such as credit screening techniques and mortgage design. More efficient screening and new credit scoring technologies can vastly improve the allocation of resources to the nonfinancial sector, which can be linked to investment-related growth (Michalopoulos, Laeven, and Levine 2009). Finally, mortgage design has also been linked to increased consumer welfare, allowing customers previously constrained in credit markets to accumulate optimal household leverage.

A similar case can be made about the growth and welfare effects of financial integration. Research focusing on capital account openness has found mixed results (see Eichengreen 2001). However, liberalization of capital accounts is less relevant for risk sharing than for equity flows, and articles focusing on equity market liberalization typically find a significant positive growth effect of liberalization (of the order of 1 percent) (Bekaert, Harvey, and Lundblad 2005). In addition, by enhancing both consumption and income risk sharing, financial openness reduces consumption growth volatility (Bekaert, Harvey, and Lundblad 2006). The same is true for banking integration, which has been shown to synchronize country-level business cycles as measured by GDP, employment, and income growth, with the evidence for that coming from both Europe and the United States (Kalemli-Ozcan, Papaioannou, and Peydró 2009; Morgan, Rime, and Strahan 2004). Finally, despite the large degree of fragmentation and disintegration they exhibited in the early stages of the crisis, interbank markets' primary role is to provide banks with an efficient risk-sharing tool.

Risk sharing in turn improves the ability of countries to specialize in their most productive sectors (Kalemli-Ozcan, Sorensen, and Yosha 2003). It allows economic agents to better smooth their consumption and investment patterns over time. And while this is mostly true for develop-

ing countries, the risk sharing provided by financial integration and increased foreign capital flows have also benefited relatively developed countries, for which the integration of Central and Eastern European countries since 1989 serves as a prime example. Precrisis research had also suggested that the cross-border diversification of large banks improves the soundness of the banking system by making individual bank failures less likely.

Another channel through which financial integration improves stability is the channel of allocative efficiency and economic diversification. Cross-border banking, for instance, tends to improve overall economic performance by making sure that productive capital is channeled toward the most efficient firms, reducing the risk of crises stemming from mispriced investment risk (Giannetti and Ongena 2009). Financial integration in general assists domestic financial systems in allocating resources across industrial sectors in a way that improves the overall diversification of the economy and lowers its volatility. As a result, an optimally diversified economy is less prone to recessions, and so its real sector responds less to the same shock than an economy that relies on just a few sectors (Manganelli and Popov 2010).

Financial Markets and Financial Fragility

The empirical evidence linking financial markets to growth has been so abundant that in 2003, in a discussion of a survey on the subject, one author was prompted to conclude that "in 1993 many people doubted that there was a relation between finance and growth; now very few do" (Zingales 2003). At the same time, however, severe global recessions driven by financial crises, like the one we just experienced, tend to throw doubt on such blissfully optimistic evidence. It appears that financial markets have a destabilizing potential. Two separate questions beg for an answer in this regard: Do financial development and integration increase the likelihood of a financial crisis? And if yes, do financial crises have a pronounced negative effect on productivity and growth?

At first sight, there are a number of theoretical arguments pointing to the fact that large and complex financial systems are associated with financial crises. One identified channel of this process is risk taking. For example, in recent work, increased risk taking before the 2007–2008 crisis has been linked to the growth of the financial industry resulting from "excess world saving" in the context of persistent global imbalances. In the wake of the dot-com bubble, the story goes, excess world saving

resulted as unsophisticated world investors, looking for assets to store value, turned to safe debt investments. To accommodate this increased demand, the U.S. financial sector manufactured debt claims out of all kinds of products, which would explain the wave of precrisis securitization (Caballero and Krishnamurthy 2009). Another theoretical perspective on the same issue offers the following argument. In a financially liberalized economy with limited contract enforcement, systemic risk taking reduces the effective cost of capital and relaxes borrowing constraints. This allows greater investment and generates higher long-term growth, but it increases the probability of a sudden collapse in financial intermediation when a crash occurs. Systemic risk thus increases mean growth even if crises have arbitrarily large output and financial distress costs, implying the coexistence of higher-level growth and more frequent crises (Rancière, Tornell, and Westermann 2008). A slightly different take, derived from excess rents in the financial sector, has allowed some authors to develop models in which higher relative productivity in the financial sector can endogenously, through the channel of risk taking, generate boom-bust episodes, with real implications for financial fragility (Biais, Rochet, and Wooley 2009).

Actual evidence suggesting that deeper and more dynamic financial markets are causally linked to financial crises was relatively sparse before the 2007–2008 crisis. While some authors had found that domestic financial development has a marginally positive effect on the probability of recessions (Easterly, Islam, and Stiglitz 2000), others had countered that the measured positive effect of finance on economic downturns disappears once institutional factors are controlled for (Acemoglu et al. 2003). Industry-level evidence had even suggested that credit market development decreases the magnitude of output declines in sectors with high natural liquidity needs (Raddatz 2006). On the other hand, recently some authors have argued that while substantially increasing long-term growth and only marginally increasing long-term volatility, financial liberalization significantly increases the left-skewness of the distribution of output growth at the industry level, implying a higher recession probability (Popov 2011). At the same time, a growing literature on early-warning signals had even before the crisis utilized simple statistical methods to link the probability of, for example, banking crises to the size of the financial sector, measured, for example, by credit growth or credit-to-GDP ratios. In hindsight, such studies did a fairly good job in "predicting" the events from 2007 to 2008 (Borio and Drehmann 2009; Detken and Smets 2004; Alessi and Detken 2009).

This mixed evidence implies important nonlinearities in the relationship between finance and crisis probability. For example, while financial integration per se is not a destabilizing force, stability risks may arise if the driving forces underlying stronger international financial integration reflect global economic imbalances. It is reasonable to argue that the precrisis boom in U.S. real estate and securitization markets reflected high foreign demand for safe U.S. assets resulting from "excess world saving" in the context of persistent global imbalances. Consequently, foreign asset demand not only pushed down the U.S. risk-free interest rate but also compressed the risk premiums on risky assets. The low cost of financing in turn fostered an increase in the level of leverage of the domestic financial sector, which exacerbated systemic risk. This interpretation of the events makes an important point: increasing the stability of the global financial system should not be done by pushing back financial globalization but first and foremost by addressing the problem of the global imbalances.

A second example of the nuances involved in assessing the destabilizing potential of financial integration is banking integration. While in principle it is associated with enhanced efficiency, surrounding circumstances, such as regulatory arbitrage and lack of transparency in transactions, can exacerbate information problems associated with cross-border banking and lead to misaligned incentives, increased risk taking, and underestimation of the social cost of contagion. It has also been observed that while banking integration benefits efficient firms through a lower cost of external finance, very rapid integration induces firms to take on excessive leverage, exacerbating the effect of financial crises on the corporate sector (Popov and Ongena 2011). Finally, cross-border banking has been shown in the context of this crisis to be associated with the transmission of financial distress from banks' balance sheets to the corporate sector of countries that were not the origins of the shock (Popov and Udell 2012).

What is the effect of such financial fragility on productivity and innovation? On the one hand, we know from standard Schumpeterian theory that recessions have a "cleansing" effect in the sense that inefficient projects, propped up by high demand during good times, are eliminated when demand declines during bad times. More recently, economists have looked at other channels, such as search (Mortensen and Pissarides 1994), technical change (Aghion and Saint-Paul 1998), and human capital accumulation (DeJong and Ingram 2001), to argue that recessions should ideally promote various activities that contribute to long-term productivity

and thus to growth. This view is derived from the notion that the opportunity cost of achieving productivity growth is lower in recessions, providing an incentive to undertake such activities in downturns. If negative macroeconomic shocks encourage growth-enhancing investments, as this view suggests, economic contractions would tend to be shorter and less persistent then they would be otherwise. Cyclical fluctuations might even contribute positively to welfare if they allow the economy to grow at a lower resource cost. Taken at face value, these arguments imply that recessions play a useful role in fostering growth, and therefore the crisis potential of financial development is not necessarily detrimental to long-term growth.

Unfortunately, recent work has also suggested that the main driver of innovation and productivity growth—R&D investment—is highly procyclical. The simple explanation for that is linked to an externality inherent in the innovation process: a new idea usually benefits rival innovators, who can improve on it or adopt it in full once the patent expires. Therefore, in deciding how much to invest in innovative activities, an entrepreneur weighs heavily the private short-term benefits that accrue to her. The lower benefits of innovation during recessions may lead to innovators failing to fully exploit downturns to carry out innovation at a lower cost. If profits are sufficiently procyclical, innovation can fall enough in recessions to turn R&D procyclical on the basis of this distortion alone. Evidence for the United States suggests a very high correlation (0.49) between R&D growth and GDP growth for the period 1958–2003 (Barlevy 2007).

Of course, there are less subtle ways in which financial crises disrupt economic growth other than by disrupting productivity-enhancing investment. The busts that follow unsustainable booms are frequently associated with falling housing prices, collapsing equity prices, and lasting declines in output and employment. Under certain circumstances, the negative impact on potential output could be longlasting rather than transitory, for example, because high and persistent unemployment leads to a deterioration of human capital. In addition, financial crises like the recent one tend to generate deteriorations in the fiscal position of many countries. Government debt explodes in the wake of banking crises, fueled not so much by the cost of recapitalizing the banking systems as by collapsing tax revenue (Reinhart and Rogoff 2009). Facing gaping budget holes, governments resort to fiscal austerity, which directly affects long-term productivity-enhancing activities such as education and publicly financed innovation.

One way in which all these considerations manifest themselves in the data is in the frequently made empirical claim that the positive relationship between finance and growth breaks down when the financial sector becomes too large. Various authors (Deidda and Fattouh 2002; Rioja and Valev 2004; Shen and Lee 2006) have found that in general, the relationship between financial development and economic growth is nonlinear: when of moderate size, financial markets strongly promote growth, but when large or when operating in relatively richer countries, their effect on growth weakens considerably.

Regulating Financial Markets: Crises, Procyclicality, and Macroprudential Policy

All this evidence points to a somewhat unsettling conclusion: while a vibrant financial industry is a necessary ingredient for sustainable long-term economic growth, it may also be associated with economic costs in terms of abnormal volatility. This trade-off between efficiency and stability may be an unavoidable fact of life, but it is, of course, still within the reach of policy makers to skew this trade-off in the right direction. Getting this balance between efficiency and stability right will be an important consideration for the newly established macroprudential regulators, such as the European Systemic Risk Board for the European Union and the Financial Stability Oversight Council for the United States.

We started this chapter by referring to the long-standing debate between Schumpeter's followers and Robinson's followers about whether finance causes growth or the other way around. While the empirical evidence supporting Schumpeter's view is abundant, the arguments we laid out in the previous sections suggest that a more relevant debate to consider may be the implicit one between Schumpeter and Minsky on the efficiency of the economic and financial cycle. Schumpeter's view was that cycles are efficient: because productive ideas do not arrive at a constant rate, economic growth tends to be associated with a boom phase, followed by recessions ensuring that the multitude of unproductive projects financed during the boom alongside the productive ones are cleansed from the economy. In this world, finance plays the beneficial role of allocating resources to credit-constrained entrepreneurs in possession of ideas that are ultimately valuable to society as a whole. Minsky, however, contended that finance tends to contribute to the boom-bust cycle. His view was that good times give rise to speculative investor euphoria, and soon thereafter debts exceed what borrowers can pay off from their

incoming revenues, which in turn leads to a financial crisis. As a result of the collapse of the speculative borrowing bubble, investors—and especially banks—reduce credit availability, even to companies that can afford to borrow, and the economy subsequently contracts (Minsky 1986; see also Kindleberger 1978).

The mutually reinforcing dynamics between the real sector and the financial sector hinted at by Minsky and Kindleberger is sometimes referred to as the procyclicality of the financial system. Consistent with this line of thinking, the Bank for International Settlements in its 2009 Note for the FSF Working Group on Market and Institutional Resilience defines procyclicality as "the mutually reinforcing mechanisms through which the financial system can amplify business fluctuations and possibly cause and exacerbate financial instability."

There are many ways to illustrate this procyclicality. Figure 9.1 plots, for the European Monetary Union period, the procyclical development

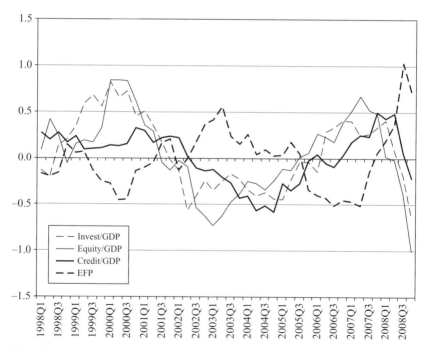

Figure 9.1
Credit, investment, equity prices, and the external finance premium in the euro area corporate investment market. *Source:* Adapted from L. Christiano, R. Motto, and M. Rostagno, "Monetary Policy and Stock Market Boom-Bust Cycles," ECB Working Paper 955 (2008), European Central Bank, Frankfurt.

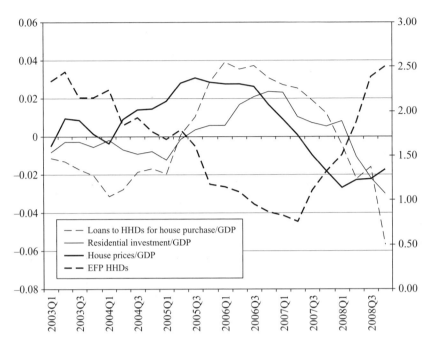

Figure 9.2
Credit, investment, house prices, and the external finance premium in the euro area housing market. *Source:* ECB calculations.

of credit, investment, and stock prices relative to GDP and the counter-cyclical behavior of the external finance premium. The vertical lines indicate the two times when the cost of finance premium reaches its minimum in this period. The first minimum is reached just before the bursting of the dot-com bubble in the first half of 2000. The second minimum is dated just before the start of the financial turmoil in the first half of 2007. So, exactly when at least ex post the risks were the highest, the premium for credit and liquidity risk is the lowest. A similar story (although less clear in the euro area) can be told for mortgage finance, house prices, and residential investment, as shown in figure 9.2.

Of course, one may argue that fundamentals are driving the boom and bust phases. The evidence we reviewed earlier suggests strongly that this is part of the story, and also the reason why it will never be very easy to identify a bubble ex ante. For example, one familiar story of the dot-com bubble is that the signs of a new economy with higher productivity and profits due to IT-related innovation lead to booming stock prices, increased investment (to benefit from the higher productivity), more

borrowing to finance that investment, and an associated increase in debt burdens. Moreover, because the outlook has improved and collateral values are up, the credit risk and the external finance premium are low. This process reverses as some of the good news turns out to be overly optimistic. While the caveat concerning the difference between a debt-based and an equity-based boom is an important one, in principle it is possible to tell similar stories about the development in mortgage markets in the United States and many other countries: good fundamentals based on innovation and benign conditions feeding on themselves.

The same two examples—the dot-com bubble of 1990s and the credit expansion of the 2000s—also make it clear that not all boom-bust episodes are the same. While both booms ended in busts, the former cycle hardly had the same negative impact on the real economy, in terms of benefits and costs. On the benefit side, it was associated with a technological boom, much like the First and Second Industrial Revolutions, which at the time were also associated with a boom-bust cycle. On the cost side, in 2000–2001 we saw nothing of the liquidity spirals, asset fire sales, interbank market freezes, and general deleveraging that we experienced in 2007–2008. The simple reason for this discrepancy is that the credit boom of the 2000s was driven by debt, while the dot-com bubble was driven by an expansion in equity ownership, and equity is not held in levered portfolios. This fairly obvious difference has prompted some academics to suggest that an institution that is engaged in "leaning against the wind" should make it a simple rule to act whenever housing prices are increasing rapidly, as such episodes are always accompanied by an accumulation of debt (Hall 2011).

Most asset price booms do build on good fundamentals. However, time and again we have learned that at some point these positive developments mutate into excessive credit expansion and risk taking owing to incentive problems, information frictions, and coordination issues (Reinhart and Rogoff 2010). This explains why, with the exception of financially repressed economies, procyclical asset price booms and busts are of all times and do not depend on the details of the financial system (see, e.g., De Bandt, Hartmann, and Peydró Alcalde 2009; Bank of England 2009).

Examples of feedback mechanisms between the real and the financial sector that have been brought into the public debate are multiple.

1. Procyclical capital requirements. As institutions incur losses and their capital cushions decline, the terms on which they can raise external funding worsen. This in turn can induce them to cut credit expansion or

dispose of assets, which weakens economic activity, raising the risk of a further deterioration in financial strength.

2. Procyclical collateral (loan to value) and margin requirements. During periods of stress, collateral requirements are likely to make it more difficult to fund existing positions, since increases in risk naturally lead to increases in margin requirements. Downturns lead to higher margin requirements and reduced market liquidity, forcing a general financial retrenchment, with obvious implications for real economic activity.

3. Endogenous procyclical financial innovation. When things are going well, firms and institutions feel confident in experimenting. They create new, untested instruments that are difficult to understand and value. Financial innovation may therefore create hidden, underpriced risks. As strains develop and the boom begins to wane, the previously unseen risks materialize, deepening the credit crunch that is already under way.

4. Procyclical behavioral mechanisms such as herding behavior, information cascades, and bouts of optimism and pessimism and confidence multiply (Akerlof and Shiller 2009).

5. Procyclical measurement of risk. Historical estimates of short-term volatility, asset and default correlations, probabilities of default, and probabilities of loss given default all move procyclically. As a result, measures of risk often spike once tensions arise, triggering strains, but may be quite low even as vulnerabilities and risk build up during the expansion phase.

6. Procyclical policies. For example, if the boom is initially driven by positive supply developments, inflationary tendencies may remain very subdued for a while, leading to low interest rates and an increased search for yields. Similarly, boom times are times of strong government revenues and an overestimation of the structural position of the government.

7. Procyclical compensation schemes and short-term horizons.

8. Procyclical risk taking due to moral hazard problems related to insurance mechanisms and "too big to fail" issues.

One implication of the fact that procyclicality has many facets is that the policy response to deal with it also must be comprehensive and multifaceted and ideally targeted to the sources of market failures and externalities. This is, of course, what the global reform agenda initiated by the G-20 and discussed by the Financial Stability Board and other multilateral institutions is all about. Some measures deal with regulation, such as

the recent agreement of the oversight group of the Basel Committee on Banking Supervision to set up a framework for countercyclical capital buffers above the minimum requirement and a minimum global standard for funding liquidity. Other measures have to do with strengthening the market infrastructure and its transparency, such as measures to enhance the transparency of new financial instruments or counteract the procyclical behavior of margin requirements by moving OTC markets to central counterparties. Still other measures, such as regulation directed at systemically important financial institutions, are geared toward reducing the problem of moral hazard related to the "too big to fail" issue.

A second observation is that because of the systemic and multifaceted nature of the procyclicality, a consensus has formed that there is a need for a new macroprudential policy framework.[3] We listed a number of challenges for a successful macroprudential policy at the beginning of the chapter: the need for one strong and independent authority rather than a fragmented set of players captured by various national interests; the need for a simple and effective policy tool; and the will of politicians and national authorities to actually implement the recommendations of that authority. In view of the discussion so far of the role of financial systems in promoting growth, we can now add to this list another challenge: what exactly would the mandate of that authority be? Is it to eliminate the incidence of rare and widespread financial crises that lead to large and abrupt macroeconomic contractions? Or is it to smooth the business cycle? Given our summary of the costs of crises in terms of growth, productivity, and consumer welfare, it looks like the former is the desirable mandate. However, it may simply not be feasible to eliminate all crises.

The establishment of a new macroprudential policy framework geared toward the surveillance of the financial system and the reduction of systemic risk is consistent with Tinbergen's assignment problem that there should be as many policy instruments as objectives. In Europe, the macroprudential policy will be pursued by the newly established European Systemic Risk Board, which will issue risk warnings and make policy recommendations. The ECB and other central banks play an important role in this risk board because of their macroperspective, their independence, their emphasis on sustainability and a medium-term orientation, and their intimate knowledge of financial markets, infrastructures, and institutions. One success factor will be the effective sharing of information necessary for a comprehensive surveillance of the financial system.

In line with Tinbergen's principle and the effective assignment of policies, monetary policy should continue to focus primarily on maintaining

price stability over the medium term. Doing anything else risks overburdening the monetary policy instrument and undermining the central banks' independence. However, this does not mean that monetary policy can ignore financial stability. First, Article 105(5) of the EU Treaty says that one of the ECB's tasks is to contribute to the promotion of financial stability. Second, monetary policy needs to take into account the effects of the financial system on the transmission mechanism and the shocks that come from the financial system. Both monetary policy and macroprudential policies affect the cost of financing and therefore will tend to interact. Third, it is also good to hear Milton Friedman's advice: Avoid monetary policy itself becoming a source of instability. Recently, there has been quite a bit of empirical evidence that keeping interest rates too low for too long encourages risk-taking behavior and therefore may sow the seeds of the next crisis. Finally, to the extent that macroprudential tools are unlikely to completely eliminate procyclical behavior, a leaning-against-the-wind strategy may not be a bad idea. Through its medium-term orientation and its two-pillar approach, including monetary analysis, the ECB's monetary policy strategy provides a natural framework to lean against credit-driven boom-bust cycles, even if this means trading off a bit of disinflation now for greater stability in the medium term. Of course, in the light of our previous discussion, a number of questions remain. Will small changes in interest rates be effective in reducing the buildup of imbalances?[4] Can we identify costly credit/asset price booms (Alessi and Detken 2009)? Recent empirical and theoretical evidence, as well as the experience with the current crisis, does suggest that the burden of the proof has shifted in favor of a leaning-against-the-wind policy.

In conclusion, based on a review of theory and evidence, we have argued in this chapter that while a vibrant financial sector contributes to sustainable, long-term growth, it may also increase the probability of financial crises associated with large economic costs. An important goal of the newly established macroprudential authorities will be to increase the resilience of the financial sector and thereby reduce the risk of a systemic collapse without endangering the vital role it plays in sustaining long-term growth.

Notes

1. The views expressed are our own and not necessarily those of the ECB or its Governing Council.

2. For a seminal empirical contribution, see King and Levine (1993).

3. See Crockett (2000) for an early exposition of this need. More recently, on the academic side, see Brunnermeier et al. (2009). On the policy side, see the report by the de Larosière Group (2009).

4. For recent evidence, see Ioannidou, Ongena, and Peydró (2009), Jiménez et al. (2009), and Maddaloni and Peydró (2010).

References

Acemoglu, D., S. Johnson, J. Robinson, and Y. Thaicharoen. 2003. Institutional Causes, Macroeconomic Symptoms: Volatility, Crises and growth. *Journal of Monetary Economics* 50: 49–123.

Acemoglu, D., and F. Zilibotti. 1997. Was Prometheus Unbound by Chance? Risk, Diversification, and Growth. *Journal of Political Economy* 105: 709–751.

Agenor, P.-R. 2003. Benefits and Costs of International Financial Integration: Theory and Facts. *World Economy* 26: 1089–1118.

Aghion, P., and G. Saint-Paul. 1998. Virtues of Bad Times: Interaction between Productivity Growth and Economic Fluctuations. *Macroeconomic Dynamics* 2: 322–344.

Akerlof, G., and R. Shiller. 2009. *Animal Spirits: How Human Psychology Drives the Economy, and Why It Matters for Global Capitalism.* Princeton, NJ: Princeton University Press.

Alessi, L., and C. Detken. 2009. Real-time Early Warning Indicators for Costly Asset Price Boom/bust Cycles: A Role for Global Liquidity. ECB Working Paper No. 1039, European Central Bank, Frankfurt.

Bank of England. 2009. The Role of Macroprudential Policy. November. Discussion paper, Bank of England, London.

Bank for International Settlements. 2009. Addressing Financial System Procyclicality: A Possible Framework. Note for the FSF Working Group on Market and Institutional Resilience. Basel, Switzerland, April.

Barlevy, G. 2007. On the Cyclicality of Research and Development. *American Economic Review* 97: 1131–1164.

Barro, R. 2006. Rare Disasters and Asset Markets in the Twentieth Century. *Quarterly Journal of Economics* 121: 823–866.

Bekaert, G., C. Harvey, and C. Lundblad. 2005. Does Financial Liberalization Spur Growth? *Journal of Financial Economics* 77: 3–55.

Bekaert, G., C. Harvey, and C. Lundblad. 2006. Growth Volatility and Financial Liberalization. *Journal of International Money and Finance* 25: 370–403.

Biais, B., J.-C. Rochet, and P. Wooley. 2009. Rents, Learning, and Risk in the Financial Sector and Other Innovative Industries. FMG Discussion Paper 632, Financial Markets Group, London School of Economics.

Borio, C., and M. Drehmann. 2009. Assessing the Risk of Banking Crises—Revisited. *BIS Quarterly Review,* March, 29–46.

Brunnermeier, M., A. Crockett, C. Goodhart, A. Persaud, and H. Shin. 2009. *The Fundamental Principles of Financial Regulation.* Geneva Reports on the World Economy 11. Geneva: International Center for Monetary and Banking Studies.

Caballero, R., and A. Krishnamurthy. 2009. Global Imbalances and Financial Fragility. *American Economic Review* 99: 584–588.

Crockett, A. 2000. Marrying the Micro- and Macro-prudential Dimensions of Financial Stability: Remarks before the Eleventh International Conference of Banking Supervisors, Basel.

De Bandt, O., P. Hartmann, and J.-L. Peydró Alcalde. 2009. Systemic Risk: An Update. In *Oxford Handbook of Banking*, ed. A. N. Berger, P. Molyneux, and J. Wilson. Oxford: Oxford University Press and Bank of England.

de Larosière Group. 2009. Report. February. De Larosière Group, Brussels.

Deidda, L., and B. Fattouh. 2002. Nonlinearity between Finance and Growth. *Economics Letters* 74: 339–345.

DeJong, D., and B. Ingram. 2001. The Cyclical Behavior of Skill Acquisition. *Review of Economic Dynamics* 4: 536–561.

Demirgüç-Kunt, A., T. Beck, and P. Honohan. 2008. *Finance for All? Policies and Pitfalls in Expanding Access*. Washington, DC: World Bank.

Detken, C., and F. Smets. 2004. Asset Price Booms and Monetary Policy. In *Macroeconomic Policies in the World Economy*, ed. Horst Siebert. Berlin: Springer-Verlag.

Easterly, W., R. Islam, and J. Stiglitz. 2000. Shaken and Stirred: Explaining Growth Volatility. Paper presented at the Annual Bank Conference on Development Economics, Washington, DC, January.

Eichengreen, B. 2001. Capital Account Liberalization: What Do the Cross-Country Studies Tell Us? *World Bank Economic Review* 15: 341–365.

Giannetti, M., and S. Ongena. 2009. Financial Integration and Firm Performance: Evidence from Foreign Bank Entry in Emerging Markets. *Review of Finance* 13: 181–223.

Hall, R. E. 2011. Presidential Address to the American Economic Association Annual Meeting, Denver, CO, January.

Hartmann, P., F. Heider, M. Lo Duca, and E. Papaioannou. 2007. The Role of Financial Markets and Innovation in Productivity and Growth in Europe. ECB Occasional Paper 72, European Central Bank, Frankfurt.

Hirukawa, M., and M. Ueda. 2008. Venture Capital and Industrial "Innovation." CEPR Discussion Paper 7089, Centre for Economic Policy Research, London.

Ioannidou, V. P., S. Ongena, and J.-L. Peydró. 2009. Monetary Policy, Risk-taking and Pricing: Evidence from a Quasi Natural Experiment. European Banking Center Discussion Paper 2009-04S, Centre for Economic Policy Research, London.

Jiménez, G., S. Ongena, J.-L. Peydró, and J. Saurina. 2009. Hazardous Times for Monetary Policy: What Do Twenty-three Million Bank Loans Say about the Effects of Monetary Policy on Credit Risk? CEPR Discussion Paper 6514, Centre for Economic Policy Research, London.

Kalemli-Ozcan, S., E. Papaioannou, and J.-L. Peydró. 2009. Financial Integration and Business Cycle Synchronization. NBER Working Paper 14887, National Bureau of Economic Research, Cambridge, MA.

Kalemli-Ozcan, S., B. Sorensen, and O. Yosha. 2003. Risk Sharing and Industrial Specialization: Regional and International Evidence. *American Economic Review* 93: 903–918.

Kaplan, S., and P. Stromberg. 2001. Venture Capitalists as Principals: Contracting, Screening, and Monitoring. *American Economic Review* 91: 426–430.

Kindleberger, C. P. 1978. *Manias, Panics and Crashes: A History of Financial Crises*. Basingstoke: Palgrave Macmillan.

King, R., and R. Levine. 1993. Finance and Growth: Schumpeter Might Be Right. *Quarterly Journal of Economics* 108: 717–737.

Kortum, S., and J. Lerner. 2000. Assessing the Contribution of Venture Capital to Innovation. *Rand Journal of Economics* 31: 674–692.

Kose, A., E. Prasad, K. Rogoff, and S.-J. Wei. 2003. Effects of Financial Globalization on Developing Countries: Some Empirical Evidence. International Monetary Fund Occasional Paper 220, International Monetary Fund, Washington, DC.

Kose, A., E. Prasad, K. Rogoff, and S. Wei. 2004. Financial Globalization, Growth and Volatility in Developing Countries. NBER Working Paper 10942, National Bureau of Economic Research, Cambridge, MA.

Levchenko, A., R. Rancière, and M. Thoenig. 2009. Growth and Risk at the Industry Level: The Real Effects of Financial Liberalization. *Journal of Development Economics* 89: 210–222.

Lucas, R. E. 1987. *Models of Business Cycles*. New York: Basil Blackwell.

Maddaloni, A., and J.-L. Peydró. 2010. Bank Risk-taking, Securitization, Supervision, and Low Interest Rates: Evidence from Lending Standards. ECB Working Paper 0000, European Central Bank, Frankfurt.

Manganelli, S., and A. Popov. 2010. Finance and Diversification. ECB Working Paper 1259, European Central Bank, Frankfurt.

Michalopoulos, S., L. Laeven, and R. Levine. 2009. Financial Innovation and Endogenous Growth. NBER Working paper 15356, National Bureau of Economic Research, Cambridge, MA.

Minsky, H. 1986. *Stabilizing an Unstable Economy*. New Haven, CT: Yale University Press.

Morgan, D., B. Rime, and P. Strahan. 2004. Bank Integration and State Business Cycles. *Quarterly Journal of Economics* 119: 1555–1585.

Mortensen, D., and C. Pissarides. 1994. Job Creation and Job Destruction in the Theory of Unemployment. *Review of Economic Studies* 61: 397–415.

Philippon, T., and N. Véron. 2008. Financing Europe's Fast Movers. Bruegel Policy Brief 2008/01, Bruegel, Brussels.

Popov, A. 2011. Financial Liberalization, Growth, and Risk. Mimeo, European Central Bank, Frankfurt.

Popov, A., and S. Ongena. 2011. Interbank Market Integration, Loan Rates, and Firm Leverage. *Journal of Banking & Finance* 35: 544–560.

Popov, A., and P. Roosenboom. 2009. On the Real Effects of Private Equity Investment: Evidence from New Business Creation. ECB Working Paper 1063, European Central Bank, Frankfurt.

Popov, A., and G. Udell. 2012. Cross-Border Banking, Credit Access, and the Financial Crisis. *Journal of International Economics* 87: 147–161.

Raddatz, C. 2006. Liquidity Needs and Vulnerability to Financial Underdevelopment. *Journal of Financial Economics* 80: 677–722.

Rajan, R., and L. Zingales. 1998. Financial Dependence and Growth. *American Economic Review* 88: 559–586.

Rancière, R., A. Tornell, and F. Westermann. 2008. Systemic Crises and Growth. *Quarterly Journal of Economics* 123: 359–406.

Reinhart, C., and K. Rogoff. 2009. The Aftermath of Financial Crises. *American Economic Review* 99: 466–472.

Reinhart, C., and K. Rogoff. 2010. *This Time Is Different: Eight Centuries of Financial Folly.* Princeton, NJ: Princeton University Press.

Rioja, F., and N. Valev. 2004. Does One Size Fit All? A Reexamination of the Finance and Growth Relationship. *Journal of Development Economics* 74: 429–447.

Robinson, J. 1952. The Generalization of the General Theory. In *The Rate of Interest and Other Essays*, ed. J. Robinson, 67–142. London: Macmillan.

Shen, C., and C. Lee. 2006. Same Financial Development Yet Different Economic Growth —Why? *Journal of Money, Credit and Banking* 38: 1907–1944.

Stiglitz, J. E. 2000. Capital Market Liberalization, Economic Growth and Instability. *World Development* 28: 1075–1086.

Wurgler, J. 2000. Financial Markets and the Allocation of Capital. *Journal of Financial Economics* 58: 187–214.

Zingales, L. 2003. Commentary on "More on Finance and Growth: More Finance, More Growth?" Federal Reserve Bank of St. Louis, *Review* 85: 47–52.

10 Financial Innovation: Balancing Private and Public Interests

Josef Ackermann

In the wake of the recent financial and economic crisis, innovation that led to the development of complex financial instruments has come under heightened scrutiny. Banks and other financial intermediaries have been criticized for developing financial instruments that work to the detriment of financial and economic stability and of society in general. A pointed yet thought-provoking critique in this respect was voiced by Paul Volcker, who stated that the only useful innovation to come out of banking in recent decades was the automated teller machine.[1]

From a general perspective, Volcker's critique reflects the perception that financial innovation, like every other economic innovation, should benefit society in a broad way. To be fair, Volcker's statement refers explicitly to the most recent developments in financial markets, that is, the products and market events that triggered or at least aggravated the crisis. In other words, it does not question the value of financial innovation per se. In fact, in many cases, financial innovation has proved to be useful to the economy and society. Long before the 1960s and early 1970s — around the time when ATMs were introduced — innovation had helped facilitate savings and investments, introduce new hedging opportunities, and significantly reduce transaction unit costs. But important advances continued to be made afterward as well.

Nevertheless, it is true that risks are generally involved in every new product and market. The recent crisis demonstrated that the improper use of financial instruments can have severe consequences, and it has been argued that these risks need to be balanced against the economic benefits of financial innovation. In this context, private sector financial institutions have a key role to play: not only are they vital facilitators of financial innovation but, together with public sector authorities, they share important responsibilities to maintain a sound and stable financial system.

This chapter explores the distinct role of banks in financial innovation as a sine qua non to conducting an informed debate on how private and public interest in financial innovation can best be balanced. The chapter starts by examining the challenges in defining the term "financial innovation." It goes on to argue that financial innovation has been around for quite a while and its economic potential must not be underestimated. By looking at how banks facilitate financial innovation, the chapter highlights the fact that innovation develops in response to clients' needs, and that the profit orientation of (private) financial institutions need not be in conflict with the (public) objective of maintaining stability and achieving economic progress. Finally, there is a discussion of how the private and public sectors can best complement each other in managing the risks that may accompany financial innovation.

10.1 Defining "Financial Innovation"

To systematically assess the risks that accompany financial innovation, a working definition needs to be established. By analogy with innovation in other industries, one can readily start by classifying a financial innovation as either a process or a product innovation. For instance, "book building," which evolved as the dominant form of price discovery in initial public offerings and capital increases, can be considered a process innovation, whereas the development of exchange-traded funds and catastrophe bonds are recent examples of product innovations. A third category can be added if one considers the creation of new financial intermediaries, such as money market funds or microfinance institutions, a form of financial innovation. The development of ATMs, mentioned by Paul Volcker, may be placed in a fourth category, that of advances in banking and financial market infrastructure, which can significantly change how markets are organized and financial services are carried out.

While categorizing the different kinds of financial innovation is fairly straightforward, it is much more difficult to distinguish between breakthrough innovation and mere modifications of existing products and processes. To make such distinctions, the novelty and uniqueness of a development must be considered, along with its potential or actual impact on the financial system. However, it is not necessarily the largest and most obvious changes that constitute the most crucial innovations. Sometimes very small changes to existing instruments can lead to breakthrough developments. A prominent example was the introduction of limited liability for company shares. Before this small but crucial change in cor-

porate law, holders of equity could be held accountable for losses that exceeded the equity capital, which in turn limited the interest in owning such stocks. With the introduction of limited liability company shares, public equity markets became an attractive option for investors to provide company financing. It has since developed into the most vital capital market segment, sparking the numerous innovations that followed.

Credit default swaps (CDSs) are another example. At first glance, CDSs seem to simply apply the swap principle to a new underlying, that is, credit risk. This would hardly qualify them as a financial innovation under a narrow definition. However, based on its economic impact, or the capacity to establish a liquid market for credit risk, the introduction of CDSs must qualify as a breakthrough development.

Therefore, a useful working definition of financial innovation would have to distinguish between innovations with a potentially high economic impact and advances that remain mere extensions of existing products or markets. However, the fact that in many cases the impact of a financial innovation is apparent only long after the new instrument or procedure becomes established poses an obvious challenge, not only for its categorization but also for its monitoring and regulation.

10.2 What Drives Financial Innovation?

Just as in other industries, innovation in the financial sector primarily arises as a response to the needs of users of financial products. Basic needs include the safe transfer of funds, the financing of private and public ventures, the facilitation of savings and investments, and the reallocating of risks. These are long-standing needs, which led, by the way, not only to the introduction of money as an abstract means to store and transfer value but also to the creation of banks to serve clients' saving and financing needs.[2]

Robert Shiller has convincingly argued that financial innovation can and should be deployed to manage society's largest economic risks (Shiller 1993). To this end, he advanced several proposals on how financial instruments can be deployed to help reduce fluctuations in peoples' lifetime income and wealth. And many of his visionary ideas have found their way into today's financial markets, including securities that can be used to hedge against inflation or house price changes. In his academic and commercial activities, Shiller addresses one of the most powerful drivers of financial innovation, the desire to reduce income volatility and insure against the occurrence of adverse events.

In fact, innovation aimed at meeting peoples' hedging needs has been around for quite a long time, even before banks came on the scene in Europe during the thirteenth century. In these early transactions, all that was needed was the understanding of two contractual partners as to how the benefits and obligations of a financial transaction were to be mutually shared. Low technical barriers combined with high potential gains for the parties involved paved the way for financial innovation in the hedging and transfer of risk, which have played key roles in commerce and finance for thousands of years. As early as 2000 BC, Chinese farmers and merchants were transacting sales of rice for future delivery. In these early forward transactions, farmers entered into the contract usually before the rice was planted, ensuring that the farmer had a market for the future harvest and the merchant would get a specific quantity of rice at a predetermined price (Hou 1997). The underlying principle is still used in today's forward contracts on the over-the-counter (OTC) derivatives market.

These markets evolved because farmers and traders understood that shielding themselves from unexpected swings in prices could be crucial for their economic success, and sometimes survival. Creating financial instruments to hedge against variable prices was among the main drivers of the financial innovations that followed. Interest rate and foreign exchange swaps, as well as CDSs much later on, were all created to hedge specific risks that could threaten the viability of a corporate or private venture.

Other innovations were aimed at facilitating or improving the transfer of funds from one account to the other, the conversion of physical cash into digital money and vice versa, or making cashless payments. Important innovations of the past few decades—apart from the ATM—include the introduction of credit and debit cards during the 1960s, which helped bank customers more flexibly transact payments and reduced transaction costs significantly. The introduction of automated clearinghouses represents another example of how the need to efficiently process a large number of financial transactions led to financial innovation (Litan 2010).

One of the central functions of the financial markets is to channel savings into investments. Innovations in this segment often develop in response to the different financing needs of corporations, sovereign entities, and households. Numerous advances made in recent years have helped address moral hazard and adverse selection problems in funding relationships. For example, borrowers who were not able to credibly commit to a verifiably prudent use of the funds were, in many cases, not able to obtain funding, or only at high costs. Financial innovation helped

overcome such barriers. For instance, inflation-linked bonds were introduced to allow countries that could not credibly commit to price stability a means of accessing capital market funding. But these bonds also provided savers with an effective hedge against inflation.

The introduction of the German covered bond (*Pfandbrief*) in the eighteenth century can be seen in the same light. Instead of issuing ordinary bonds, a mortgage bank may choose to issue debt securities backed by mortgages or public sector loans, such as the German covered bond, which is a tightly regulated product ensuring that only high-quality collateral is used while providing excess coverage. Buyers of such bonds can thus acquire a mortgage investment and risk without having to devote time and money to selection and monitoring. In most cases, this arrangement results in a lower risk premium for the bank issuing the securities, as the bondholder has recourse to the loan portfolio should the original lender become insolvent.

Finally, the tranching of asset-backed securities works in a similar manner. Not only can investors choose a specific risk tranche according to their individual risk preferences, they can also select a tranche that best suits their ability to overcome information discrepancy problems. For the issuer, this can result in a reduction of the funding costs, as the entire range of investors can be addressed and offered tranches that optimally match their preferences. Of course, the overall value of the transaction depends on how the resulting incentive problems can be mitigated.

The concrete needs of potential users of financial innovations are a necessary but not a sufficient condition for financial innovation to take place. The potential suppliers of such innovations must have the ability to create such products. Over the last thirty to forty years, breakthrough developments in financial theory and IT have been among the most powerful drivers of more recent financial innovations.[3] For instance, thanks to new insights in theory and increased data-processing capacities, modern portfolio management is no longer guided solely by a mean and variance analysis but also takes into account correlations between different securities and different types of financial instruments and events. In other words, theoretical concepts of efficient asset allocation have been successfully implemented in today's portfolio management industry. In recent years, financial theory has become a key driver of commercially applied financial innovation. Similarly, as progress in asset pricing and credit risk models allowed new products to be priced and risks to be handled, limits were virtually eliminated for the design of new derivatives, making it possible to offer every desired payoff structure for every

possible underlying risk. Complexity in these instruments stems not only from the desire to create investment and hedging solutions ideally suited to the diverse needs of investors and clients but also from the ability of market participants to price and handle the risks involved.

Apart from users' needs, major impulses for financial innovation often come from financial liberalization, that is, the deregulation of financial markets, and from market participants' attempts to avoid or circumvent taxation and regulation. In fact, taxation and financial regulation can trigger the development of transactions geared to optimize tax and regulatory charges. Realistically, such developments may be impossible to avoid and should be recognized as part of a functioning market economy. The tax and regulatory regime in turn needs to be sufficiently robust and adjusted on a frequent basis to optimally achieve its public objectives.

In this context, innovation based on regulatory arbitrage, like every other innovation, should be judged on the basis of its added value to the economy, which in turn is a function of the usefulness of the underlying regulation. It cannot be assumed that the (ex post) assessment always leads to a negative judgment, as the following example demonstrates: The invention of money market funds and the eurodollar market both owe their origins to a U.S. rule known as Regulation Q. The regulation placed a ceiling on the rate of interest that U.S. banks could offer on their time deposits. Since the restrictions of Regulation Q did not apply to investment funds or to Western European branches of U.S. banks and their foreign competitors, these institutions were able to offer short-term dollar-denominated accounts (Miller 1986). The fact that both markets continue to thrive even though Regulation Q has long ceased to exist suggests that money market funds and the eurodollar market have in fact added some value that does not depend on regulatory arbitrage.

10.3 Banks Facilitate Financial Innovation

Two factors drive the speed and power of innovation at financial institutions. On the one hand, banks are in constant dialog with their clients. This leads banks to continuously think about the specific demands of their clients and how these demands can best be met by services and products the bank offers. To this end, banks strive to identify areas for improvement and work together with their clients in order to provide them with superior solutions. In many cases, tailor-made solutions subsequently lead to the development of new products as the idea proves valuable to other clients, too. On the other hand, banks are constantly

being challenged by their competitors. In a competitive environment, innovation is considered to be an effective means to raise margins, increase operating efficiency, and build a unique selling proposition.[4]

Innovation at banks is not restricted to the marketing of new products but extends across the entire value chain. For instance, modernizing internal processing standards through process innovations can help reduce the marginal costs of existing business lines while raising productivity. Likewise, innovation in connection with internal risk management processes, such as credit scoring models, stress testing, and the introduction of extreme value theory into credit risk models, can help decrease delinquency rates and raise profitability.

In addition to direct cost and revenue effects, there are further (positive) externalities that add to the attractiveness of an innovation strategy: It is not only the long-standing relationships with its clients that allow a bank to sell innovative products but also the reputation it enjoys in the market. Of course, reputation is earned from previous successful transactions. Banks that have established themselves as market leaders in a certain segment may find it easier to market new products in this segment, too. An innovative bank's positive reputation derived from intellectual leadership in a certain field of expertise can thus help shield it from competitive pressure.

In developing new products, banks and their clients regularly form a symbiotic relationship: banks play a key role in the development of workable solutions to help satisfy their clients' funding and risk management needs. The emergence of new instruments can frequently be observed in the OTC derivatives market, which is one of the most flexible and innovative market segments. The OTC derivatives market has gained widespread acceptance among companies with international operations as they rely on OTC instruments to hedge specific business risks. Industrial corporations that are exposed to the international commodity markets, for example, can combine commodity and foreign exchange forwards to hedge their input costs. Internationally operating airlines use foreign exchange swaps to hedge their exposures from anticipated ticket sales, just as an international trading firm will want to hedge its receipts from the sale of goods. More complex financing and hedging requirements on the part of corporate end-users require more flexible financial solutions, and this has been one of the main drivers of financial innovation during the past few decades.

To gain a better understanding of how banks facilitate innovation, it is instructive to look at how innovations evolve in the OTC derivatives

market. Three phases can be distinguished: the innovation, diffusion, and standardization of financial products.

10.3.1 Innovation

A financial institution's product development process is generally fed through two possible channels. Key account managers and salesmen are in constant dialog with their clients to find out how the bank can best serve clients' needs. Also, many ideas are directly voiced by the clients themselves or developed in discussion with the bank's staff. But other channels also involve analysts, product managers, and financial engineers, who constantly think about how to best meet clients' needs.

Once an idea is born, the new product is often developed by combining and modifying different building blocks from existing instruments. Product innovations aim to achieve a unique risk and payment profile that could not be achieved to a similar extent with traditional products. Variability in a bank's existing components and the ability to individually structure new products are essential to achieving a better alignment with a client's preferences. The better the issuer is able to meet its clients' needs, the more likely the clients are to accept a somewhat higher price, for example, if they feel that the product offers a superior hedge for the targeted risks. In the absence of a liquid market, the innovator has some pricing power for the new product, which can be reflected in a higher bid-ask spread for innovative products compared to established products. Ideally, the innovation creates a true and lasting economic rent, for example, because the new instruments allow for a more efficient allocation of risk or help overcome frictions in financial transactions.

During the innovation phase, structuring banks are able to capture a larger share of the value created by the new product. However, the time span in which a potential innovation rent can be captured is very limited, not least because financial innovations are generally not patentable. At the same time, the innovator needs to be prepared to handle a number of risks that usually accompany the creation and marketing of new products. For instance, the bank issuing a new product may be directly exposed to the underlying market risk if it serves as a permanent counterparty to its clients. In flow business, the issuing bank may not be able to sell off the warehoused products, again leaving it with the underlying market risk. Moreover, the issuing bank may face heightened uncertainty in pricing new products. This can affect not only initial transactions but also any subsequent collateralization or market-making activities.

To adequately deal with these risks, banks that wish to become active innovators need to meet certain criteria: They should have well-founded research, structuring, and pricing know-how—in other words, the expertise to manage the challenges that accompany the design and marketing of new products. Moreover, they should possess an effective risk management system, also to ensure a systematic approach to all risks involved in novel transactions. Finally, these banks need to maintain close relationships with their clients, as developing and marketing innovative products requires a great deal of mutual trust and understanding. For their part, clients need to have the assurance that the counterparty they are dealing with is capable and ready to deliver suitable solutions, so that only banks with excellent reputations can hope to receive the necessary acceptance among potential clients.

10.3.2 Diffusion

The innovator who brings a new product onto the market has an interest in raising the attractiveness of the product. For many products, attractiveness increases with its widespread use and the possibility of trading it in a liquid market: clients benefit from prices that are observable on a frequent basis, but also from the possibility of more easily terminating a contract by just selling it off. Innovators are faced with a trade-off in this situation: They must weigh safeguarding their proprietary knowledge against the need to cooperate with other (competing) market participants in order to increase the product's attractiveness.

Once the innovation becomes public, competitors start imitating the new product, while more and more clients learn how to make use of it. Sophisticated corporate end-users may further contribute to the diffusion of new products. Large international corporations often maintain a high level of financial expertise, and some even operate their own trading units. Such clients usually gain extensive insights into banks' overall production processes and may engage in the active promotion of a new market segment. There is a positive side effect from the diffusion of innovation: When the innovation is used to distribute risks more efficiently or to overcome prior frictions, market efficiency increases accordingly.

10.3.3 Standardization

If commercially successful, a financial innovation finally enters the third phase of market development, standardization. Although not all products are suitable for standardization, it is easier to efficiently organize

trading as well as pre- and post-trade processes for standardized products. While standardized products can be more easily traded, collateralized, and cleared at central trading and clearing facilities, many custom-made derivatives products continue to be traded OTC. Only if the frequency and volume of trades pass certain thresholds will new products start migrating onto centrally organized trading platforms.

As the new product becomes increasingly commoditized, the number of dealers, traders, and end-users, as well as the volume traded, rises significantly. The higher trading volumes and the more efficient market organization that tend to accompany standardization lead to a significant reduction in the transaction cost scales. Again, clients benefit from this development, as they have to pay less for their financial transactions. The resulting reorganization of the market also leads to a different business case for the initial suppliers of the new instruments. Innovators must decide whether they are able to continue operating in this new cost-competitive environment or whether they should turn their attention to other segments that are less developed and still promise high innovation margins. Of course, large institutions may be able to follow a twofold strategy comprising innovation as well as volume-based business models.

10.4   Balancing Private and Public Interest

Financial innovation can be considered economically useful if it addresses legitimate hedging, funding, saving, transaction, investment, or informa-tion needs that can potentially be handled by the financial markets. In so doing, financial innovation helps to complete the market, creating a lasting economic benefit for everyone participating in the market. When looking at some of the more obvious cases, it would be hard to contest the economic usefulness of early financial innovations, such as the intro-duction of money, bank deposits, letters of credit and bills of exchange, the bond and stock markets, and, later on, the trading of standardized financial contracts intended to hedge the price risks of certain goods. All of these innovations have proved to be extremely valuable over time.

Many of the instruments that were created or that experienced a breakthrough in terms of issuance or trading volumes over the past twenty years also qualify as economically useful according to the criteria presented above. This applies to many OTC derivatives—including CDSs—and securitizations that have helped complete the market and now provide effective means to manage the credit risk of commercial banks. In fact, the lending business of traditional commercial banks

would be infeasible without these innovative financial instruments. Simply assuming on-balance-sheet risk is incompatible with the demands posed by today's risk management requirements. Banks need to actively manage their risk and capital positions on a continuous basis, which is only possible by means of innovative financial instruments such as CDSs and securitizations. Moreover, the funding that was needed to finance growth in the larger global economy, encompassing industrial countries as well as transitional and emerging market economies, would have been impossible if traditional, on-balance-sheet commercial banking had not evolved to also comprise innovative forms of financing using instruments developed for the capital markets.

Nonetheless, the crisis has shown that not every financial innovation deemed economically worthwhile at the level of the individual financial institution (or its internal business divisions) turned out to be desirable if social costs had been taken into account. And in retrospect, not every product marketed over the past few years was economically successful.

10.4.1 Useful Innovations Can Entail Risk

Recent experiences made with credit securitizations and derivatives have demonstrated that financial innovation bears great economic potential but also creates uncertainty that may translate into real financial or economic risk. It goes without saying that we would like to accept only the financial innovations that are economically useful but entail low risk. In reality, most innovations involve some risk, which can be of a transitory nature, for instance from temporary market setbacks, or of a lasting nature, owing to an inherent fragility of the instrument in question.

Callable bank deposits, for example, represent an economically useful innovation with a risk that could not be handled for a long time. Demand deposits certainly marked a great leap in financial history, offering a unique form of liquidity storage to banks' clients and facilitating liquidity transformation on a large scale. Still today, bank deposits are generally considered to be an economically useful instrument, but one that comes at the cost of a certain degree of financial fragility. It took several hundred years to figure out how the risk of a "run on the bank," a risk that is inextricably linked to the benefits of liquidity transformation, can be reduced to a manageable size—although this risk will perhaps never be entirely eliminated.

Credit derivatives and securitizations are a much different case. The costs to society incurred during the recent crisis were extremely high,

even though the difficulties in assessing and managing the underlying risks are probably of a transitory nature. While some of the more complex products, such as CDOs-squared, are of questionable economic value, most of the instruments complement the market in a reasonable manner and come with economic benefits that are potentially huge. One of the greatest challenges, however—and most likely a permanent phenomenon—remains the interdependencies between financial institutions across markets and countries generated through the advances in financial instruments.

But how does one assess whether a new financial instrument is disproportionately risky? Without the possibility of conducting adequate field tests, theoretical underpinnings become essential. In principle, financial innovation could be tested in a model-based world derived on the basis of economic theory. It can be argued that instruments that do not work in theory should not work in practice, either. The reverse, however, does not always hold true: not everything that works in theory does so in practice. And many products that could be considered harmless if judged on an individual basis may turn out to be dangerous in an environment marked by a toxic combination of market developments. In many cases, a useful theory is developed only after the fact to explain what was previously observed in the market. Again, the recent crisis provides a case in point. Only after a long series of real-time "testing" and only after the first problems emerged did market participants and regulators become aware of the systemic risks that had been building up during the preceding years. The financial crisis that started in 2007 has sparked a host of new research projects aimed at explaining what went wrong. Research is likely to continue for many years until final conclusions can be reached.

10.4.2 Financial Innovation Is an Evolutionary Process

The financial crisis has demonstrated once again that the effects of any type of innovation cannot easily be foreseen, neither the positive nor the negative effects. Advances in financial innovation often build on each other, evolving to some extent erratically and by no means according to a master plan. The resulting process may therefore best be described as evolutionary. There are new products that fail shortly after their inception and others that experience a landslide success in a relatively short period of time. Many of the innovations still in use today have survived various crises and were adjusted afterward. Securitization, for example, continues to be an integral part of today's financial markets, though

without some of the more complex product structures, while many other securitization instruments are being modified to incorporate the lessons learned from the crisis, namely, to fulfill the need for more transparency on the underlying assets.

Others fared extremely well for quite a long time, such as the German covered bonds. Back when *Pfandbriefe* were first introduced, the authorities could not have imagined that these bonds—in a slightly modified form—would continue to thrive several hundred years later, becoming the predecessor of asset-backed securities. The lasting success of these covered bonds clearly illustrates how hard it is to predict not only the risk but also the opportunities inherent in financial innovations.

In this sense, innovation in the financial sector is just like innovation in many other industries. It involves to some extent a market-driven search process, with the possibility of failure ensuring market discipline. A regulatory regime that intends to limit the risk of financial innovation by slowing down the pace of innovation or by making concrete decisions on which specific new instruments are desired and which are not runs the risk of passing up valuable developments along the way.

10.4.3 Financial Institutions Have a Key Role in Mitigating Innovation Risk

Given the chances and risks inherent in financial innovation, market participants as well as regulatory and supervisory authorities find themselves faced with a situation in which they have to constantly balance the need for safety with entrepreneurial freedom. Banks and other financial institutions have a key role to play in safeguarding their clients and the wider economy from unintended consequences of their commercial activities.

Financial institutions can and actually do contribute substantially to mitigating the downside risks of financial innovation. To this end, senior management teams of financial institutions must ensure that a robust risk management culture prevails in the creation of new products and the development of new markets. At the operational level, financial institutions maintain robust control infrastructures that enable them to identify, evaluate, and address the risks associated with their business activities. Within well-defined procedures that are often assigned to special committees, new products are examined for their economic usefulness, for their compliance with existing rules, and for their suitability to serve the clients' needs before they are marketed. In such product approval processes, banks first develop an understanding of the risks the

new products will bring to the institution. Of course, when a financial institution markets a new product, it bears the usual market, credit, and operational risks associated with the transaction, but in some cases it may also face heightened legal and reputational risks arising from its involvement in untested markets. In a second step, the committee in charge considers measures to mitigate the risk. The range of possible measures includes internal risk management procedures, but also restrictions on how and to whom the products can be marketed. Taken to the extreme, an envisaged new line of business will be canceled altogether if the risks are deemed to be too high.

The procedures in place are potentially well-suited to shield clients from badly designed products. They are also useful in protecting financial institutions from legal, reputational, operational, and other risks. However, they are insufficient to detect systemic threats and prevent crises, since financial institutions primarily focus on the impact the new products might have on clients and their own companies. It will be difficult for them to assess systemic implications owing to the lack of data, but also owing to their specific incentive structures.

Instead, safeguarding systemic stability is the task of public authorities, as they can more easily assume a systemwide perspective. Regulatory and supervisory authorities not only have a different objective function, they also have access to a much wider range of data, enabling them to better assess systemic risk. Make no mistake, this is not to say that banks themselves, as part of their product approval processes, should not also consider the potential systemic repercussions of new products. However, banks have neither the right incentive structures nor the proper tools to fulfill that role to the extent required.

10.4.4   Designing an Adequate Regulatory Response

One of the problems prior to the crisis was that investors relied heavily on third-party judgments and did not fully understand the risks involved in some of the new structures. Systemic risks in particular were sometimes underestimated or even neglected. In some cases, issuers did not make sure that the structures were sufficiently transparent to allow risks to be assessed by both the sellers and the buyers of the products. But regulatory and supervisory authorities also found it difficult to grasp the systemic implications of the use of these new instruments. The problem, it seems, was not necessarily the products but the ways in which the parties involved used and assessed them. For instance, the fact that many

investors in structured products relied exclusively on third-party assessments (i.e., ratings) instead of performing their own due diligence on the quality of the assets involved does not actually reflect an inherent weakness in the products themselves but the deficiencies in risk management structures and processes.

When discussing an adequate regulatory response, the question arises as to whether ad hoc product-specific regulation is well-suited to contain systemic risk. Policy makers are currently discussing additional guidelines for the testing of new products before they can be marketed to clients. One of the proposals is that an official body be established with the mandate to assess products before they can be released to the market. The approach is used in the clinical testing of pharmaceuticals and in safety inspections of mechanical devices, areas in which people's lives and health can be at risk.

With respect to financial innovation, there are a number of challenges that accompany a product-specific approach, which question the feasibility and usefulness of such an approach. First, it would be difficult to come up with a working definition of financial innovation at the product level. Second, it would often be impossible to identify potentially dangerous instruments beforehand, as there is basically little to no empirical evidence to draw on in new markets. Furthermore, systemic risk is also a matter of size, and even potentially high-risk instruments do not pose a systemic threat unless they are widely distributed. Third, a product-based approach fails to address the behavior of financial market participants, as risks that stem from the systematic misjudgment and misbehavior of market participants are not taken into account. Most important, in this regard, the risk attached to the instruments is subjective: What may be a high-risk product for an undercapitalized bank may be perfectly safe in the hands of a sound and well-managed institution. Finally, the evolutionary nature of the financial market leaves much room for potential error, for example, by letting a potentially risky product through to the market or by forgoing the opportunity to develop a desirable market.

An instrument-specific approach would do more harm than good, as it would not only neglect the opportunities that accompany financial innovation but would also be ill-suited to achieving its ultimate goal. The better alternative to regulating financial innovations is a principles-based approach aimed at achieving a diffusion of the risks at the system level. Enabling investors to make good choices would be one of the building blocks of such an approach, and this is, to no small degree, a function of the product issuer's information policies. But such information needs to

be well targeted and designed to avoid an "information overload." For newly introduced products, a concise summary of the risk factors would help investors to independently evaluate the products. In the early phase of a market, the innovation phase, it must be ensured that access to the new products is limited exclusively to investors who are able to assess and cope with the accompanying uncertainties. At a later stage, the standardization and harmonization of market definitions and structures will be essential for the ongoing development of the market and to allow a wider, less sophisticated investor base to have access to such products.

To monitor systemic risk, it will be useful to establish a comprehensive data set on the volumes of new and existing financial products, as well as the net risk at the level of individual institutions. Ideally, there will be an internationally coordinated effort to collect such data in a consistent and comprehensive manner. Here it may be helpful to gather data from existing trade repositories. Additional data collection efforts may be necessary, since not every transaction can and should be reported to a trade repository, depending on the maturity of the respective market as well as the transacted volume. Supervisory authorities should be granted access to such data to help policy makers gain a clear overview of the volumes outstanding, as well as the risks market participants have assumed. Enhanced transparency on these key risk indictors will allow policy makers to monitor the buildup of possible risks, while allowing market activities to proceed. With such an approach, regulators would be expected to intervene only if potentially negative consequences could be reasonably expected on the basis of actual data, precluding the necessity to decide on the viability of new product innovations without being able to refer to a sound body of empirical data.

In addition, robust market infrastructures have a key role to play in this context. Although financial innovation is by no means restricted to certain market segments, the OTC derivatives market is currently one of the most active segments where new products are constantly being created. In this segment, adequate collateralization and improved management of counterparty risk can help form a more robust financial system. Again, it is important to strike the right balance between prudence and realizing economic benefits. Forcing newly created instruments onto central trading or collateralization platforms would be an improper impairment of innovative forces. As long as trading in a new product has not attained a sufficiently high volume, central counterparties will find it difficult to assess the amounts necessary for adequate collateralization, but systemic threats from the product will also remain limited.

A final consideration relates to one of the key drivers of financial innovation, namely, attempts to evade regulatory restrictions. In light of financial innovation's relevance for the industry, any direct restriction placed on the process of innovation will have an immediate, adverse impact on the competitive position of a financial institution that operates under the restrictive regime. It will therefore be essential to accord financial institutions equal rights and duties across the globe and to maintain an internationally level playing field with respect to controls on innovation.

10.5 Conclusions

Going forward, financial innovation is set to continue. Extending the set of available hedging and investment opportunities will benefit investors, corporations, and households alike. However, to improve the risk-bearing and information-processing capacities of capital markets, numerous technical and intellectual challenges need to be addressed. The private sector can significantly contribute to adequately meeting these challenges and help facilitate innovation that is useful to society. To this end, it will be important to foster the forces that help lever the economic potential of future financial innovation while maintaining market integrity and stability.

In working toward establishing a more efficient and robust financial system, public and private interests in financial innovation need to be consistently balanced. At first glance, there appears to be a lack of clarity regarding the respective objective functions—but, as outlined above, it is possible to align, although perhaps not to perfectly match, public and private interests. Finding the appropriate tools to mitigate the risks that accompany any individual financial innovation will remain a challenge that will inevitably have to be handled on a case-by-case basis. A differentiated view of financial innovation is necessary to meet the intellectual and practical challenges in designing an adequate response. A principles-based approach that addresses the risk caused by a lack of understanding and the improper use of financial innovations seems to be preferable over ad hoc instrument-specific interventions.

Notes

1. Paul Volcker, according to *The Times*, London, December 9, 2009 (Hosking and Jagger 2009).

2. Peter Tufano (2002a) provides an instructive overview of why financial innovations arise from a financial economics perspective.

3. Peter Bernstein (1992) provides a vivid description of how advances in financial theory have helped transform the finance business.

4. Empirical evidence seems to confirm that there are early-mover advantages to financial innovation. Among others, see Carrow (1999) and Tufano (2002b).

References

Bernstein, P. 1992. *Capital Ideas*. Hoboken, NJ: Wiley.

Carrow, K. A. 1999. Evidence of Early Mover Advantages in Underwriting Spreads. *Journal of Financial Services Research* 15 (1): 37–55.

Hosking, P. and S. Jagger. 2009. "Wake Up, Gentlemen", World's Top Bankers Warned by Former Fed Chairman Volcker. *Times (London, England),* December 9.

Hou, V. L. 1997. Derivatives and Dialectics: The Evolution of the Chinese Futures Market. *New York University Law Review* 72: 175.

Litan, R. 2010. In Defense of Much, But Not All, Financial Innovation. Washington, DC: Brookings Institution. Mimeo.

Miller, M. H. 1986. Financial Innovation: The Last Twenty Years and the Next. Selected Paper Number 63, Booth School of Business, University of Chicago.

Shiller, R.J. 1993. *Macro Markets: Creating Institutions for Managing Society's Largest Economic Risks*. Oxford: Oxford University Press.

Tufano, P. 2002a. Financial Innovation. Harvard Business School, Boston. Mimeo.

Tufano, P. 2002b. Financial Innovation and First Mover Advantages. *Journal of Financial Economics* 25: 213–240.

11 Market Efficiency, Rational Expectations, and Financial Innovation

Maria Vassalou

While the financial crisis that intensified around the time of the Lehman Brothers collapse has dominated discussions in academic, policy, and practitioners' circles, a by-product of these events has been a rigorous debate over the implications of the crisis for market efficiency, the rationality of investors, and the merits of financial innovation. Since much of the discussion that dominated the media has been against market efficiency and critical of financial innovation, in what follows, I venture to make the case in support of market efficiency and the merits of financial innovation, as well as provide my own views.

The Market Efficiency Hypothesis and Its Implications

The market efficiency hypothesis has its roots in the random walk hypothesis. Kendall (1953) was probably the first statistician to show empirically that the prices of stocks and commodities follow a random walk, that is, that successive changes are independent of each other. Those observations subsequently led to the formulation of the efficient markets hypothesis (EMH), which states that prices fully reflect all available information. Eugene Fama, the first recipient of the Deutsche Bank Prize in Financial Economics, has devoted a large portion of his research to further developing and refining the concept of market efficiency, as well as to identifying and testing its implications.

One of the most significant implications of the EMH is that testing it involves a joint-hypothesis test of market efficiency and the validity of the asset pricing model used to test it.

To borrow from Campbell (2000), the most basic and fundamental equation in asset pricing is the one that expresses an asset price as a function of the asset's random payoff and the stochastic discount factor (SDF):

$$P_{it} = E_{it} (M_{t+1} \times X_{t+1}) \tag{11.1}$$

where P_{it} defines the price of asset i at time t, E_t is the expectation conditional on today's information set, X_{t+1} is the random payoff of asset i at time $t + 1$, and M_{t+1} is the SDF. The SDF generalizes the concept of the discount factor in the presence of uncertainty. The origins of this representation are credited to Cox and Ross (1976), Ross (1978), and Harrison and Kreps (1979). An empirical application of its discrete-time representation was first provided by Grossman and Shiller (1981).

If prices of assets are nonzero, one can divide both sides of equation (11.1) by P_{it} to obtain:

$$1 = E_t [M_{t+1} (1 + R_{i,t+1})], \tag{11.2}$$

where $(1 + R_{i,t+1}) \equiv X_{i,t+1}/P_{it}$. Empirical asset pricing relies on equation (11.2), and the literature of multifactor asset pricing models revolves around the specification of the SDF. In particular, the SDF is assumed to be a linear function of K common factors $f_{k,t+1}$, $k = 1, \ldots, K$, and each asset pricing model differs from others in the functional form of the SDF. To test market efficiency, we need an asset pricing model, but to obtain an asset pricing model we need to specify the SDF. In other words, any test of market efficiency is effectively conditional on the validity of the SDF used to test it. This is an insight discussed in Fama (1970).[1] It follows that it is easy to reject market efficiency if the SDF implied by the asset pricing model used to test it is misspecified or simply incorrect.

Much of the empirical asset pricing literature from the late 1960s to the early 1990s is centered on tests of the capital asset pricing model (CAPM) of Sharpe (1964) and Lintner (1965). The CAPM expresses the expected excess return of a risky asset as a linear function of its beta with the market portfolio, often proxied in practice by a value-weighted index of U.S. stock returns. While the CAPM has been a useful starting point in our quest to characterize the discount factor, the academic asset pricing literature has moved well beyond the CAPM in the past fifteen years or so, but it still has a long way to go.

Over the years, a number of asset pricing anomalies have been identified in the asset pricing literature. "Anomalies" are price behaviors that cannot be explained within the structure of a particular asset pricing model. Most of the popular anomalies, such as the size effect, the book-to-market effect, and the momentum effect, have been identified within the context of the CAPM. Empirical work has shown that the CAPM

cannot explain why, for instance, small-market-capitalization stocks out-perform large-market-capitalization stocks, after adjusting for their beta exposures with respect to the market portfolio. Similarly, it cannot explain why high book-to-market stocks outperform low book-to-market stocks on a market-beta risk-adjusted basis, or why stocks that performed well in the past tend to outperform stocks that performed poorly, again after adjusting for their market beta exposure.[2]

Given the joint-hypothesis nature of market efficiency and the valid-ity of the asset pricing model used to test it, it is tempting to attribute to a failure of the EMH the identification of a price behavior that cannot be explained within the context of the prevailing asset pricing model of the time. The implication of attributing a price behavior to market inefficiency is the belief that any excess return generated from that price behavior is unrelated to a failure of the asset pricing model used itself.

Such a stance could have very negative implications, not only for academic research but also for financial practice. Suppose the excess return is not due to market inefficiency but rather to a source of risk not captured by the asset pricing model used to determine the anomaly. Active asset managers may attempt to exploit the anomaly in order to earn the excess return, assuming that this will not add any further risk dimension to their portfolio. While the beta exposures of their portfolio with the factors considered by the prevailing asset pricing model may remain unchanged, the excess return on the anomaly may in fact be a risk premium with respect to a new and perhaps little understood risk factor. The worst part of this possibility is that the active manager, being unaware of the presence of such a risk exposure in his portfolio, may fail to manage it appropriately as part of his risk management process.

Viewed differently, a true asset pricing anomaly is a phenomenon by which an excess return of an asset is unrelated to systematic risk. To the extent that this asset can be freely traded and held either long or short, it should be easy for at least skilled investors to arbitrage this anomaly away. Indeed, one of the most puzzling facts about these so-called anom-alies is that they are stubborn; they persist through time, even though they are widely known and the related assets are fully and freely traded. Even if they subside temporarily, they tend to reappear with vengeance. In my view, this is an indication that something other than mispricing drives the observed price behavior. And that something is likely to be risk.[3] I return to this point in the next section.

Beyond the Single-Factor CAPM: What Types of Risk Factors Could Explain Those Persistent Anomalies?

There are two main shortcomings with the single-factor CAPM. First, it is a static, two-period model that does not take into account the dynamic nature of the world economy in which global markets operate. Second, and related, it is a partial equilibrium model that does not link asset prices to fundamental risks in the economy. As Cochrane (2001) mentions, it prices assets relative to other assets. This is unsatisfactory, as the first assets need to be priced somehow, too. There are alternative asset pricing formulations that remedy, at least partially, the above shortcomings. To have a good chance in discovering asset pricing relations that explain the so-called anomalies, we need to have asset pricing models that link effectively the real side of the economy with the financial markets. Several directions to that end have been explored over time, with some success.

Merton's (1973) Intertemporal Capital Asset Pricing Model

The intertemporal CAMP of Merton (1973) addresses the static nature of the single-factor CAPM and has the potential of also mitigating its partial equilibrium aspect.

In simple terms, Merton's model says that investors' assets demand is influenced by the uncertainty related to the future investment opportunity set, which in turn is likely to influence the relative attractiveness of the various investment alternatives. Rational investors would want to be able to hedge such uncertainty by holding portfolios of assets that protect them against adverse changes in the future investment opportunity set. As a result, in Merton's model, an asset earns a risk premium not only because of its systematic risk but also to the extent that it can be used as a hedge against uncertain future economic conditions. Merton's model does not identify the state variables that track changes in the investment opportunity set, although it proposes the short-term interest rate as a potential such state variable. While theory can guide our search, the identification of the state variables is essentially an empirical task.

For the asset manager, this research area can be of great importance in terms of managing the positions and risk exposures of his portfolio. If we can model the evolution of the investment opportunity set over time, then it is possible to structure the portfolio positions in such a way that subgroups of them mimic certain economic scenarios likely to unfold going forward. If the asset manager holds appropriate weights in these mimick-

ing portfolios, he can hedge undesirable scenarios while maintaining exposures to beneficial economic outcomes, within his permissible investment
universe.[4] To that end, we need to have a clear understanding of how
the macroeconomy affects the whole spectrum of financial assets.

What are some of the macro-risk factors that traditional asset pricing
models do not capture? To draw from my own work, Vassalou (2003)
uses news about future GDP growth as a factor to capture important
changes in the economic environment likely to affect the prices of risky
assets.[5] This work shows that a model that contains the market factor
together with a mimicking portfolio of news about future GDP growth
can explain the cross section of equity returns as well as the three-factor
Fama-French model. This is despite the fact that it is only a two-factor
model and it is tested on the difficult-to-explain Fama-French size- and
book-to-market-sorted portfolios.

Similarly, Vassalou and Xing (2004) create a default likelihood indicator (DLI) that captures variations in the aggregate default risk of the
equity market. They show that this formulation again does a very good
job in explaining the cross section of the Fama-French size- and book-
to-market-sorted portfolios. They also show that their DLI fully explains
the small-cap effect and substantially explains the book-to-market effect.
On the asset pricing side, their work potentially implies that much of the
ability of news related to future GDP growth to explain the cross section
of equity returns has to do with variations in the aggregate default risk
in the economy. It is certainly true that DLI rises significantly during
recessions and therefore it is negatively correlated with GDP growth, as
figure 11.1 shows. It is interesting to note, in particular during the recent
recession of 2007–2009, which coincided with the financial crisis, the
aggregate DLI increased to unprecedented levels compared to what was
observed during the other five recession periods covered by the sample.

Let's go briefly through the implications of this recent dramatic rise
in aggregate default risk from the perspective of an asset manager who
invests in the small-cap effect. Table 11.1 updates some results from Vassalou and Xing (2004) to the recent period. As we can see, there is certainly a small-cap effect in the whole sample of U.S. equities, of the order
of 1.45 percent per month or 17.4 percent per annum (p.a.) (Panel A). If
we subdivide the sample into quartiles according to the DLI of the individual stocks, we clearly see that the small-cap effect is concentrated in
the stocks with the highest DLI, that is, the ones that are most likely to
default.[6] This result is provided in Vassalou and Xing (2004), and table
11.1 shows that it continues to hold when the data sample is extended to
the present time.

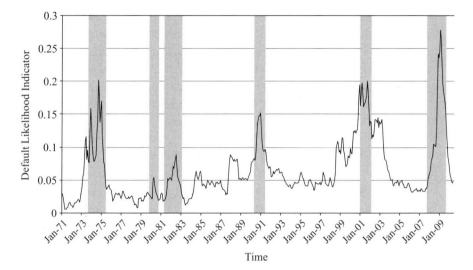

Figure 11.1
Aggregate default probability, January 1971 to June 2010. Aggregate default likelihood
indicator. This graph extends figure 1 in Vassalou and Xing (2004) to the period up to June
2010. As noted in Vassalou and Xing (2004), the aggregate DLI is computed as the simple
average of DLIs of all firms in our sample. The shaded areas denote recession periods as
defined by the National Bureau of Economic Research.

If we look at the pre–financial crisis period, that is, the period from
1993 to the end of 2006 (Panel B), the small-cap effect remains prominent
in the whole sample, although it stems entirely from the outperformance
of small caps with high DLI. However, if we examine the same effect
during the subsequent period, which overlaps with the recent recession
and the financial crisis, we see that the small-cap effect has disappeared
(Panel C) both from the quartile with the highest DLI and the whole
sample. Even if we lump together the two recent recessions represented
in the sample at hand, the same result is obtained (Panel D).

This makes sense if the excess return of small caps relative to large
caps is due to default risk. When the default risk in the economy is low,
investors can earn the risk premium associated with it without realizing
the risk. But when default risk rises, especially as dramatically as we
observed during this last crisis and the last two recessions combined,
investors in the small-cap effect will be negatively affected by the realization of the high default risk. This will render the trade unprofitable,
especially after factoring in the transaction costs and other realistic
trading constraints. It would be dangerous to assume that the small-cap
effect has disappeared because it got arbitraged away. If the small-cap

Table 11.1
Size Effect Controlled by Default Risk

Panel A. Total Period: 1993/2–2010/6

	Small			Big		
	1	2	3	4	Small–Big	t-stat
Average Return of Equally Weighted Portfolios						
High DLI 1	5.6672	1.0830	0.7601	0.6939	4.9733	(7.7925)
2	1.1176	0.9674	0.7759	0.6549	0.4628	(1.4607)
3	1.0803	0.8949	0.9843	0.8336	0.2468	(0.9917)
Low DLI 4	1.1031	1.0912	0.8713	0.7987	0.3044	(1.5660)
Whole sample	2.2037	1.0127	0.8496	0.7451	1.4586	(5.0273)

Panel B. Subperiod: 1993/2–2006/12

High DLI 1	6.1442	1.3707	0.8855	0.6283	5.5158	(8.2630)
2	1.4833	1.3368	1.0094	0.8278	0.6555	(1.8559)
3	1.4040	1.2360	1.1886	1.0565	0.3475	(1.2839)
Low DLI 4	1.3547	1.3913	1.0982	1.0344	0.3204	(1.5186)
Whole sample	2.5611	1.3393	1.0484	0.8874	1.6736	(5.3003)

Panel C. Subperiod: 2007/1–2010/6

High DLI 1	3.7708	−0.0609	0.2616	0.9548	2.8160	(1.6348)
2	−0.3364	−0.5016	−0.1525	−0.0327	−0.3037	(−0.4264)
3	−0.2066	−0.4616	0.1720	−0.0530	−0.1537	(−0.2496)
Low DLI 4	0.1024	−0.1022	−0.0309	−0.1383	0.2406	(0.4944)
Whole sample	0.7830	−0.2860	0.0592	0.1792	0.6037	(0.8558)

Panel D. Recent Recession Periods Only: 2001/3–2001/11 and 2007/12–2009/6

High DLI 1	3.2684	−1.7921	−0.8714	−0.5222	3.7906	(1.5027)
2	−0.9378	−1.4075	−0.8692	−1.2897	0.3519	(0.2859)
3	−0.4460	−0.8000	−0.5386	−1.4908	1.0448	(1.2470)
Low DLI 4	−0.0650	−0.5459	−0.8715	−1.1067	1.0417	(1.5259)
Whole sample	0.3915	−1.1373	−0.7885	−1.1084	1.4999	(1.3850)

Notes: This table extends results published in table 4 of Vassalou and Xing (2004). The main difference here is that stocks are sorted into quartiles instead of quintiles to make the market capitalization of the stocks in the small-cap portfolios more meaningful and relevant for practical purposes. Sorting stocks into quintiles results in small-cap portfolios populated by too small firms. The results, however, remain qualitatively the same whether the sorting is done in quintiles or quartiles. As noted in the notes to table 4 of Vassalou and Xing (2004), from 1993 to 2010, and at the beginning of each month, stocks are sorted into four portfolios according to their DLI in the previous month. For a detailed discussion on the computation of DLI, please see Vassalou and Xing (2004). Subsequently, and within each of the quartiles, stocks are sorted into four size portfolios based on their market capitalization in the previous month. The returns below are from equally weighted portfolios and are reported in percentage terms. Please note that the results are qualitatively the same when portfolios are value-weighted. "Small–Big" is the return difference between the portfolio of the smallest market capitalization stocks and the portfolio of the largest market capitalization stocks, within the DLI quartile. The rows labeled "Whole Sample" report results using all stocks in our sample. *T*-values are reported in parentheses.

effect disappears during recessions and reappears during expansions, then, in my view, the driving force behind it is risk, not an anomaly.[7]

The Consumption and Investment CAPM

Breeden's consumption CAPM (Breeden 1979) provided an early exploration of the interrelation of financial assets and the macroeconomy. Its empirical success has unfortunately been limited, mainly because consumption generally varies too little over time to explain the level of volatility typically associated with most risky assets.[8]

A formulation that I find far more appealing than consumption CAPM is Cochrane's (1996) investment CAPM. Cochrane's model links asset returns with the investment side of the economy, which is much more volatile. In particular, it shows that the expected excess return of a risky asset is a linear function of its sensitivity to the economy's investment growth rates. In his empirical formulation, he uses residential and nonresidential investment growth rates as factors to explain returns. While this choice did not result into a large degree of cross-sectional explanatory power for the model, Li, Vassalou, and Xing (2006) showed that a three-factor sector investment growth specification can dramatically improve the empirical success of Cochrane's investment CAPM and fully explain the size- and book-to-market-sorted test portfolios. The reason is that each sector of the economy may receive different productivity shocks that will affect returns on capital at the firm level differently. This differentiation across sector investment growth rates allows the model to explain a substantial part of the cross-sectional variation in equity returns.

Market Efficiency and Investors' Rationality

What is the distinction between market efficiency and rational expectations? None, really! When prices reflect all available information, it means that investors evaluate all publicly available information and trade on it, and therefore it gets reflected in asset prices. This is the reason why I have not spent any time discussing rationality per se so far.

Does market efficiency mean that all investors act rationally all the time? Not necessarily. It is possible that some investors exhibit irrational behavior sometimes or all the time. What is important for market efficiency is that the marginal investor be rational. Indeed, the literature of behavioral finance is full of interesting anecdotes of investors' irrationality (Barber and Odean 2001, 2008). However, none of the behavioral studies that I am aware of has demonstrated that any identified devia-

tions from rationality have any lasting or prolonged effect on prices.[9] Furthermore, as Merton (1987) eloquently noted more than twenty-three years ago, the increasing emphasis on anomalies "has been institutionalized by responsible and knowledgeable journal editors who understandably look more favorably upon empirical studies that find anomalous evidence with respect to a widely accepted theory than upon studies that merely serve to confirm that theory yet again." He continues by stressing that this emphasis on the anomalous is given with "little control over the number of tests performed, creates a fertile environment for both unintended selection bias and for attaching greater significance to otherwise unbiased estimates than is justified."

Some market observers and participants point to bubbles as evidence of market irrationality. Recent examples of often discussed bubbles are the Internet bubble in the late 1990s and the housing bubble of the 2008–2009 recession and financial crisis. It is important to stress that bubbles are phenomena identified ex post. We do not have theories that predict bubbles. Therefore, I view it as pointless to discuss bubbles as evidence of irrationality. Investors act on the basis of the information they have at each point in time. This is the rational thing to do, irrespective of how their decisions look ex post in the presence of additional information not available to them ex ante.

Popular asset pricing anomalies can be used as evidence of irrationality by the proponents of behavioral theories. However, as we have discussed earlier, it is possible to provide risk-based explanations for many, if not all, so-called asset pricing anomalies. In addition, as Brav and Heaton (2002) have shown, it is in several cases impossible to empirically distinguish between a risk-based and a behavioral explanation for a given price behavior branded as an anomaly. It therefore becomes, to some extent, a matter of taste. Would you rather have as your prior that investors are irrational and consequently markets are inefficient, or would you rather believe that any excess risk-adjusted return is due to sources of risk missing from, or as yet unknown to, the asset pricing model used to assess it?

I personally believe that the second choice is more appealing. My view is that it is never a good idea to underestimate the collective wisdom of the market. It can also be dangerous for all practical matters, if it leads to less stringent risk management practices that can prove disastrous in certain states of the world.

There is also, in my view, something fundamentally unsatisfactory about behavioral asset pricing. While it is possible to define deviations from rational behavior that will help explain a particular asset pricing phenomenon, it is often necessary to alter the nature of the deviations

from rationality in order to explain a different asset pricing phenomenon. In other words, there does not seem to be consistency across behavioral theories as to the form of irrationality that investors exhibit over time. Therefore, there is a lack of a consistent framework within which all asset pricing observed patterns can be explained.

While rational expectations may appear rigid to those versed in behavioral sciences, they do provide a clearly defined framework within which asset pricing theories have been developed and have evolved over the past fifty or more years. In my view, for behavioral finance to provide an attractive alternative to rational expectations it needs to specify a comprehensive framework of mutually exclusive deviations from rationality. It should then aim to explain all asset pricing phenomena of interest within that framework. Only then does it stand to gain serious and longlasting ground over rational expectations theories of asset pricing. It is in that event that it can also have a more profound and beneficial effect on shaping asset management practices, which is one of the ultimate goals of the asset pricing literature.

Financial Innovation

Financial innovation is the means by which capital markets move closer to completeness, and therefore risk sharing improves across market participants around the world. In that sense, financial innovation is a necessity in order to improve the functioning of capital markets.

An example of financial innovation relevant to the discussions of the previous sections is Robert Shiller's MacroMarkets. Shiller (1998) greatly contributes to this field through his intellectually stimulating and innovative work on MacroMarkets. Shiller recognizes that uncertainty related to personal income and living standards can significantly affect the demand side of the economy and therefore by extension the investment opportunity set faced by market participants. His book discusses extensively the desirability of hedging long streams of income, related either to national income or to personal labor income.

Shiller has also put his ideas to practice through the creation of MacroShares. MacroShares are fully collateralized exchange-traded securities that allow investors to express either optimistic or pessimistic views about key economic variables and asset classes.[10] In many respects, MacroShares can be viewed as a vehicle to trade mimicking portfolios of state variables that describe likely changes in the future investment opportunity set.[11] The full development of a market for such instruments can

significantly increase the level of market completeness and facilitate risk sharing across market participants around the world. The set of instruments or variables that can be traded in the MacroShares' fashion is limited only by our creativity and imagination. It can certainly be fueled and supported by the research produced on empirical asset pricing and the links uncovered through this process between the real economy and financial markets.

There should be no expectation that all financial innovations will be deemed useful or successful ex post. Progress, whether in science or in financial engineering, is the result of experimentation, trial and error. In science, it is common to discard a portion of innovations over time, as better approaches to tackle the same issue emerge and the shortcomings of existing methods become apparent.

The same should be expected from financial innovation. The fact that certain assets, produced through financial engineering, were shown during the recent crisis to be badly structured, or even harmful to a subset of investors, does not speak to the usefulness of financial innovation per se. It speaks to the shortcomings of those specific asset structures. At the very least, the experience gained during the crisis should help improve aspects of those financial instruments that proved to be defective or problematic. It should not be used as an excuse to stifle financial innovation going forward. Without financial innovation, the financial markets will be unable to keep up with the liquidity demands of an ever increasingly globalized world economy.

Conclusions

In this chapter, I aimed to provide a brief discussion of my views on market efficiency as it relates to asset pricing. A lot of these views have been apparent in my own research over the years, which can be summarized as an effort to uncover economically motivated sources of risk that affect asset returns. In the process, I also provided some closely related references to other studies. The list is by no means exhaustive. The asset pricing literature is vast and ever evolving. It is impossible to do justice to it in a few pages. This chapter should be viewed as an opinion piece rather than as an attempt to provide a review of the literature.[12]

I believe in the value of trying to understand the complexity of the return structure through the identification of economic risk factors that link the real side of the economy with the financial markets. While groups of investors may exhibit elements of deviation from rationality

at times, it is yet to be proved that such behavior renders the financial markets materially inefficient. Successful financial innovation has the potential of further improving market efficiency by improving risk sharing and liquidity in the markets, and by extension, the speed with which information is incorporated into prices. And while some assumptions of rational expectations theories of asset pricing may appear too restrictive or even unrealistic, to paraphrase Milton Friedman, a theory has to be judged by the strength of its predictions and not by the validity of its assumptions.

Models are tools. Any tool or invention in the hands of the wrong user can be dangerous and harmful. Nuclear power is a wonderful discovery if used for peaceful purposes. It can, however, be catastrophic if used for warfare. It is not the rational models that failed us. It is some users that misused them.

Acknowledgments

I would like to thank Yuhang Xing for providing me with the data used to update the DLI estimators and related analysis, as well as Ming Cen for excellent research assistance. All views expressed in this chapter are mine and do not necessarily represent those of my current or past employers. I remain responsible for any errors.

Notes

1. Eugene Fama shows that the joint-hypothesis property is related to the submartingales of Samuelson (1965) and Mandelbrot (1966). See also Fama (1976, 1991) for further discussion of this point.

2. Empirical papers that discuss these effects include Banz (1981), Jagadeesh and Titman (1993, 2001), and Fama and French (1992). Please also see references herewith. There is also a host of other asset pricing anomalies identified in the empirical asset pricing literature over the years. A comprehensive review is beyond the scope of this discussion.

3. The anomalies I have in mind are those that persist over very long periods of time, such as the size, book-to-market, or momentum anomalies. There are other types of potentially true anomalies that are short-lived and often related to market microstructure issues. Typically, those are exploited quickly by intraday or high-frequency traders.

4. Of course, one may also benefit from betting on adverse economic scenarios, usually by shorting a set of relevant assets. However, this approach is not always fully available to all categories of asset managers.

5. See also Liew and Vassalou (2000) for a precursor of this work.

6. For a description of these tests and their methodology, please refer to Vassalou and Xing (2004).

7. Similar statements can be made about the book-to-market effect. Owing to lack of space, I refrain from elaborating on it here.

8. Tests of the consumption CAPM include Breeden, Gibbons, and Litzenberger (1989), Campbell (1996), and Cochrane (1996), among others. An example of a more recent conditional test of the consumption CAPM is Lettau and Ludvigson (2001). For a discussion of the poor performance of the consumption CAPM, see Campbell and Cochrane (2000).

9. As noted earlier, short-term deviations from rationality or market efficiency can exist but should be arbitraged away to the degree possible, and be eliminated as a result.

10. See the product description on the MacroMarkets website, http://www.macromarkets .com/macroshares/index.shtml.

11. See the article on Robert Shiller in *Fortune*, July 7, 2009, "Bob Shiller didn't Kill the Housing Market," Katie Benner, writer-reporter.

12. The reader is referred to Campbell (2000) and Cochrane (2001) for a thorough and critical discussion of the asset pricing literature.

References

Banz, Rolf W. 1981. The Relation between Return and Market Value of Common Stocks. *Journal of Financial Economics* 9: 3–18.

Barber, Brad, and Terrence Odean. 2001. Boys Will Be Boys: Gender, Overconfidence and Common Stock Investment. *Quarterly Journal of Economics* 116 (1): 261–292.

Barber, Brad, and Terrence Odean. 2008. All That Glitters: The Effect of Attention and News on the Buying Behavior of Individual and Institutional Investors. *Review of Financial Studies* 21 (2): 785–818.

Brav, A., and J. B. Heaton. 2002. Competing Theories of Financial Anomalies. *Review of Financial Studies* 15 (2): 575–606.

Breeden, Douglas T. 1979. An Intertemporal Asset Pricing Model with Stochastic Consumption and Investment Opportunities. *Journal of Financial Economics* 7: 265–296.

Breeden, D. T., M. R. Gibbons, and R. Litzenberger. 1989. Empirical Tests of the Consumption-Oriented CAPM. *Journal of Finance* 44: 231–262.

Campbell, John Y. 1996. Understanding Risk and Return. *Journal of Political Economy* 104: 298–345.

Campbell, John Y. 2000. Asset Pricing at the Millennium. *Journal of Finance* 55 (4): 1515–1567.

Campbell, John Y., and John H. Cochrane. 2000. Explaining the Poor Performance of Consumption Based Asset Pricing Models. *Journal of Finance* 55: 2863–2878.

Cochrane, John H. 1996. A Cross-Sectional Test of an Investment-Based Asset Pricing Model. *Journal of Political Economy* 104: 572–621.

Cochrane, John H. 2001. *Asset Pricing*. Princeton, NJ: Princeton University Press.

Cox, John C., and Stephen A. Ross. 1976. The Valuation of Options for Alternative Stochastic Processes. *Journal of Financial Economics* 3: 145–166.

Fama, Eugene. 1970. Efficient Capital Markets: A Review of Theory and Empirical Work. *Journal of Finance* 25 (2): 383–417.

Fama, Eugene. 1976. *Foundations of Finance*. New York: Basic Books.

Fama, Eugene. 1991. Efficient Markets II: Fiftieth Anniversary Invited Paper. *Journal of Finance* 46: 1575–1617.

Fama, Eugene, and Kenneth R. French. 1992. The Cross-Section of Expected Stock Returns. *Journal of Finance* 47: 427–465.

Grossman, Sanford J., and Robert J. Shiller. 1981. The Determinants of the Variability of Stock Market Prices. *American Economic Review* 71: 222–227.

Harrison, John M., and David Kreps. 1979. Martingales and Arbitrage in Multiperiod Securities Markets. *Journal of Economic Theory* 20: 381–408.

Jagadeesh, N., and Sh. Titman. 1993. Returns of Buying Winners and Selling Losers: Implications for Stock Market Efficiency. *Journal of Finance* 48: 65–91.

Jagadeesh, N., and Sh. Titman. 2001. Profitability of Momentum Strategies: An Evaluation of Alternative Explanations. *Journal of Finance* 56: 699–720.

Kendall, M. G. 1953. The Analysis of Economic Time Series: Part I. Prices. *Journal of the Royal Statistical Society. Series A (General)* 96: 11–25.

Lettau, Martin, and Sydney Ludvigson. 2001. Resurrecting the (C)CAPM: A Cross-Sectional Test When Risk Premia Are Time-varying. *Journal of Political Economy* 109: 1238–1287.

Li, Qing, Maria Vassalou, and Yuhang Xing. 2006. Sector Investment Growth Rates and the Cross-Section of Equity Returns. *Journal of Business* 79 (3): 1637–1665.

Liew, Jimmy, and Maria Vassalou. 2000. Can Book-to-Market, Size and Momentum Be Risk Factors That Predict Economic Growth? *Journal of Financial Economics* 57: 221–245.

Lintner, John. 1965. The Valuation of Risky Assets and the Selection of Risky Investments in Stock Portfolios and Capital Budgets. *Review of Economics and Statistics* 47: 13–37.

Mandelbrot, B. 1966. Forecasts of Future Prices, Unbiased Markets and Martingale Model. *Journal of Business* 39: 242–255.

Merton, Robert C. 1973. An Intertemporal Capital Asset Pricing Model. *Econometrica: Journal of the Econometric Society* 41: 867–887.

Merton, Robert. C. 1987. On the Current State of the Stock Market Rationality Hypothesis. In *Macroeconomics and Finance: Essays in Honor of Franco Modigliani*. Cambridge, MA: MIT Press.

Ross, Stephen A. 1978. A simple Approach to the Valuation of Risky Streams. *Journal of Business* 51: 453–475.

Samuelson, Paul. 1965. Proof That Properly Anticipated Prices Fluctuate Randomly. *Industrial Management Review* 6: 41–49.

Sharpe, William. 1964. Capital Asset Prices: A Theory of Market Equilibrium under Conditions of Risk. *Journal of Finance* 19: 425–442.

Shiller, Robert J. 1998. *Macro Markets: Creating Institutions for Managing Society's Largest Economic Risks*. Oxford: Oxford University Press.

Vassalou, Maria. 2003. News Related to Future GDP Growth as a Risk Factor in Equity Returns. *Journal of Financial Economics* 68: 47–73.

Vassalou, Maria, and Yuhang Xing. 2004. Default Risk in Equity Returns. *Journal of Finance* 54 (2): 831–868.

Contributors

Ackermann, Josef, Dr., Chairman of the Management Board and the Group Executive Committee, Deutsche Bank AG, josef.ackermann @db.com

Barberis, Nicholas C., Ph.D., Stephen & Camille Schramm Professor of Finance, Yale University, nick.barberis@yale.edu

Campbell, John Y., Ph.D., Harvard College professor and the Morton L. and Carole S. Olshan Professor of Economics, Harvard University, john_ campbell@harvard.edu

Case, Karl E., Ph.D., Professor of Economics Emeritus, Wellesley College, kcase@wellesley.edu

Greenwood, Robin, Ph.D., Associate Professor of Business Administration, Harvard University, rgreenwood@hbs.edu

Haliassos, Michael, Ph.D., Professor of Macroeconomics and Finance at Goethe University Frankfurt and Director of the Center for Financial Studies, haliassos@wiwi.uni-frankfurt.de

Issing, Otmar, Dr., President of the Center for Financial Studies, and Honorary Professor at the University of Würzburg (1991) and Goethe University Frankfurt, issing@ifk-cfs.de

Popov, Alexander A., Ph.D., Economist, Directorate General Research, Financial Research Division, European Central Bank, alexander.popov @ecb.europa.eu

Shiller, Robert J., Ph.D., Arthur M. Okun Professor of Economics, Yale University, robert.shiller@yale.edu

Shleifer, Andrei, Ph.D., Professor of Economics, Harvard University, ashleifer@harvard.edu

Smets, Frank R., Ph.D., Director General of the Directorate General Research, European Central Bank, frank.smets@ecb.europa.eu

Smith, Susan J., D.Phil., Professor and Mistress of Girton College, Cambridge University, mistress@girton.cam.ac.uk

Viceira, Luis M., Ph.D., George E. Bates Professor, Harvard Business School, lviceira@hbs.edu

Vassalou, Maria, Ph.D., Head of Asset Allocation, MIO Partners, Inc., subsidiary of McKinsey & Company, maria@maria-vassalou.com

Name Index

Subject Index